LIB051005 R3/78

SIMON FRASER UNI

Unless recalled

due on last date stamped

D0450249

S.F.U.   MAR 2 0 1980

---

11 1 1 1   DEC 13 1984

REC'D DEC 1 1984

THE SCIENTIFIC ESTATE

DON K. PRICE

THE BELKNAP PRESS OF
HARVARD UNIVERSITY PRESS · Cambridge, Massachusetts

1965

© Copyright 1965 by the President and Fellows of Harvard College

All rights reserved

Distributed in Great Britain by Oxford University Press, London

Library of Congress Catalog Card Number: 65-22047

Typography, binding and jacket design by Burton Jones

Composition, printing and binding by
The Riverside Press, Cambridge, Massachusetts

FOR GAIL

Preface

MARK TWAIN ONCE OBSERVED that in writing his *Pudd'nhead Wilson* he was unable to follow his original plot because several of the characters developed wills of their own, and did things quite different from those he had planned for them. When I wrote this book my original plan was complicated less by my subjects than by my audiences. Several years ago, I was doing my best to continue some earlier studies of the administration of scientific programs in government. But my hope of doing a quick and workmanlike job on that practical problem was frustrated when I was invited to speak to audiences at the University of Virginia and the American Philosophical Society. For I found it impossible to discuss the relation of science to governmental affairs in lectures at those two institutions, which are still haunted for any scholar by the ghosts of Thomas Jefferson and Benjamin Franklin, without facing up to much more fundamental issues than the influence of science on current problems of administration, or the methods by which government agencies finance research projects.

Jefferson and Franklin were politicians as well as scientists, and were interested in science not merely for its intellectual aspects, nor even for its material benefits, but also for the liberating effect it would have on the politics of all nations. A little after their time, American scientists quit taking part in politics, and scientific institutions came to be thought of as something apart from, if not in opposition to, the political and constitutional system. The middle of the twentieth century brought science back into the main stream of political affairs, but with no theory of its proper role. Instead of a theory we had only a vague and uneasy feeling that although we were sure that the claim that Communism was based on scientific principles was bogus, we were not quite sure why, and by no means sure that we knew what was happening to our own constitutional system as a result of our pragmatic development of scientific programs.

And so I felt impelled to tackle the problem of the relation of science and scientists to the political ideas and the constitutional system of the United States, not as Jefferson and Franklin thought it would turn out to be, but as it has developed since their time partly as a result of the work of institutions that they were the foremost in creating.

I therefore wish to express my appreciation to the University of Virginia for the honor of its invitation to deliver the Page-Barbour Lectures at Charlottesville in March 1963, and—almost as important—for its generosity in permitting me not to publish the lectures as delivered, but to take time to expand and rewrite them for later publication. The opportunity to prepare the original lectures challenged me to face the subject in its broader aspects. The opportunity to revise and extend my remarks let me take advantage of the helpful criticism of friends and colleagues in both Charlottesville and Cambridge.

As a result, this book turns out to be quite different from my earlier effort in the same general field—*Government and Science* (New York University Press, 1954). That book represented the point of view of a government official and reflected my experience in the Bureau of the Budget and the Department of Defense. This one adds the perspective of my experience in a private foundation with a world-wide program, the Ford Foundation, where it was painfully clear that the development of newly independent nations in the direction of political freedom does not depend altogether on technical assistance or the skills drawn from the sciences. It adds, too, the perspective of collaboration with colleagues from a number of academic disciplines, who have forced me to see the problem of the new political status of science in relation to more fundamental questions—the nature of scientific knowledge and the way in which that knowledge bears on human purposes and human freedom.

Since all these subjects are far beyond my professional competence, I have leaned heavily on the advice of my academic colleagues, especially those with whom I have been closely associated in the Science and Public Policy Program at Harvard. From Harvey Brooks, Dean of the Division of Engineering and Applied Physics; I. Bernard Cohen, Professor of the History of Science; and Carl Kaysen, Littauer Professor of Political Economy, I obtained not only invaluable guidance on particular problems but helpful criticism of the manuscript itself.

I am grateful to Rowland Egger, until recently Dean of the Faculty of Arts and Sciences at the University of Virginia, and now at Princeton, not only for his initial encouragement, but also for his criticisms and suggestions.

John W. Gardner, President of the Carnegie Corporation of New York, and Gerald Holton, Professor of Physics at Harvard and Editor of the American Academy of Arts and Sciences, read and criticized most of the manuscript in early drafts, as did my Harvard colleagues Merle Fainsod and Louis Hartz in a later draft, and their critical advice was invaluable to me.

Among the many other present or former Harvard colleagues to whom I am grateful for advice on particular problems or parts of the manuscript are J. Stefan Dupré, William Y. Elliott, Carl J. Friedrich, Arthur Maass, Robert G. McCloskey, Edward S. Mason, Ernst Mayr, Roger Revelle, and James Q. Wilson. I am similarly obliged for advice or for critical readings of parts of the manuscript to Caryl P. Haskins, President of the Carnegie Institution of Washington; to Major General James McCormack (USAF Ret.), Vice President of the Massachusetts Institute of Technology; to Harrison Brown, of the California Institute of Technology; to Albert Wohlstetter of the University of Chicago; to Clifford L. Berg, of the U.S. Bureau of the Budget; to Edward Wenk, Jr., Chief of the Science Policy Research Division of the Legislative Reference Service; and to several staff members of the RAND Corporation, notably Burton H. Klein and Andrew W. Marshall.

I shall of course personally blame any error of fact or opinion in this book on one or more of the friends whom I have named above, but, fortunately for them, they are numerous enough so that each can easily evade public responsibility.

I wish to thank the Rockefeller Foundation for its generous grant to Harvard University for the Science and Public Policy Program, which supported much of the preparation of this volume. The Foundation, of course, has had nothing to do with the conduct of the research nor with the writing of this book, and accordingly is not responsible in any way for its contents.

Much of Chapter 3 was first published in the *Proceedings of the American Philosophical Society,* to which I am obliged for permission to include it in this volume. I am similarly grateful to the editors of *Daedalus,* which first published an abridged version of Chapter 4.

I owe especial thanks for their help in the preparation of the manuscript to Mrs. Shirley F. Brooks, Miss Angelina Caneles, and Miss Jeanne Brown.

Max Hall, Editor for the Social Sciences at Harvard University Press, has shown a determination far beyond the call of friendship to make the author's meaning clear to the reader. In my working with him, the partnership has been as pleasant as the discipline has been rigorous.

Don K. Price

Graduate School of Public Administration
Harvard University

March 1965

CONTENTS

d) propos sci
y) prog. soc.

CHAPTER 1

Escape to the Endless Frontier

THE UNITED STATES was founded at a time when philosophers were beginning to believe in the perfectibility of mankind. Ever since Benjamin Franklin and Thomas Jefferson, Americans have been inclined to put their faith in a combination of democracy and science as a sure formula for human progress.

Today that faith burns much less bright. Since the Second World War it has seemed to many, and especially to scientists, that the faith was dimmed by the mushroom cloud of the atomic bomb. The scientists who found themselves, to their great surprise, caught up in the political troubles of the contemporary world are tempted to blame their fate on their success in discovering nuclear fission: they see their tragedy, like that of Prometheus, as the result of seizing the secrets of the gods. But it seems more realistic to remind them that their own faith in inevitable progress had been dampened before Hiroshima—during the Great Depression or even before.

The earlier creed of progress had two main articles of faith, one relating to the progress of science, the other to the progress of society. The first was that men's desire for material benefits would lead society to support the advancement of science and technology, just as the profit motive would encourage the development of the economy. The second was the corollary that the advancement of science would lead society toward desirable purposes, including political freedom.

The depression gave the general public reason to doubt these beliefs, as many scientists and philosophers had already come to do. After economists and politicians lost their confidence that the individual profit motive would automatically guarantee economic progress, and that technological innovation would necessarily further social welfare, it became easier for the general public to share the skepticism of scientists. The leaders of the scientific world, of course, had already come to understand that science makes progress less by the effort of inventors to find solutions for the practical problems of industry or government, than by the formulation of abstract theory and the search for basic knowledge. And they had much earlier given up their faith that science was certain to further either divine purpose or political progress.

At the end of the Second World War, the scientists' skepticism became a basis not for despair, but for vigorous action to guarantee the progress of science. Under the leadership of Vannevar Bush, the scientists undertook to teach the nation that basic research would not be produced automatically by the efforts of industry or government to apply science and technology to their own purposes, and that as a matter of policy the government should support basic research without regard to its application. The United States had been weak in basic science, and had had to rely on Europe for the fundamental knowledge that guided the development of the spectacular new weapons during the war. Now, knowing that "basic research is the pacemaker of technological progress," the United States must provide support from government funds for the advancement of fundamental science. This argument, presented to President Roosevelt by Dr. Bush in his famous report, *Science the Endless Frontier,* reversed the traditional policy of the United States in two ways: it persuaded universities and private research institutions that they had to ask the government for financial aid, and it persuaded the government that basic science, as well as applied research, deserved support.

But although the report abandoned the traditional faith in automatic progress with respect to science, and proposed deliberate governmental policies to encourage that progress, it did not undertake to deal with the second and more general aspect of the problem—progress in social and political affairs. The relation of science to political purposes was set aside with the assurance that the progress of science is essential to "our health, prosperity, and security as a nation," and the disclaimer that science alone would provide no panacea for social problems.[1]

The Bush report thus dealt—as, of course, Dr. Bush was asked by the President to do—with only half of the total problem of science in its relation to politics. On that half of the problem, it taught its lesson well, and the electorate learned it thoroughly. The results can be graded, in a crude way, by looking at what Congress was persuaded science is worth to the taxpayer: we are spending more dollars today on research and development than the entire federal budget before Pearl Harbor. If the lesson was an incomplete one, no one should single out the scientists for blame. Dr. Bush was not asked by the President to revise our political philosophy, but only to present a plan for the support of science. It is curious, in retrospect, that the political questions were not raised, but the fault was not that of the scientists, but of the politicians and political scientists. There were, indeed, some arguments about such questions as how the officials should be appointed who were to make grants to scientists, and what the procedures should be for accounting and overhead payments. But these were applied details, and hardly anyone stopped to ask the fundamental question: how is science, with all its new power, to be related to our political purposes and values, and to our economic and constitutional system?

By ignoring this question, we have been trying to escape to science as an endless frontier, and to turn our backs on the more difficult problems that it has produced.

For more than a decade, this escape seemed a sound strategy for science. Plenty of money was being provided, although there were indeed some minor inconveniences, as well as some worries in principle, about the way in which basic research was subordinated to certain applied programs. But then it began to be clear, in two ways, that troubles were sure to arise in the relationship between science and politics. The first way has now become clear to everyone in practice; the second is more theoretical, and therefore more important, but less obvious.

The practical trouble has arisen because practical politicians came to doubt that the identity of purpose between government and the scientific community should be taken for granted. "Health, prosperity, and security"—it was an argument, in a more sophisticated form, that what's good for science is good for the nation. This is surely true, in a general sense, but it is no longer completely persuasive as unfriendly members of Congress begin to look for conflicts of interest between the scientific community and the nation as a whole.

Conflicts of interest appear first in petty problems, such as those of accounting for federal grants to universities. But then they appear in graver problems, like the degree to which scientists as such should have a voice in policy decisions, or government should control the direction of research and the use of its results. The simple reassurance that science is bound to be good for you is not likely to be adequate, especially in view of the new potentialities for both good and evil of the biological and social, as well as the physical, sciences. Our popular worries about intercontinental missiles and radiation fallout, in which our alarm can be directed against an alien enemy, are bad enough. But to these worries we have added the fear that scientists are about to use chemistry to poison our crops and rivers, biology to meddle with our heredity, and psychology to manipulate our ideas and our personality.

So we are about to reach the point when both scientists and politicians begin to worry not merely about specific issues, but about the theoretical status of science in our political and constitutional system, and no longer rely on the assumption—which was acceptable enough to the general public when Dr. Bush presented his memorable report—that science and democracy are natural allies. Especially since some scientists have never believed it: some have been profoundly suspicious of the American version of democratic politics, rather preferring the status of science in the more conservative and traditional societies of Western Europe, and a few have been persuaded that science would prosper better under some form of socialism.

But most scientists, of course, like most politicians, have not thought very much about the problem at all. Indeed, any reasonable foreign observer would be obliged to conclude that we have socialized our science at best in a fit of absence of mind, and at worst with the purpose of subordinating it to the purposes of military power.

Accordingly, the scientific community and the United States generally are in even deeper trouble for their lack of a theory of the politics of science, than for their failure to solve practical problems of organization or policy. The nation that was born of the first effort in history to marry scientific and political ideas—the political heir of Franklin and Jefferson—is apt to speak of the relationship of science and politics with an air of apology; while throughout Asia and Africa the missionaries of Marxism teach the developing intelligentsia that the Communist system is the only approach to politics that is firmly grounded on the scientific method.

The clearest example of this contrast, as it has percolated down from the scholarly elite to the general public, may be found in science fiction. This is a form of literature unwisely neglected by students of politics. On something like the theory that if I could write a nation's songs I would be glad to let someone else write its laws, I am inclined to think that it is the space cadets of the comic strips—and their fictional counterparts back to Jules Verne or even Daedalus—who have fired our enthusiasm for the race with the Russians to the moon. That enthusiasm is certainly shared on both sides of the Iron Curtain. But with a difference, and a difference that may be more important to the future of our political system than the amount of money that we spend on space exploration.

The difference is that the Soviet space cadet, in sharp contrast to his opposite number in Western science fiction, seems to be very conscious not only that he is in a race for prestige or power with another country, but that he has discovered the key to the use of the scientific method in human affairs. This is the materialist dialectic, which is supposed not merely to let the Communist system make the best use of science in technical matters, but to give the scientific intellect a generally dominant role in the society of the future.

This notion began to appear in Soviet space fiction long before the first Sputnik. Forty years ago Aleksei Tolstoi, with some technical help from the pioneering rocket engineer Tsiolkovski, used a new propellant to put a heroic Red Army man on Mars, where he proceeded to help organize a proletarian revolution against a decadent Martian society.[2] More recently, it has become even clearer that the Soviet conquest of space will be a means of extending to the cosmos the spread of Marxist philosophy. Thus, as one space ship rushes through the void to its first meeting with beings from another solar system, the hero reassures his colleagues that sympathetic communication will surely be possible: "Thought, no matter where it is found, will inevitably be based on mathematical and dialectical logic." (Incidentally, the hero does not rely entirely on such spiritual comfort, for he goes on to issue tranquilizers to all hands on board.) And his comrade replies with a sententious expression of confidence that they will be congenial with the beings they are about to meet, since it is inevitable that on other worlds, as on the Earth, "humanity has been able to harness the forces of Nature on a cosmic scale only after reaching the highest stage of the communist society."[3]

In the West, of course, the science fiction hero is a good deal less sure that science is about to bring the cosmos to a state of perfection. As Isaac Asimov has noted, most contemporary science fiction in America is not utopian, but anti-utopian.[4] If the hero is not full of complexes from his infancy or frustrated by romantic difficulties, he is likely to be upset by the feeling that the social system in which he lives is not all it should be. The clear-eyed young hero in his space suit (like the clear-eyed cowboy or the earlier pioneers and pathfinders) is all too likely to be betrayed by selfishness or weakness in high places. Or in the more recent and more apocalyptic stories, the hero, if any, is likely to be struggling in a world that is about to be ruined, or has been ruined, by the inability of politicians to understand and control the powers released to mankind by modern science.[5]

A generation ago, the popular utopias were mainly in the tradition of Edward Bellamy's *Looking Backward,* which in turn was still in the tradition of Francis Bacon's *New Atlantis:* the world remade to the heart's desire by the rationalism and the power of science. But today, the few scientific utopias are not calculated to inspire much hope for humanity. Even a Marxist scientist like J. D. Bernal finds some of them repulsive because "a lack of freedom consequent on perfect organization" leads to a society in which the "Utopian seems, notwithstanding his health, beauty, and affability, to partake too much of the robot and the prig."[6] The anti-utopian theme, on the other hand, appears in serious pronouncements by scientists as well as in science fiction; even at meetings of scientific societies, speeches are likely to be made gloomily predicting disaster from our advance in scientific knowledge, and calling for a revival of something like traditional faith.[7]

And if the utopias have changed, so have the horror stories. A generation or two ago the traditional symbol of political oppression had not changed since before the days of Thomas Jefferson: it was the rack of the Inquisition. If you were brought up on *Westward Ho!* and Browning's dramatic monologues, to say nothing of Jefferson and Macaulay and later political historians in the liberal tradition, you were likely to believe that the main historic threat to human freedom had been averted from the English-speaking world by the defeat of the Armada, and destroyed in America by the disestablishment of the church in

Virginia. About all that was necessary to perfect the possibility of human freedom (one could learn from *Huckleberry Finn* or *Elmer Gantry*) was to destroy the last vestiges of enforced conformity in our society.

But within a few decades, the popular symbol of oppression had changed completely. The techniques of torture in *Westward Ho!* had been replaced by the more scientific methods of Orwell's *1984* or Zamyatin's *We*. A society founded on technology, rather than superstition, had become the most plausible system of tyranny.

The difference between the democratic and Communist camps in the popular attitude toward the political significance of science might be dismissed as the product of frivolous fiction if it did not also appear in the writings of eminent scientists. It is tempting to hope that the Soviet scientists are really dedicated only to their science, and eager to join in an international community with their Western colleagues. But it is hard to write off completely the official point of view, as expressed by Academician S. I. Vavilov, that Lenin had correctly comprehended the philosophical significance of science in general, and physics in particular, when he had "pointed out that the crisis in physics could be overcome by mastering the science of dialectical materialism. This provided a sure way for physics to surmount every kind of crisis and develop further." As a result, it is supposed to be the obligation of Soviet physicists to take the dialectic as their guide not only in their approach to politics and philosophy, but also to physics itself.[8]

In practice, all the evidence suggests that this has very little to do with the way physicists actually work in their laboratories; if they make a few rhetorical gestures in the direction of political orthodoxy in an introductory paragraph of a scientific paper, they can write as they please on scientific subjects.[9] But Marxist dialectic is still the orthodoxy; like other authoritarian orthodoxies, it cannot stamp out skepticism and cynicism, but it can stamp out open dissent.[10]

The scientists of democratic nations, even if they are ardent anti-Communists, take no such confident view of the role of science in their political systems. Some of this pessimism comes out when leading scientists take to science fiction as a medium. Fred Hoyle, the Cambridge University astronomer, has his hero in *The Black Cloud* sum up the British political system thus: "Politicians at the top, then the military, and the real brains at the bottom . . . We're living in a society that contains a monstrous contradiction, modern in its technology but archaic in its social organization . . . We [scientists] do the thinking for an archaic crowd of nitwits and allow ourselves to be pushed around by 'em in the bargain."[11] And the late Leo Szilard, University of Chicago physicist, seems to sum up his view of American politics when he has his delightful dolphins, who are surely the most engaging heroes in recent science fiction, tell why politicians fail to solve modern problems:

> Political issues were often complex, but they were rarely anywhere as deep as the scientific problems which had been solved . . . with amazing rapidity because they had been constantly exposed to discussion among scientists, and thus it appeared reasonable to expect that the solution of political problems could be greatly speeded up also if they were subjected to the *same kind* of discussion. The discussions of political problems by politicians were much less productive, because they differed in one important respect from the discussions of scientific problems by scientists: When a scientist says something, his colleagues must ask themselves only whether it is true. When a politician says something, his colleagues must first of all ask, "Why does he say it?"[12]

The same themes come out when scientists undertake to write explicitly about the relation of science to politics. The difference that Dr. Szilard's dolphins noted between science and politics is indeed a major difference, and one that could be a starting point for a political theory. Why, indeed, do politicians, unlike scientists, have to worry about the unstated purposes of another politician, or another government? But a great many scientists do not like to follow up on the implications of that question. It is more satisfying to argue that the straightforward scientific approach of the scientist should replace the devious and prejudiced ways of politicians, and to wonder whether the scientific revolution has indeed not made obsolete the institutions of modern democracy, or at least the present way in which they are organized and managed.

Thus a federal research administrator may complain of the scientists' lack of influence by comparison with lawyers and politicians, and argue that the federal government should have a Secretary of Science to mobilize the nation's scientific resources and coordinate all its policies from a scientific point of view.[13] Or a great German physicist and Nobel prize winner may summon his colleagues to international discussions of their difference in ideology, and to international cooperation to end the race in atomic armaments, arguing that they need to apply to politics the methods of thinking used successfully in physics—"to think out these problems, which have arisen out of our research, in our own simple realistic manner."[14] And one of his colleagues in those international discussions, Dr. Eugene Rabinowitch, poses the central problem directly: "The capacity of the democratic, representative systems of government to cope with the problems raised by the scientific revolution is in question."[15]

Dr. Szilard and Dr. Rabinowitch probably represent a distinct minority of American scientists, rather than the majority who are (or wish they were) consultants to corporations and members of Rotary Clubs, and who do not trouble their heads about political theory. But the question that this minority poses about the relation of representative government to the scientific revolution cannot be brushed off lightly. For the scientific revolution has changed not only the basic sciences themselves, but their consequent ability to produce new technology; it is this ability that has led to their new financial support by government, and changed the nature of military strategy and even of the economic and political system. It is accordingly very difficult, when speaking of the social effects of science, to distinguish it from technology; even those who keep accounts on government expenditures for research and development admit that the distinction they make between basic research and applied technology is not a precise boundary. (I will try later to distinguish the roles of science and technology a little more clearly, but at first I must discuss some of their joint effects.)

The relationship of the scientific and technological revolution to our system of representative government is a cogent question, both in its own right and because it has been raised with such urgency not only by those who seek to strengthen the political influence of scientists, but by others who are worried about the way in which such influence may be used.

During the early 1960's, it was a rare scientific meeting that failed to discuss two pronouncements on the relation of science to politics. The first was Sir Charles Snow's vivid story about the wartime rivalry of Tizard and Lindemann as scientific advisers to the British government. That "cautionary tale" warned us that democracy was in danger from the great gulf in understanding between the Two Cultures of science and the humanities, and from any possible monopoly on scientific advice to high political authority.[16] The second was the farewell address of President Eisenhower, warning the nation that its public policy might "become the captive of a scientific-technological elite."[17]

It is easy to appreciate why President Eisenhower felt as strongly as he did. His administration had started out to cut back on expenditures for research and development, but had ended by quadrupling them. This increase was by no means for defense alone; during his eight years in office the Congress multiplied the appropriations for the National Institutes of Health more than ninefold, giving them each year more than he had recommended. Science seemed clearly to be getting out of hand. It was almost enough to make one try to apply to the budgeting process the theory of Henry Adams that science, as it becomes more abstract, increases in geometrical progression the physical power that it produces.[18]

The President's statement was a great shock to the scientists, especially to those who had been working with the administration rather than criticizing it in the columns of the *Bulletin of the Atomic Scientists.* President Eisenhower, indeed, quickly explained that he was not talking about science in general, but only those parts allied with military and industrial power.[19] Nevertheless, to the typical American scientist who still believed that science had helped to liberate man from ancient tyrannies, it was disconcerting to be told by a conservative president that he had become a member of a new priesthood allied with military power.

Yet it had begun to seem evident to a great many administrators and politicians that science had become something very close to an *establishment,* in the old and proper sense of that word: a set of institutions supported by tax funds, but largely on faith, and without direct responsibility to political control. The terms under which this support is now given to science do not seem to many politicians to fit into the traditional ideas of Jeffersonian democracy.

From the point of view of scientists and university administrators, on the other hand, the growing dependence of science on government brings a great many problems, especially the danger of increasing government control over universities. It is hard to turn money down, but more and more scientific spokesmen are beginning to worry about the conditions that come with it.[20] From the point of view of government, the sentiment in Congress now seems to be considerably more critical of the terms on which money is provided for scientific research. Edward Gibbon summed up the cynical eighteenth-century attitude toward a religious establishment by remarking that all religions were "considered by the people, as equally true; by the philosopher, as equally false; and by the magistrate, as equally useful."[21] And now, it seems that all sciences are considered by their professors, as equally significant; by the politicians, as equally incomprehensible; and by the military, as equally expensive.

So we are beginning to observe in the Congressional attitude toward science some of the symptoms of friction between an establishment and a secular government. The symptoms showed up, for example, in Congressman L. H. Fountain's investigations of the National Institutes of Health, wherein he sought reform by uncovering abuses in the administration of the cloistered but tax-supported laboratories. And they showed up in Congressman Wright Patman's attacks on the tax-exempt foundations—institutions which by a modern kind of *mortmain* give science a range of political initiative outside the control of politics.

These attacks do not get at the main issues. They have so far been only a minor nuisance to scientific institutions, with an effect measured mainly in the time taken to fill out accounting forms. But they are a threat because they may reflect a more fundamental uneasiness in the intellectual as well as the political world. This is an uneasiness not merely about the terms of the financial relationship between government and science, but about the question whether the growing influence of science can be kept compatible with representative government. It is, in short, the same question asked by Dr. Rabinowitch—can democratic government cope with problems raised by the scientific revolution?—but from the opposite point of view.

These attitudes, as yet, may have very little to do with the way most American scientists think, either on or off duty, and practically nothing to do with the amount of money their laboratories get in government grants. They are only a small cloud on the intellectual and political horizon of the United States. But they correspond to a much greater intellectual disturbance, over the past century and a half, in Europe, where the political faith in the alliance of science and reason with free government that was characteristic of the Enlightenment gave way in the late nineteenth century to various forms of scholarly despair. In America, a faith in the political rationalism of the Enlightenment tended to persist in the political thinking of scientists, even after the depression shook their confidence in the inevitability of progress. Right up to the present, American scientists have shown singularly little interest in either the conservative political theorists who tell them that scientists cannot deal with basic values or solve the major human problems, or the radical theorists who tell them that science can do so if it will only join in a political system, like Marxism, that will give it real power over society.[22]

Even the strongest critics of the government and its scientific policies—for example, many of the contributors to the *Bulletin of the Atomic Scientists*—are surprisingly traditional in their approach to the political system. They may question the capacity of our representative institutions to cope with the scientific revolution, but they tend to propose as remedies more international good will and cooperation, adequate scientific education of political leaders and the electorate, and unbiased scientific advice for members of Congress.

It is hard to quarrel with any of these ideas. But they are a little like the remedy that was most often proposed for corruption in government during the late nineteenth century: more good men should go into politics. That exhortation surely did some good, but probably less than the effort to adjust our political and economic institutions to the realities of the industrial revolution. That adjustment required a great many changes, by Congress and the judiciary and administrators, but it did not follow the prescriptions of any of the single-minded political prophets. It came instead from a new way of looking at the problem: we gave up thinking about politics merely in terms of the formal Constitutional system, which had been based on an analogy with Newtonian thought—a mechanistic system of checks and balances. In the latter part of the nineteenth century, students of politics (if they had not given up their interest in science) might have noted with interest a new analogy: as science penetrated the structure of the molecule, and identified its elements, politicians were becoming preoccupied with the elements of politics—with parties and economic classes and pressure groups—as well as its mechanistic Constitutional balances.

The scientific revolution in nuclear physics and in such fields as genetics is carrying us into a third stage of complexity. That revolution seems certain to have a more radical effect on our political institutions than did the industrial revolution, for a good many reasons. Let us note three of them.

1. *The scientific revolution is moving the public and private sectors closer together.*

During the industrial revolution, the most dynamic economic interests were more or less independent of the political system. They might depend on it, as many American corporations did by relying on tariff protection, and they might try with some success to control it, but they were not incorporated into its administrative system, they did not receive support from taxation, and the main directions of their new enterprise were controlled by their owners and managers. Today, our national policy assumes that a great deal of our new enterprise is likely to follow from technological developments financed by the government and directed in response to government policy; and many of our most dynamic industries are largely or entirely dependent on doing business with the government through a subordinate relationship that has little resemblance to the traditional market economy.

2. *The scientific revolution is bringing a new order of complexity into the administration of public affairs.*

The industrial revolution brought its complexities, and relied heavily on new forms of expertise, but it did not challenge the assumption that the owner or manager, even without scientific knowledge, was able to control the policies of a business. And the same general belief was fundamental to our governmental system: the key ideas, if not the lesser details, could be understood by the legislature and debated before the public, and thus controlled by a chain of public responsibility. In one sense this was never true; in another and more fundamental sense, I think it is still true. But it is much less apparently true today than it was, and a great many more people doubt it. The great issues of

15

1. lest govt. research institutes. 2. Govt. Corpor.
3. Govt. expand. (public sector)

life and death, many people fear, are now so technically abstruse that they must be decided in secret by the few who have the ability to understand their scientific complexities. We were already worrying about the alleged predominance of the executive over the legislature; now we worry lest even our elected executives cannot really understand what they are doing, lest they are only a façade that conceals the power of the scientists—many of whom are not even full-time officials, but have a primary loyalty to some university or corporation—who really control the decisions. If (as I believe) this is not really true, it is nevertheless true that the scientific revolution has upset our popular ideas about the way in which policies are initiated and adopted, and in which politicians can control them and be held responsible for them. We have to reconsider our basic ideas about the processes of political responsibility.

3. *The scientific revolution is upsetting our system of checks and balances.*

From a moral or ethical point of view, the industrial revolution raised problems that were relatively simple. Everyone admitted that it was possible for economic interests to control politics, but the remedy seemed to be clear: regulate business to prevent abuses, and keep selfish business interests out of the political process. This seemed clearly the basic formula for dealing with the obvious conflict of the public interest with the special interests of business. And the formula of separation of business and government was analogous in a comforting way to the formula for the separation of church and state. A church that was not dependent on government support was able to provide an independent source of moral judgment which could help to control the ethical standards of our politics and our business. As the problems began to seem a bit complex for unaided theological opinion, the universities began to provide an additional source of more scientific, but equally independent, advice to the public on the basic value judgments that should govern our policies. This was the fundamental system of checks and balances within our society: the check on practical political affairs imposed by sources of utterly independent criticism, based on a system of values that was not corrupted by the political competition for wealth or power.

But the scientific revolution seems to threaten to destroy this safeguard in two ways: First, it has gradually weakened the moral authority of religious institutions by the critical skepticism that it has made predominant in Western intellectual life, most notably in the universities. Second, it has made the universities themselves financially dependent on government, and involved them deeply in the political process. Thus, after helping to disestablish churches and free most universities from ecclesiastical control, science has now made those universities dependent on a new form of establishment, in the guise of government grants, and allied them more closely with a military power that is capable of unlimited destruction.

These three developments make some of our traditional reactions—our automatic political reflexes—unreliable in dealing with our present problems. We are automatically against socialism, but we do not know how to deal with an extension of governmental power over the economy that technically leaves ownership in private hands. It is almost an instinct with us to distrust the political bosses who, by controlling the votes of the ignorant masses, seek personal profit or power without accepting official responsibility. But we do not know how to deal with irresponsible influence that comes from status in the highest sanhedrin of science, untainted by any desire for personal profit. And we are fanatically against the public support of any institutions that might impose religious values on public policy, but when the institutions of organized skepticism tell us what science believes or how much money science needs, we have no reliable procedure for questioning their infallibility, or even for criticizing their budgets.

Science has thus given our political evolution a reverse twist.

problem of Medieval estate.

The Scientific Estate

It has brought us back to a set of political problems that we thought we had disposed of forever by simple Constitutional principles. These are the problems of dealing not only with territorial subdivisions of government, and not only with economic interests and classes, but also with various groups of citizens which are separated from each other by very different types of education and ways of thinking and sets of ideals. This was the problem of the medieval estates.

The three estates of the realm, whose customary privileges grew into constitutional functions, were the clergy, the nobility, and the burgesses—those who taught, those who fought, and those who bought and sold. In our impatience with privilege at the time of the American Revolution, we abolished the estates in our political system so thoroughly that we have almost forgotten what the word meant. To abolish the first estate, we disestablished the church and provided secular education through local governments. To abolish the second, we forbade titles of nobility, made the military subordinate to civil authority, and relied on a popular militia rather than a standing army. To abolish the third, we did away with property qualifications on voting and exalted freedom of contract and competition above legislative interference.

But now the results of scientific advance have been to require federal support of education and the appropriation of a tithe of the federal budget for research and development, to set up the most powerful and professional military force in history, and to make free competition a minor factor in the relationship to government of some of the major segments of the economy.

Thus we are left to face the second half of the problem which we were afraid to face during the depression, and tried to escape at the end of the Second World War: the necessity for discovering a new basis for relating our science to our political purposes. We learned half of our lesson from the scientists: the lesson that we could not have a first-rate scientific establishment if we did not understand that first-rate science depended on fundamental theoretical work and required the support of basic

| 18

tithe

research for its own sake, and not merely as a by-product of applied science. Now the outlines of the second, or political, half of our problem are becoming more clear. Basic science as such became steadily more powerful as it freed itself from the constraints of values and purposes. As an institution in society, it had to free itself in an analogous way from subordination to the applied purposes of the industrial corporation or the government bureau or the military service. And in the unpredictability of its progress it challenges the old notion that in matters of public policy the scientist must be controlled completely by purposes defined by politicians. So we must face the possibility that science will no longer serve as a docile instrument toward purposes that are implicit in a system of automatic economic progress, or even toward purposes that are defined for scientists by business and political leaders. In short, we can no longer take it for granted that scientists will be "on tap but not on top."

Accordingly, we need to consider not only the practical relation of scientific institutions to the economy and the government, but also the theoretical relation of science to political values, and to the principles that are the foundation of the constitutional system. Only with the help of scientists can we deal with the great issues of war and peace, of the population explosion and its effects in the underdeveloped countries, or of the dangers to our environment from our technological advances not only in weaponry but also in civilian industry and agriculture. But before we are likely, as a nation, to let science help us solve such problems, we are sure to want to know the full terms of the bargain. For although some of the political reflexes that we have acquired by several centuries of constitutional experience may be out of date, one of the most automatic is still useful: we want to know not only whether some political pronouncement is true, but why the speaker said it, having a healthy suspicion that we need to know whose interests it would further, and what its effect would be on our capacity to govern ourselves, or at least to hold our governors responsible.

The scientific community in the United States is not an organ-

19

ized institution, or a group with definite boundaries. It is not a hierarchical establishment. But its existence as a loosely defined estate with a special function in our constitutional system is becoming apparent, and we would do well to assess its political significance.[23] If we do, we may find that a deeper understanding of the basic relation of science to government will help us to give it the kind of support it needs for its own purposes, as well as use it more effectively for the practical ends of public policy. And if we are willing to renounce the utopian hope that science will solve our problems for us, we may find that science by its very nature is more congenial to the development of free political institutions than our anti-utopian prophets would have us believe.

CHAPTER 2

The Fusion of Economic
and Political Power

IF SOME HISTORIAN a hundred years hence is interested in tracing the influence of science on the complex of economic and political power in the United States of the twentieth century, he may well single out Congressman "Tip" O'Neill as the hero of a turning point in history. For in January 1963 Thomas P. O'Neill, United States Representative from Cambridge, Massachusetts, demanded that an executive agency *not* offer jobs to his constituents.

Congressman O'Neill may have been the first member of Congress in history to make such a demand. But he was not violating the traditions of Massachusetts Democracy by refusing patronage for his area. The jobs were about to be offered, as a matter of fact, by the National Aeronautics and Space Administration in Washington to scientists and engineers on a strictly merit and nonpartisan basis. He was objecting because he had been persuaded, as a matter of applied economics and practical politics, that the presence of large numbers of scientists and engineers in his area would attract additional business and more government contracts. If he turned down Washington jobs on behalf of his constituents, it was because he was interested in a far more substantial form of patronage: contracts in Boston for industrial corporations and universities.[1]

We may well reflect on this incident if we wish to understand what the development of science is doing to our system of political responsibility in general and to the relation between economic and political power in particular.

When Congressman O'Neill made his protest to NASA, he was merely translating into political action what the economists had been writing for a decade or more. Throughout the nineteen-fifties more and more economists had begun to be impressed by the contribution that technological advances were making, along with capital investment, to the processes of economic growth.[2] More recently, this idea has become a part of official policy. The Secretary of Commerce, on the same day that Congressman O'Neill was letting the Boston press know that he had repelled the NASA invasion, was telling the Chamber of Commerce of the United States that research and development were "the lever of rising living standards and economic growth," and proposing a new program for federal aid to civilian technology.[3] Within the week President Kennedy, in a message to Congress on education, based his proposal for the development of new centers of graduate instruction and research on the belief that "new industries increasingly gravitate to or are innovated by strong centers of learning and research."[4]

With these ideas in the air, there were plenty of politicians who shared Congressman O'Neill's interest in the government's scientific and technological programs. For example, Lyndon B. Johnson, then Vice President, chose to make the exploration of outer space his main political interest, and as chairman of the Space Council assured Texas that the new space center at Houston was only the beginning of a series of technological advances that would let the Southwest take the lead in the nation's economic development.[5] Senator Clinton P. Anderson of New Mexico resigned the chairmanship of the Senate Committee on Interior and Insular Affairs, which was once the highest ambition of any Western Senator because of its influence over irrigation and grazing and mining programs, to become chairman of the Committee on Aeronautical and Space Sciences.[6] And state governors got aboard the technological bandwagon; the governments of New York and California established special official delegations in Washington to help their states' industries

| 22

problem of
geog. economy here.
" axe to grind "

get government contracts, and the governors of New York, Ohio, Illinois, Wisconsin, Georgia, Oklahoma and other states began to talk of the creation of new centers of scientific research as an inducement to the location of new industry. "Simply in terms of our own economic self-interest," the Republican governor of Ohio told the annual Governors' Conference, "our only proper course is to increase our investment in science, technology and research just as fast as we can—to a limit not yet known."[7]

Though many businessmen continued in principle to disapprove of federal grants, in practice most of them agreed with the chairman of the Area Development Committee of the Committee for Economic Development, Walter H. Wheeler, Jr., who undertook to persuade his business associates that they could no longer depend on privately financed laboratories for the advancement of productivity and economic growth. He said it was therefore important for each region to "have its full share of government research contracts."[8] Acting on the same idea, many businessmen in regions formerly weak in advanced research have been engaged in building up institutional programs for the advancement of science, such as Oklahoma's "Moving Frontiers of Science" program and the Graduate Research Center of the Southwest at Dallas.

Some still see this new involvement of science and technology in our economic and political systems from the traditional point of view of the conservative businessman or the laissez-faire economist: from this point of view, these new developments are part of the corrupting influence of politics, which is leading us toward socialism. There are also those who have another reason for deploring the unprecedented federal support of private corporations: they see it as evidence of political reaction, in which private interests benefit at the expense of the government. But some of these new programs of government subsidy for science are different in their political significance from government subsidies for the dredging of harbors, or the building of roads, or the advancement of particular industries, or the reclamation of

23

desert lands. This means that science is beginning to alter the basic relation of political and economic power, at least in certain important segments of our economy, and that the direction of this new development cannot be plotted in terms of the traditional dimensions of conservatism and radicalism.

THE BREAKDOWN OF BOUNDARIES

The United States Constitution was drafted in the period of the Enlightenment. The political ideas that shaped that document were influenced in part by the English legal tradition; in part by political theorists like Locke; in part, of course, by practical circumstances like geography and the nature of economic interests; but in part too by the new scientific ideas of the age. It may have been only by crude analogy, but some of the Founding Fathers were certainly conscious of the correspondence between their proposed system of constitutional checks and balances and Sir Isaac Newton's system of mechanics, in which the universe was held together and kept in order by a balance of counteracting forces set in motion by a Prime Mover, but working endlessly thereafter by a sequence of cause and effect.[9]

At the same time, the most influential among the framers of the Constitution had a very realistic appreciation of the fact that the political forces that had to be kept in balance were largely economic in their origin, and the different political ideas of the period grew out of different views of the kind of economic system that was desired. Jefferson and his followers, preferring a homogeneous agricultural society, had a different notion of checks and balances from that of Adams or Hamilton, who wanted constitutional powers distributed so as to protect the interests of the several "orders" of men in a nation devoted to commerce and industry.[10] But they all hoped that a proper constitutional mechanism would maintain a balance between private economic interests and the various branches and levels of government. And the notion began to grow that the system would work automatically and guarantee permanent economic progress, provided the politicians realized they were merely Prime Movers. That is, they were supposed to establish the Constitution, guaranteeing the rights of property and contract, and then refrain from meddling with the economy, so that the forces of the market could maintain a balance as automatic as that of universal gravitation.[11]

This analogy between the physics and the politics of the late eighteenth century may have some substantial meaning, or it may be only one of those superficial similarities in style between different aspects of the culture of an age that tantalize the intellectual historian. But even if it is only a superficial analogy, it is interesting to note a similar analogy in the development of science and politics since that time. It can be summed up best by looking at the way men manage their careers in the two fields.

In the late eighteenth century, Mr. Jefferson was at the same time an engineer and a meteorologist and a paleontologist and an agronomist, and several other things besides. He was able to maintain an active interest in all of these fields, and attain a certain amount of distinction in all of them. Nevertheless, it would never have occurred to him to think that they were not separate fields of knowledge. In France, of course, a Laplace might assert that all phenomena were governed by the same system of universal mechanics, but in both science and politics everyone knew that the French carried the process of abstract reasoning to unreasonable extremes.

Similarly, George Washington during his lifetime had great agricultural and business interests, and a role in local government, and a military career, and a role in national political affairs. He would, however, certainly have assumed that these several categories of activity not only called for quite different types of skills, but involved quite distinct interests, and ought to continue to do so.

Obviously the boundaries between these several aspects of public affairs have been blurring, if not breaking down entirely, during the past century and a half. Industrialism and the Civil

War unified our national governmental interests and destroyed Jefferson's hope that an agrarian society could maintain the independence of state and local governments. More recently, the boundaries between the interests of government and business have been breaking down, and (this is even more shocking to those concerned) between government and the universities.

To the surprise of those who identify the progress of science with endless specialization, an analogous process has been going on in the sciences. Science has indeed continued to specialize at an accelerating rate; scientific societies are continually dividing and subdividing to take care of the special interests of their members. But in their basic concepts or techniques they are growing more and more together. It is not always easy to tell a biologist from a physicist by the work he does; either one is likely to turn out as a biophysicist before he is through. The disciplines, of course, have differences but the boundaries between them are no longer so clear and the interconnections between them are now just about as important as their peculiar interests.

The layman notices one result of the breakdown of the boundaries between sciences as he hears of the practical jobs they work on together. When it comes to space travel, for example, the astronomer's domain is invaded not only by the various kinds of astronautical engineers, but by the astrobiologist and the astropsychologist—at any rate the National Aeronautics and Space Administration is now spending quite a lot of money for applied research in the biological and social sciences.

But, to the scientist, the more important manifestation is that the inner workings of the basic sciences are becoming almost indistinguishable. The many interconnections in their concepts and techniques began to emerge when they went beyond their interest in merely describing and classifying their several types of phenomena and explored the basic processes that affect those phenomena—in short, when they became more abstract and got down to fundamentals.[12] The breakdown of boundaries has taken place in an even more spectacular way between the basic sci-

26

ences and engineering; for the "applied" fields have tried to base themselves more firmly on fundamental science—to reach beyond practical experience into a common set of scientific principles.

So if Mr. Jefferson were alive today, the progressive specialization of the sciences would probably oblige him, in the interest of his scientific career, to decide to be either a paleontologist or a meteorologist or an engineer or an agronomist, and not to try to be all at once. But no matter which he chose to be, he would find that all of these sciences were drawing much more on a fundamental set of operational concepts and techniques than they had a century or two before. Similarly if General Washington were alive today he would be under a little more pressure, at least at any particular time, to concentrate on being either a general or a businessman or an engineer or a political leader. But he would find that in the actual things he did, any role today would be much more like the others than in the old days when he might play all the roles at once. As a general, he would today be not on a horse in the field, but in the Pentagon politicking with the Congress, and planning a research and development program with the engineers, and making sure with the businessmen that he had an effective industrial base for his weapons procurement program.

This is not to say, of course, that in the days of General Washington there were no connections between the interests of the army, the merchants, the engineers, and the politicians. Obviously there were, and the Founding Fathers were keenly aware of them. But to the extent that a man chose to stay within one of those occupational fields, the work that he did and the skills that he used bore comparatively little resemblance to those of the other fields. Today, the higher a man rises in any of these fields, the more his work begins to resemble the work done in the others, much as the scientists and engineers who come closest to talking a common language across disciplinary boundaries are those who are the most advanced in their specialized disciplines.

There is an effective connection between the gradual breaking down of the boundaries in the sciences and that of the boundaries between government and private institutions. It is not a mere accidental analogy. This study is concerned with science and its economic and political influences, and if it undertakes to describe some of those influences it may seem to claim that science alone has caused everything important that has happened in the modern world. A strong disavowal is in order: social problems are too complex ever to be explained so simply. But I think there is no doubt that the changes within science have helped to push the changes in the political economy, in ways that may escape our attention either because they are almost too obvious to be noticed, or because they do not conform to our conventional notion of science as a process of endless specialization.

SCIENCE AND ENGINEERING

The first thing to emphasize is that the main change in science over the past century or two has been the change in the direction of greater abstraction. The scientist deals less and less with the specific objects of everyday experience, in all their complicated and concrete reality; he is more interested in their abstract qualities that can be measured and related in new ways to other abstractions. The layman can appreciate this idea, and its practical consequences, by looking at the history of scientific associations. We started in the United States with the American Philosophical Society; it was a comprehensive association, but there was comparatively little to comprehend, either in the content of knowledge or the number of scientists. Indeed the word "scientist" had not yet been invented, and science itself was still considered a subordinate branch of philosophy, as the Society's name suggested—even though the Society took an active interest in very mundane projects like how to clear smoky chimneys or improve ships' pumps.

A few generations later, the greatest activity was in the specialized organizations of scientists with something to contribute to our national economic development, especially the geologists, who were helping to explore our mineral resources, and the naturalists, interested in our biological resources. These were sciences that did their work by observing and classifying types of minerals and plants and animals, and then proceeding to experiment with them. They shared a general approach to scholarship; they were interested in dealing with the material world by observation and experiment, and not in the classical arts or literature or history. But the geologist did not have much to contribute to the study of zoology, or vice versa. And when the associations of geologists and naturalists merged in 1848 to found the American Association for the Advancement of Science, it was more in the nature of a defensive alliance within the academic world than a merger of interests.

If we then jump ahead a few more generations, from the mid-nineteenth to the twentieth century, we find the leading influence within the sciences in quite different hands. The chemists, by getting inside the molecule and discovering the processes by which elements combine with each other, laid the basis for fundamental changes in industry. The geologists could discover new mineral deposits, but the work of the chemists made radical advances in their industrial exploitation. The individual prospector and the small mine owner, selling his products on the general market to small manufacturers, could (with the help of the U.S. Geological Survey) do business within a laissez-faire competitive economy and a governmental system devised for an agrarian society. But that day was done after the chemists brought us into a technological era in which you could not tell, when you mined coal or pumped oil, whether it might be used most profitably as fuel or as the raw material for the manufacture of nylon stockings or ammunition, and you could take advantage of such opportunities only by operating on a scale adequate to support a considerable laboratory.

This is not to say that the growth of great corporations was initially caused by advances in pure science. But most of them were dependent on some kind of technology, which came to be dependent on science for its continued improvements. The great competitive advantage of the industrial corporation over the small businessman was often based on its ability to support a new technology which was being developed, even if it had not been created, by a more abstract science. This kind of science did not stop with observation and classification, or the improvement of the practical man's techniques, but went on to use analytical and experimental methods to create new and unforeseen products, which only a great corporation could have the versatility to exploit.

It therefore followed that the dominant form of industrial organization became the giant corporation, large enough to support the research to provide it with a range of products that were either entirely new or were improved in ways that the routine engineer could not have foreseen. And it followed, too, that the most powerful scientific association of the period between the two world wars was the American Chemical Society, having an extensive membership from industry as well as from universities.

The next step, of course, came with the increasingly abstract and mathematical concepts of physics, which led scientists into the nucleus of the atom. The result was not merely to release physical forces many times as powerful as those which the chemists had been able to produce, but to create *political* energies of a comparable degree of superiority over anything imagined before. Within the scientific world, the lesson was rapidly learned. The several societies of physicists, which were intimate clubs of theoretical academicians before World War II, began to find that their members had moved into positions of managerial importance in a great academic-industrial complex, and were deeply involved in the affairs of government. More important, the abstract concepts of physics and mathematics began to pervade the other sciences; chemistry and geology began to use the techniques of physics, and to insist that their people be trained in its more fundamental and apparently less practical ways of thinking.

Consequently, even politicians who did not pretend to understand the inner workings of science became persuaded that the real magic lay in the more theoretical approach. They accepted the idea that it was worth investing large amounts of government money in the support of research without having the slightest idea of its practical purpose. It was enough to know that this was the approach that had been getting the most powerful results, and at a rate of speed that was accelerating so rapidly that, like the Red Queen, we had to keep on running faster and faster in order even to stand still. The stakes had become too high, in this gamble for more and more physical power, for anyone to ante up except the national government. The progressive abstraction of the sciences had not only broken down the boundaries between the several disciplines, but had involved first industry and then government in their support and in the application of their results—and finally had obliged industry and government to merge their interests.

This process has, of course, depended on advances in engineering as well as science. The recent history of our major engineering schools makes plain the extent to which the old boundary between science and engineering has broken down. The practical problem of these schools has been to adapt themselves to the new velocity of scientific change. Since "the useful life of technical information has become so much shorter than the professional lifetime of an individual," the engineering school has to teach the engineer not how to do a particular kind of job, but how to keep up with the effects on his field of the advancement of science. It was the failure of engineering schools to appreciate this fact, a committee for the study of engineering education reported to the president of Yale University in 1961, that made them lose undergraduate students to courses in science and mathematics: "The intelligent student has not failed to notice that, in the professional world, it has been much easier for the scientist to convert himself into an engineer than for the trained engineer to master the new science required for a dynamic technology."[13]

If intelligent students noticed that fact, it was because their elders had observed it under the dramatic conditions of the Second World War. Karl T. Compton went back to the Massachusetts Institute of Technology, James B. Conant went back to Harvard, and Lee A. DuBridge became president of the California Institute of Technology after service in the Office of Scientific Research and Development. In that agency it was plain that the most conspicuous advances in weapons technology—on the atomic bomb, on radar, and all the rest—came from the work of young men trained in the basic sciences. As a result, the leading engineering schools began to convert their curricula to give a greater emphasis to abstract science and less to applied techniques. As C. Richard Soderberg, Dean of the School of Engineering at M.I.T., summed it up in 1959, it was once possible to train engineers how to build things by teaching them the current practice, but "when an engineer sets out to build something today, he frequently builds something . . . never built before." It used to be possible to let an engineer think that what he "learned in school would remain valid during his entire professional life." But engineering today must assume that the basic sciences will make obsolete in a very short time any specific practical skills. The engineer, therefore, has to be trained in those basic sciences which will give him the greatest degree of "competence in facing the unknown future."[14]

But the M.I.T. dean went even further. This competence must run beyond the boundaries of the natural sciences alone. For the engineer is becoming "the efficient cause of rapid change in the economic, social, and cultural environment that has been built on technology." This carries us a step further than what was accomplished in the late nineteenth century by the industrial corporation's systematic support of research. The greatest invention of nineteenth-century Germany, as A. N. Whitehead noted,[15] was that of the method of invention itself: how to organize a research program with the deliberate purpose of inventing new products and techniques for a particular industry. But what the great engineering schools of today are interested in is a more ambitious business; they are learning the techniques of what the M.I.T. dean called "the organized forcing of development change," the economic and managerial arrangements that may lead to a continued increase in the velocity of technical and social change within society as a whole.

As soon as engineering came to be a profession based more on the fundamental sciences than on the routine applied techniques of particular industries, a major change was sure to take place in the relation of that profession to industry. The velocity in the advancement of science and the unpredictability of its direction, to say nothing of its increasing expense, made it poor strategy to tie the engineering profession to the coat tails of business alone. The old arrangement was for a corporation to hire a development engineer; it got its money back by having the patent rights to anything he invented. He worked, accordingly, along lines dictated by the company's requirements. This is still a very common arrangement, but not the one that is growing in influence. What more and more engineers now think about is not how to improve the efficiency of present products, or even to create new products, but how to develop new markets and new industries.

In some of the large and technologically advanced industries, patents are no longer the principal way of maintaining a lead over the competition. At any rate, they are merely defensive tactics, which are becoming less important as technological change becomes more rapid and unpredictable. The important thing is to keep on the aggressive with an ample supply of scientific talent, and to be able to follow where its new developments lead. So we see in various sectors of industry a good many corporations spring up and flourish with very little capital other than the knowledge and talents of a group of scientists and engineers; property may be becoming a less influential form of capital than brains. This statement does not mean much for the purposes of econometrics, for, although you can measure capital in dollars, and buy it and sell it, brains are not so easy to deal with. A Ph.D. is not a very precise unit of measurement, and you cannot buy scientists or sell them, even though a number of defense industries do their best to stockpile them at government expense.

SCIENCE AND PRIVATE PROPERTY

Within a decade after the Second World War ended, economists were beginning to call the attention of politicians to the role of research and development in economic growth. Thus Alvin H. Hansen, who had been known during the depression as a leading advocate of deficit financing, told the Congressional Joint Committee on the Economic Report in 1955 that scientific research and invention provided a more important basis for long-term growth than capital accumulation.[16] And Sumner H. Slichter told a National Science Foundation conference in 1958 that research, by creating new competitive products and new industries, was preventing the stagnation of the economy, the stratification of society, and the emergence of the class struggle predicted by Marx and his followers.[17] From a more conservative point of view, Dexter M. Keezer, vice-president of McGraw-Hill Publishing Company, told the same conference that McGraw-Hill had concluded that "what goes on in research and development has a key bearing on what is going to go on later in the field of business investment," and had accordingly begun to make annual surveys of research programs, as a guide to business predictions.[18]

The technological advances that are forcing economic growth and social change are certainly not all the result of basic scientific research by men with Ph.D. degrees. Until a half-century or quarter-century ago, most development engineering was done by the self-trained inventor, or the operating man interested in product improvement. But the significant point is that some of the most rapidly developing industries have been those allied with the most rapid advances in the abstract sciences, and this lesson has not been lost on the others.

Nevertheless, no matter how much a businessman may believe that science is really an endless frontier, he has to ask himself not only whether a research program would help the country but whether it would provide returns for his stockholders. It costs a lot more money to keep up a research laboratory than to employ a few engineers on routine product improvement. There is something like a critical economic mass—a minimum size below which it is hard to maintain an effective laboratory. This is big enough to keep the smaller firms out of the competition. Then, too, the inherent uncertainty of research comes into the picture. Most manufacturing firms have to have some kind of engineering or product improvement laboratories, and many can support work for the development of specific products. But if we are talking about fundamental research, of the kind that may lead to radically new and unexpected developments, very few companies can afford it, both because it costs a lot of money and because no one can say whether what comes out will be of any benefit to their particular products or whether they can maintain exclusive control over its benefits. As a result, it is mainly the industrial giants with a wide range of products, like Du Pont or General Electric, or firms with a near monopoly in a given field, like Bell Telephone, that can afford to keep up substantial basic research programs at their own expense.

And here, of course, is where government comes in. The federal government, by 1963, was paying for nearly three fifths of the more than twelve billion dollars spent annually for industry for research and development. The amount spent by industry for research and development out of its own funds doubled between 1953 and 1960, but the amount of research and development it actually conducted nearly tripled, for during these eight years industry's use of federal funds for these purposes went up more than fourfold. Industry, in short, was during the Eisenhower administration accelerating its reliance on federal research funds, and the process slowed down only a little during the Kennedy administration.[19]

Some impression of the magnitude of the expense involved may be given by the testimony in 1962 of the Defense Department comptroller, Charles J. Hitch, who told the House Committee on Government Operations that there were then under development seventeen weapons systems big enough to cost over a billion dollars.[20] All this would have very little effect on the internal structure and operations of business if these government funds were purchasing items that could be specified in advance, like shoes or rifles. But the key point here is uncertainty, requiring continual collaboration between the government officials and the corporate executives.

Very few complex systems are ultimately developed along the lines laid down at the beginning; for example, more than half the aircraft developed since the Second World War were finally built with engines quite different from those originally planned for them.[21] Some idea of the extent of uncertainty was suggested in the same testimony by Mr. Hitch, who remarked that "about 40 percent of our total development appropriations are going into the funding of cost overruns,"[22] that is, into expenditures beyond the amount originally planned. About 60 percent of the contracts, in any case, are not fixed-price contracts, since neither the government nor the corporation can even pretend in legal form that it knows just what is to be done and what it should cost, and formally advertised competitive bidding has become the exception rather than the rule.[23] The very uncertainty of the research and development process requires the government and business to work out a joint arrangement for the planning and conduct of their programs; the relationship is more like the administrative relationship between an industrial corporation and its subsidiary than the traditional relationship of buyer and seller in a free market.

Although this system is a part of a much older stream of political and constitutional development (see next chapter), its immediate origins were in the weapons research programs of the Second World War. In the Office of Scientific Research and Development, and in the atomic energy program that grew out of that office and was carried through by the Manhattan District of the Army Engineers, the basic operating system was one of enlisting industrial corporations and universities in the war effort under contractual arrangements, rather than setting up a centralized system of military laboratories.

The outlines of the postwar development, which in the main continued the wartime pattern, are well known. Through a continuation of this system of administering research and development programs by grant or contract, the Atomic Energy Commission, which was hailed by the draftsmen of the Atomic Energy Act as a triumph of socialism,[24] supports a program in which some nine tenths of the employees work for private corporations. The adamant arguments of many scientific leaders of the 1930's against federal support of science now seem as ancient and irrelevant as debates over infralapsarianism or supralapsarianism; no major university today could carry on its research program without federal money. The Massachusetts Institute of Technology, California Institute of Technology, Chicago, and Johns Hopkins, of course, all administer special military or atomic energy programs and consequently draw from three fifths to five sixths of their budgets from government. Harvard, Yale, and Princeton now get a larger proportion of their operating revenues from federal funds than do land-grant colleges like Illinois, Iowa State, and North Carolina.[25]

In dollar volume, the biggest contracts are between the military services and industrial corporations. Though most of this money goes for procurement, much of it goes for research and development, and for the systems analysis and the direction and supervision of subcontractors that in a simpler age would have been done by the technical services of the Army and Navy. And even in the business of procurement, the contractual relation is not the traditional market affair: the contract is not let on competitive bids, the product cannot be specified, the price is not fixed, the government supplies much of the plant and capital, and the government may determine or approve the letting of subcontracts, the salaries of key executives, and a host of other managerial matters. A sizable proportion of the government's (and nation's) business is done this way; each of five industrial corporations spends more than a billion dollars a year from federal taxes—which is more than any one of five of the executive departments.[26]

In the industries in which this process has gone furthest, such as aircraft and electronics, the result is a striking change in the internal composition of their production systems. As the Bureau of the Budget pointed out in "Government Contracting for Research and Development," a study made for the President in 1962, the older industries were organized on mass production principles and used large numbers of production workers, but "the newer ones show roughly a one-to-one ratio between production workers and scientist-engineers." Between 1954 and 1959, the number of scientists and engineers in the aircraft industry went up by 96 percent while the number of production workers went down by 17 percent. This is the industry in which the corporation least dependent on government business had less than a third of its sales to nonmilitary buyers, and the Martin Company had less than one percent.[27]

These developments led the Bureau of the Budget to ask in the same report, "In what sense is a business corporation doing nearly 100 percent of its business with the Government engaged in 'free enterprise'?" and to note that "the developments of recent years have inevitably blurred the traditional dividing lines between the public and private sectors of our Nation." The House Committee on Government Operations, after a general review of the relation of the federal government with its contractors, had decided a year before that "if we look at the nature of the function, there are no clearcut criteria for determining what should be done by Government personnel and what by outsiders under contract."[28] The study by the Budget Bureau in effect replied by recommending useful general criteria, but they were certainly not the clear-cut rules that we once would have expected to distinguish the public from the private sector of the economy.

This rapid mixture of government and business interests depended, of course, on the realization of what had happened as a result of the advances in the sciences, their marriage with engineering, and the consequent acceleration of technological change. At the same time its immediate political motivation was obviously a military one. One of the basic reasons for the blurring of the boundaries between business and government was the earlier blurring of the boundaries among the sciences, and between the sciences and engineering; but the more urgent reason was the need to advance weapons technology in the interest of national defense.

But this reason, too, was a result of the changes in the sciences. For science, by making possible hydrogen weapons and intercontinental missiles, had made obsolete the old habit of relying for defense on an industrial mobilization after the outbreak of a war. Another boundary was blurred: the boundary between war and peace. So we had to turn not merely to a state of constant armament and psychological warfare, but to a process of looking a decade ahead with respect to the production of the scientists who were to carry on the basic research that would serve as the technological basis for future weapons systems. Industry was no longer to be mobilized by government only in time of a hot war and then demobilized as quickly as possible. The mobilization had to be a permanent arrangement. It had to be organized and professionally staffed. It required the continuous managerial supervision by government of a large segment of private industry and the continuous subsidy by government of the higher education of scientists and others.

For a time the support and supervision by the Defense Department of the research and development programs of large segments of American industry seemed tolerable because people could see that the civilian economy benefited considerably from this infusion of technology. No matter how scrupulously a corporation may obey security regulations, a great deal of technological progress is unclassified in nature and is bound to seep over into the civilian side of its business. It was obvious that many specific developments financed largely by defense appropriations had proved to be of great benefit to industry in general, for example, the jet aircraft and the electronic computer.[29] And, of course, a corporation obtained intangible benefits from having a large team of scientists trained and exercised at government expense.

More recently, a good many economists and politicians have begun to criticize this "trickle down" theory, and to argue that domination by military programs has distorted the purposes of research and development. Robert A. Solo, for example, has argued that our rising expenditures for research do not ensure faster economic growth and may even be inhibiting it; that the civilian and military sectors are now interested in radically different types of products; and that the transfer of scientific advance from the military and space sector to civilian purposes is now more difficult than it was in the days of simpler weapons systems.[30] The development of a bomber plane a decade ago taught industry lessons that were easily transferred to the business of civilian transportation; it is a little harder to see the possible commercial application of intercontinental missiles or space vehicles.

Or, as Secretary of Commerce Luther Hodges put it, it is wrong to assume that "research and development for any purpose—space, military, or whatever—automatically fosters economic growth . . . Of the total effort, overwhelmingly oriented to defense, relatively little is directed to the creation of new consumer products, or to improved machines to make the products, or to improved processes to use in the machines."[31] It was for this reason that Secretary Hodges, with the support of President Kennedy, proposed a Civilian Industrial Technology program. He asked federal aid for groups of industries that need to develop their research capacities and the inauguration of an industry-university extension service to do for small business what the Department of Agriculture had done for farmers. The Eisenhower administration had proposed to deal with the same problem by authorizing the Small Business Administration to lend funds to groups of businesses which organize to support cooperative research programs.[32] Now the Kennedy administration was proposing to take a leap ahead from loans to subsidies and direct governmental operations. Both parties, in effect, had acknowledged a governmental responsibility for aid to business in the use of science and technology for civilian purposes, and the issue was one of means rather than ends.

Congress, during 1963, was distinctly cool to Secretary Hodges' Civilian Industrial Technology proposal;[33] but it was clear that the question of the government's support of scientific research and development directed especially toward civilian problems had gone on the political agenda of the future. It is surprising, indeed, that the question had been kept off the active agenda for so long, for Secretary Hodges had only revived the main outlines of the proposal first presented to Congress in various versions from 1942 to 1945 by Senator Harley M. Kilgore of West Virginia. That was the original proposal for a National Science Foundation, which in Senator Kilgore's version was expected to go much more into applied research and development, and into active assistance to industry, than was desired by the counterproposal submitted in 1945 by Vannevar Bush with the support of most of the scientific community.

If we look at the federal expenditures for all research and development, of course, the Defense Department easily leads all the rest in the dollar volume of support to private institutions, especially to industrial corporations. But most of this money is for applied weapons development. If we look at federal support for basic research in educational institutions, the Defense Department is well down in the list; it provided in 1963 only a little more than one eighth of the total, which puts it below the National Aeronautics and Space Administration; the Department of Health, Education, and Welfare; the Atomic Energy Commission; and the National Science Foundation.[34] Clearly the contractual merger of public and private interests, through support of the sciences, is a strategy that is beginning to seem useful for civilian as well as military purposes—and in respectable financial dimensions.

But the significance of this system of grants and contracts, which has seemed so congenial to the scientists and their professional colleagues, does not turn on the sheer quantity of money that it distributes, but on the possibility of institutional development. Sir Henry Maine, who believed that progress was measured by the change from status to contract, would be intrigued to note that we have not stopped with the discovery that the Air Force can contract with a private corporation to develop a new bomber system; it can contract with another to maintain its bombers and its missile ranges. If the contractual system will work for scientists and engineers, why not for others? So the Joint Chiefs of Staff and the Senate Foreign Relations Committee alike contract for studies of our fundamental strategy questions and our foreign policy, and the State Department turns over to universities and engineering firms the administration of technical assistance programs all over the world.

And if a contract can be made with an *established* academic or industrial corporation, why cannot a new one be set up for the purpose? Accordingly, we have seen the creation, under government auspices, of new private corporations to do government business. Most of them have been not-for-profit corporations, chartered under the law of some state—for example, the RAND Corporation, which makes technical and strategic studies for the Air Force; the Aerospace Corporation, which is the Air Force's systems engineer for the development of ballistic missiles; and the Institute for Defense Analyses, which evaluates weapons systems in relation to strategy for the Joint Chiefs of Staff and the Secretary of Defense. Now we have moved on to a new stage, as Congress itself has chartered a special corporation to enable the telephone and radio companies to pool their resources in a profit-making company, open to public investment, which will work with the Space Administration in the operation of telecommunications satellites.

If we carried our thinking on this problem only so far, most Americans would be likely to conclude, rather pessimistically, that the federal government, having long since found ways to break down the Constitutional defenses of states' rights, has now developed a complete range of techniques for breaking down the independence of private business. It has learned, in short, how to socialize without assuming ownership. Many people will find it a little depressing to think that in the most dynamic sectors of our economy—those in which science and technology are producing the most rapid advances—the Executive and Congress alike have given up trying, by the traditional approach of assigning functions as a matter of legal right or fundamental principle, to maintain the proper balance between government and business.

We are sentimentally attached to the tradition that our political freedom is dependent on the protection of particular kinds of property. Until a century or so ago, the main source of economic strength was the land, and political freedom depended on the ownership of land by the small farmer—political freedom and the human virtues that went with it. We are still stirred by the traditional memories of the yeoman with his longbow breaking the power of the feudal chivalry, or of the long rifles of Kentucky farmers opening the Mississippi to the free use of the new republic. Even in the vicinity of the concentration of electronic industries on the outskirts of Boston—the industries that help make possible intercontinental missiles—the village of Concord proposes to call its civil defense forces, set up to guard against the hazards of fall-out, Minute Men.[35]

But that tradition was made obsolete by the growth of great corporate concentrations of industrial power, based on the technology of the late nineteenth and early twentieth centuries. There was no question that their command of technology was the most important component in our national military strength and the greatest safeguard of our national security. There was somewhat more question about the great corporation's assumption of the legal status of a person, and the same right to use property without governmental interference that the Constitution had undertaken to guarantee to human beings; but in general its claim that its free enterprise helped strengthen the freedom of society as a whole was accepted.

But then science changed the picture with remarkable suddenness, and we have scarcely had time to appreciate the effects of that change on the role of property in politics. The key item in the competition for power (whether competition in the international arms race or in industrial markets) became not land, and not current industrial production, but the science of the future. And this is something that you cannot build a fence around, or organize on a production line. It is traditionally a proper function for support by the government, as well as by industry and education. Its new costs are so massive that only the government can pay them, and its benefits so unpredictable that no one can say in advance how they should be allocated.[36]

Accordingly, the new basic sciences, by their inherent nature, have carried forward by a large jump the change in the nature of property that had been made by the old industrial technology. The old technology fostered the growth of private corporations, and made their stocks a new kind of liquid property. The new science has made some property almost ethereal. Or, in less metaphorical terms, it has based some very fast-growing forms of property on brainpower, and on the terms and conditions under which the humans who have that asset are related to public authority. In short, they have made it more obviously a political force. So it is hardly surprising to find that you can no longer tell, by identifying an institution as a private corporation in legal form, whether it competes in the market economy, or is simply a new type of government agency, or is somewhere along a highly varied spectrum in between.

SCIENCE AND BUREAUCRACY

But if science has reduced the independence of business from politics, it has helped to create a much greater degree of independence within government itself, and a new kind of autonomy at many points within the vast complex of mixed government-business interests. Perhaps we should not tie our hopes for a free system too exclusively to the obsolescent forms of material power, but look for the ways in which those hopes may be fostered by the new ones.

The old working model of the political system for most people was one in which the President and Congress, as representatives of the people, would determine policies, and the executive departments and agencies would carry them out. The ideal organization of the administration was one in which there was no overlapping of function, no vested interests, no competition, and no effort to influence the policy-making function of political leaders. Policy was supposed, by the unsophisticated, to be made by statesmen in the public interest; by the cynical, to be the result of either a class struggle or a scramble among a great many pressure groups and local interests.

It is getting harder and harder to believe that these are the ways government actually works, or even should work. The sciences and the new technology that they have stimulated, just as they have helped to change the nature of economic power, have also affected the nature of political power—and have indeed made the two seem much more like each other, and more nearly interchangeable. This is a matter of degree; it is not completely true in any department or agency, and the degree to which it is true depends on how much a particular program is influenced by the development of the sciences. But it shows up in two ways.

First, the executive agencies acquire an amount of initiative and autonomy that makes them somewhat harder to treat as passive agents of political authority, servants of the policies determined by the traditional processes of legislation; this amounts to a blurring of the old boundaries between the legislative and executive branches. Second, their programs become harder to distinguish from each other in advance, and the boundaries between their policy interests, and even between their operations, break down completely.

The more closely a federal agency's program is related to scientific advance, the more difficult it is to control it in detail by statutes or executive orders. You cannot order things to happen when you cannot know what the main outlines of the problem are going to be, and it is irritating to the politician to have to wait for the scientist to tell him. More and more things have to be left not to administrative discretion, but to scientific discovery, or to the judgment of the scientists and their professional colleagues. And in making their judgments, the scientists are likely to be influenced by the opinion of their fellow scientists, especially as it may develop through the many advisory networks that now link public and private interests.

That is to say, people with scientific training, or any other kind of professional training and status, are hard to make over into passive agents of either a bureaucracy or a political machine. This has had interesting effects on the nation's constitutional system of political responsibility, to be discussed in the next chapter. The point here is that specific agencies of government develop doctrines and policies of their own, either on the basis of bureaucratic habit, or professional expertise, or scientific and technical knowledge. And when all three bases coincide, as they do in the programs of the military or the public health or the forest and conservation services, they will have a profound influence on policy decisions, and the political parties and Congressional committees and the White House will find it hard to move them. Policy will be developed as the result of forces generated within the management of the service itself, and growing out of its relationships with the scientists and professional personnel concerned, both inside and out of government. That is to say, as science has forced many business corporations to become more political, it has added to the tendency of government agencies to become vested interests that guard their programs as if they owned them.

The central fallacy of Marxism has been that it recognized the dangers of only one kind of power, industrial capital, which during Marx's lifetime happened to be the power of the most aggressive new element in society. The effort to counteract or destroy the power of capitalism by putting power into the hands of a bureaucracy or a single political party, as any political theorist should have predicted, merely transferred the foundation of power to a basis other than property, and thus created a New Class.[37] Members of Congress are fortunately not abstract theorists, but they were forearmed on this point, being trained by the way Congress works to look on a civil servant or military officer not as the representative of a unified bureaucracy, but as a spokesman for the interest of a particular agency.

The attitude of the orthodox liberal in Congress a generation ago was distrust of the power of the selfish industrial corporation; today the liberal is more likely to look on the businessman and the bureaucrat as in theory almost equally subject to an obligation to serve the public interest (although their tests of performance and the penalties for delinquency are quite different), and equally likely to be obstinately committed to the interests of his own organization, rather than the broader purposes of public policy. Representative Chet Holifield, for example, was probably making a straightforward comparison and intending no irony when, at the hearings in 1962 regarding the way in which the Space Technology Laboratory made large profits while serving as a systems manager for the Air Force, he suggested that commercial motives could distort the objective judgment of a business executive in the same way that service loyalty could for a military officer.[38]

Science has made executive agencies not only more independent but also more interdependent. The difference is no longer clear between departments that used to be thought of as domestic in their interests and those that were international; or, among the latter, between the military and the diplomatic agencies. What the agricultural scientists do to increase our domestic farm surpluses has just as obvious and immediate effect on our international relations as do their efforts, through international technical assistance, to help the underdeveloped countries increase their own productivity. The very title of the "National Defense Education Act" indicates a combination of the interests of federal agencies that would have been unthinkable a generation ago, as well as a merger of federal and state responsibilities that would have been even more unthinkable. And of course the problem of working out an international treaty for the control of nuclear tests was one which made it impossible to distinguish between diplomatic and military interests—and which involved university laboratories and industry as well.

As it becomes clear that executive departments and agencies have professional personalities of their own, and are not to be treated as automatic transmission belts of political decisions, it follows that political leaders will find it desirable to think of the problem of organizing and administering them in patterns that are different from those of the traditional bureaucratic hierarchy. The first systematic argument—or at least, the most systematic argument on scientific grounds—against those traditional patterns has come from some of those concerned with the military research and development programs. They have come to reject the old logic of administration in which a large-scale organization achieves efficiency by marshaling all technical efforts under the guidance of centralized planning. Their main reason is that the sheer unpredictability of scientific development, and the velocity of technical change, make it much more efficient to rely instead, within the structure of government, on much the same sort of free competition that is supposed to prevail within the private economy.[39]

This theory was not a bad description of the way in which

the military research and development programs were already being administered in practice, but it became more politically respectable when one of its main authors, Charles J. Hitch, became comptroller of the Department of Defense in 1961. That appointment called the attention of economists and students of government to the ways in which similar approaches had already been influencing the conduct of federal administration. There was the action taken by an earlier comptroller, Wilfred J. McNeil, to set up many of the procurement and supply programs of the Defense Department with "revolving funds" of their own. The idea was that the men in charge of those programs would be able to buy and sell in their dealings with other parts of the department, and thus be subject to some of the discipline of the traditional economic market. There was the effort, pushed valiantly by the two Hoover Commissions, to contract out to private firms functions that did not need to be performed directly by government. And there was the disposition of a political virtuoso like Franklin D. Roosevelt to maintain his effective leadership not by maintaining clear-cut lines of administrative responsibility, but by keeping his principal subordinates and their agencies in competition with one another.[40]

THE SHIFTING OF BATTLE LINES

Private property is, as the old legal maxim puts it, a bundle of rights. Government is a bundle of traditional powers and functions. The scientific approach, and the unsettling effect on society of the technological changes that science has made possible, have helped us see that we can abstract certain rights of property and put them under the control of government, and abstract certain functions of government and assign them to private institutions. This opens up an infinite range of possibilities. Theoretically, it makes the old arguments about socialism versus private enterprise a series of obsolete abstractions. Practically, it suggests that some new abstractions might be very fruitful indeed.

It is interesting to remark how many new types of institutions are being invented, or proposed, that do not fit within the traditional bundles of either government or private enterprise. The scientists and engineers have been prolific of them, as suggested by the wide variety of government-university research centers and of organizations in operations research and systems management. More important, they have begun to think about the problem of new organizations systematically: "We need to find . . . new institutional patterns and relationships to provide research facilities adequate to deal with modern research techniques," as Dr. James R. Killian, Jr., told a Conference on Research and Development and Its Impact on the Economy in 1958.[41] And today, we have a wide range of proposals under active consideration for the establishment of new hybrid forms of private-public enterprise.

Congress has shown that it understands the extent to which our economics and politics are merging, not by enacting any new theories but by what it does at the grubby level of law enforcement and legislative investigations. This comes up most clearly in the conflict-of-interest problem. The conflict-of-interest statutes on the books a few years ago were based on the technology of the Civil War, and were designed to protect the government from the rapacity of the salesmen of blankets and shoes and rifles and fodder. That protection, naturally, was to take the form of an enforced separation of the powers of economics and politics: no government official was to have any connection with any private contractor in doing work for the government. But the new nature of science and technology makes our weapons systems depend on a considerable fusion of private contractors (universities as well as industries) with the government. And this means that many positions having great influence on strategic decisions must be filled by men who are valuable *because* they have a variety of interests—indeed, a formal conflict of interests.

It was the plight of the scientists, above all, that forced both the White House and the Congress to revise their notions of conflict of interests. Both did so by moving in a direction that was analogous to the change in modern science; they became less interested in labeling men as either private citizens or public officials, and more in asking how they operate. Thus a recent statute and a recent set of executive regulations do not forbid an industrial or university scientist to serve as a government official and advise on matters of interest to his business or his university; they insist instead that his particular interests be made plain and that his function be restricted to advice and not responsible decisions.[42]

Both the Executive and Congress now seem to be interested primarily in learning how to discriminate among the functions of various types of corporations, sorting out the appropriate roles of manufacturing concerns, systems engineering firms, research and advisory institutions, and university laboratories along lines that would prevent the professional motives of any one institution from being detrimental to the purpose that it is supposed to serve.[43] But the most significant development is a negative one, like the evidence of Sherlock Holmes' watchdog that did not bark: no Congressman chose during the 1950's to make political capital out of an investigation of the interlocking structure of corporate and government interests in the field of research and development.

It would be intellectually very satisfying, of course, to be able to measure in some precise way the extent to which economic and political power have been split into their basic elements—or perhaps even into their nuclear particles—by the pressure of scientific change, and then recombined into a new type of power. This job is ready at hand for one of the many social scientists with the skills and the taste for quantification. He might well start with a grand and simple abstraction, such as the notion that although economic power and political power have always been in interaction, the new factor that is responsible for their fusion is the velocity of scientific change. So he might come out with some basic equation like this: political Energy equals economic Mass multiplied by the square of the velocity of scientific Change, or E equals MC². But if our behavioral Einstein works out some such equation, it will probably not stay true very long, since the human beings who are the refractory ultimate units of the problem would soon find some way to change the economic elements and the political combinations with an eye to asserting their autonomy, or advancing their interests.

Even without quantification some broad trends seem clear enough.

I have already noted how the attitudes of the liberal wing of Congressional opinion seem to have changed over the past generation. In the early nineteenth century—before Karl Marx—the essential purpose of liberal political theorists was to keep economics and politics as distinct elements, with as little interaction as possible. It was conservatives like Hamilton and Adams and Clay who wanted tariffs and a national bank and internal improvements, and Andrew Jackson who fought them on all counts. Later on, and much later in the United States than in Europe, the left wing of politics became committed to government regulation or ownership of parts of the economy, while the right wing took up the cause of the separation of business and government. Now it appears that the new velocity of social change, in which scientific development plays so large a part, is bringing about another reversal in the alignment of political forces on economic issues.

At any rate, the point of view of business seems to be changing, in practice if not in theory. In theory industry is still against government planning, but it wants a rational system for the allocation of government contracts, and it wants the kinds of government services in fields like statistics, and public works, and transportation that will let industry get on with its job. Industry has of course won its main battle: nobody wants government ownership of business, as long as the rich variety of contracting and regulatory techniques gives the government an ample choice of policy tools to direct the economy in whatever degree of detail the Congress and the President want to direct it. And that, of course, is where the issue now really arises: in what degree of detail? A report made by some three dozen private corporations to the director of the Budget Bureau in 1962—in effect a competing report to the official one on "Government Contracting for Research and Development"—very significantly did not object to the essentials of policy and program control, but mainly to the detailed techniques of administrative supervision.[44] Its authors were quite properly eager to be given a broad range of delegation, rather than supervised in niggling detail by government contracting agencies.

And in this desire, industry is enthusiastically joined by the universities. The days have long since ended when you could with some color of realism portray American business as anti-government and universities as harboring a lot of socialists. The presidents and business managers of big universities have as strong a set of motives, and then some, as those of big corporations for wanting as much freedom as they can get, along with their government grants. (The "then some" derives, of course, from the principles of academic freedom, which academic types tend to rate considerably higher than free enterprise as a value to be given nearly absolute respect by society.) And among the scholars and scientists, the commitment to free basic research, and the very internal structure and system of incentives of academic institutions, lead to a demand for freedom in practice even by those who want planning in theory. In theory, indeed, the strongest new currents of political thought seem to be strongly in the direction of the basic merits of freedom as a condition for both scientific and political advance.[45]

Now obviously we have been looking at trends that are not peculiar to science as practiced in the laboratories. It is not only the nuclear physicists, but the American Medical Association and the United Electrical Workers, that have increased their share of power over the economy by political influence, as a result of technological change. It is obvious, too, that these trends are not evenly distributed throughout the political economy; in the main they have occurred in the growing segment of American society that is most heavily influenced by science and most extensively supported by the government. Is all this merely a military aberration rather than something inherent in the influence of science on politics? Certainly, the fusion of economics and politics has happened faster in the weapons business than anywhere else. Just as certainly, no one should expect that the same kind of things will happen in a great deal of American business in the near future.

But it is well to recall what has been going on in another sector of the economy, agriculture, under the steady pressure of a less spectacular technology. There, it is hard to separate the forces of the market from those of the crop support laws; it is impossible to separate the interests of a man as an individual farmer from those that he has as the trustee of a soil conservation district, or to tell whether a county agent is a public or private functionary; and the land-grant colleges continue to enjoy the best combination of public support with independence of policy initiative. If our agricultural scientists do not slow down, the embattled farmer's dependence on a combination of government programs and scientific techniques will soon be even greater than the astronaut's.

So there is a twin lesson in our administrative and scientific history: (1) the lesson of the weapons and space programs, that the most advanced technologies can be supported by government and directed to public purposes; (2) the lesson of the agricultural program, that scientific advance can be used even to help ordinary human beings at home. And we are beginning to get hints that political leaders may be drawing a moral from this twin lesson.

Mr. Jefferson's farmers and Adam Smith's manufacturers had a common interest. Jefferson and Smith were fully aware of the political significance of economic power, but as liberals they wanted the economy freed as much as possible from governmental control. Hence they favored the independence of private busino way !!

ness, and of the state and local governments that dealt most directly with business. But by the time of, say, the First World War, the state of technology had made possible the creation of giant corporations which seemed to be identified somewhat less with the cause of the common man than had the small farmer or the family manufacturing firm, and indeed seemed to have passed from the control of their owners to their managers. Hence the liberal changed his position; he moved in the direction of greater power to the national government and more government control or ownership of major segments of the economy. In this respect, he was reluctantly following Karl Marx, no matter how much he disapproved of Marx's political purposes.

But now science has again changed the nature of the property that is of the most strategic importance to politics, and the position of the liberal has shifted with it. When politicians became persuaded that basic research held the key to our future security and material welfare, the basic relation of government to private institutions changed. The breakdown of the boundary between the basic sciences and engineering—which in turn had depended on the discovery of common ground among the basic sciences—made it impossible for the businessman to defend the old boundary of private ownership that he had fortified so carefully between economics and politics, and unnecessary for the government to attack it.

So whether one is fearful of central authority and eager to protect individual and local interests, or fearful in an era of international danger of the weakness that comes from too feeble a national authority, the battle lines have shifted. We have completely forgotten the issue of government ownership; the other ways of accomplishing the same purpose are so much less troublesome. We are likely to argue less about whether government should have a broad responsibility for economic policy and the direction of economic effort. But we are likely to argue a great deal more about the terms of the relationship under which private corporations and institutions maintain a degree of autonomy while working within a framework of limited governmental support and direction.[46]

In short, we are now obliged to think about the political functions of various types of people not on the basis of the property they own but of what they know, and of the professional skills they command.

CHAPTER 3

The Diffusion of Sovereignty

"FACELESS TECHNOCRATS in long, white coats are making decisions today which rightfully and by law should be made by the Congress," said Senator E. L. Bartlett of Alaska as he urged that Congress set up its own corps of scientific advisers.[1] His complaint reflects a fear that is probably shared by many citizens. In view of the esoteric nature of the scientific processes that now seem to dominate our policies, can the elected representatives of the people maintain control over the major decisions of the government?

The typical liberal who supported the extension of governmental control over business in the early twentieth century was not very greatly worried about weakening the independent status of private property as a check on centralized power. To protect his freedom, he was inclined to trust the responsible processes of representative government. No matter how much power might be vested in the government, it would still be under popular control; the experts in the civil and military services would function only as the agents of policies that had been initiated by the processes of party leadership and legislative debate.

But now that great issues turn on new scientific discoveries far too complicated for politicians to comprehend, many people doubt that representative institutions can still do their job. The fear that the new powers created by science may be beyond the control of constitutional processes, and that scientists may become a new governing clique or cabal of secret advisers, has begun to seem plausible. The intellectual world in general, especially in Europe, is tempted to believe that modern man faces a political dilemma and is now obliged to choose between the two kinds of authoritarian governments that have taken over the control of many countries. One is the type that is guided by military or clerical leaders who affirm traditional values; the other is the type of dictatorship based on the materialist dialectic, professing science as its basic faith.

If American scientists, like American politicians, have generally not been persuaded that they had to choose either horn of this dilemma, it was probably because their actual experience was quite different from that of their counterparts in many other countries. In most of Europe, the reactionaries and the radicals shared a basic assumption not only with each other, but also with the parliamentary liberals against whom they rebelled. That assumption was the idea of sovereignty, the notion that the government of a nation was in some sense an expression of a single authoritative national purpose, and the embodiment of a unified will. This sovereign will, or the parliament that expressed it, would define a set of policies, based on a coherent set of principles, to be administered by a coordinated and disciplined bureaucracy.

To any newspaper reader, it should be obvious how little this ideal of sovereignty corresponds to the actual nature of the American political system, although some scholars try to make the facts fit the ideal. Some of the most obvious differences appear in the different role of scientists, and in the organization of the new programs they have initiated. For American scientists have played a significant role in the development of a system of political responsibility that does not work on the principles of parliamentary government and does not work on the principles of the new dictatorships of either the right or the left that have been supplanting the parliamentary system in many countries. It is a system that—along with some considerable disadvantages—has one great advantage: it does not assume that within the government there must be a single sovereign will, and therefore additional functions can be given to government without adding to the concentration of power within society.

We need a theory of the relation of science to political authority that will more accurately reflect the American experience. Before we Americans try to outline such a theory—or at least an approach toward it—we need to take a careful look at the facts. We cannot understand science in relation to politics unless we understand the way scientists behave in relation to politicians, both individually and in the organizations to which they belong. We should therefore ask three elementary questions that seem relevant to any theory of political responsibility, and take special note of the role of scientists as we answer each of them: (1) What kind of men make a career of running the government? (2) Who initiates new policies? (3) Who controls the organization and procedures of the government departments?

SCIENTISTS AND PROFESSIONALS IN ADMINISTRATION

The classic parliamentary system is based on the collective responsibility of a cabinet to an elected assembly. Since that responsibility is collective—that is, all members of the cabinet are equally responsible for the policies of the government as a whole—it is necessary for the actual administration of the government to be under the coordinated control of a single disciplined administrative corps. It is hard to imagine such a corps composed of men whose education and early careers had been devoted to the intense specialization of the modern sciences. At any rate, none of the major nations whose governments are set up on the parliamentary model have ever tried to do without an elite corps of career administrators, and in such a corps scientists are rare indeed.

In the United States, on the other hand, men trained in the sciences, and in the professions based on the sciences, find it easy to move up into high administrative positions.

In Great Britain, which is the classic example of a parliamentary government, the Administrative Class, the top corps of the civil service, is still dominated by men trained in the humanistic and historical studies; not one man in twenty among these guardians of public policy has had a scientific or technical education. In spite of recurrent criticism of its role, the Administrative Class still maintains a professional monopoly (though in a studiously amateur and nonscientific way) over the organization of the government departments, and a major share of influence in the formation of national policy. It thus has no great interest in making it easy for scientists to move up into its membership, or the universities to work closely with it on its major policy problems.[2]

Now that we are both constitutional democracies, it makes much less difference that Great Britain has a king and the United States a president, but a great deal of difference how we set up the professional group of men who actually run the government. Our Jacksonian revolution indeed destroyed the hopes of John Quincy Adams for a continuation of the Jeffersonian alliance between science and republicanism. At the same time, by wiping out the beginnings of a career system, it prevented the development of an elite administrative corps and thus cleared the channels of promotion for the scientists who, decades later, were to begin to move up in the civil service. The frontier radicalism of the day distrusted all forms of Establishment; this was the era in which state constitutions forbade clergymen to hold public office and prohibited educational qualifications for admission to the bar. But as the business of government got more complicated, the frontier had to admit that certain skills were necessary. Its essentially pragmatic temper insisted, as it became necessary to hire civil servants for merit rather than patronage, that the requirements be defined in terms of the needs of the specific jobs, rather than by general educational status. It was easiest to prove the need for special skills in technical fields, partly on account of the objective nature of the problem, partly because scientific societies were determined to raise and maintain their professional standards in the civil service as well as in private practice.[3]

As a result, it was in the scientific and professional fields that the career civil service system was first pushed up to the higher ranks. As we developed our top civil service, we made it something quite different from a career Administrative Class; most of its members are not only nonpolitical, but nonadministrative as well, and they are not career officials in the same sense as a U.S. Navy officer or a British Civil Servant.

In recent years, scientists and engineers, though rare among those in high political office, have done reasonably well in the civil service. The program of Rockefeller Public Service Awards, recognizing distinguished achievement in the federal civil service between 1952 and 1960, gave two fifths of its awards to men engaged in scientific or technological programs, and having scientific or technical educations.[4] Similarly, a recent study of 7,640 federal civil servants in the top ranks showed that as undergraduates a third of them had specialized in engineering, and nearly a quarter in the physical or biological sciences. By contrast, only 16 percent had specialized in applied studies like business, education, and administration, 16 percent in the behavioral sciences, and only 9 percent in the humanities. One tenth of them had doctors' degrees, and one quarter masters' degrees; among those who did graduate work, the proportion with training in the physical and biological sciences was even higher than at the undergraduate level. On their way up to administrative responsibilities, whether in government service or private life, many of these officials had served at length in the sciences and related professions; as late as fifteen years after starting their careers, 18 percent had been engineers, 8 percent scientists, and 2 percent medical doctors; only 3 percent had been lawyers.[5]

The top positions within the career civil service, for administrative continuity and bureaucratic power, are those of the bureau chiefs. A study in 1958 of the 63 bureau chiefs showed that 9 of them had advanced degrees in the natural sciences, and 17 others had been trained in lesser ways as engineers or technicians. By comparison with these 26 from various branches of technology, there were 9 economists and only 8 lawyers, and 20 from miscellaneous administrative or business careers.[6] Aside from the positions of bureau chief, the top career positions are the so-called "supergrades," which were added above the regular civil service grades to let the government compete for scarce talent.[7] The favorite justification for creating these positions is the need to employ capable scientists and engineers, notably in the technical branches of the Defense Department and the National Aeronautics and Space Administration. Administrators have ridden along to higher salaries on the political coat tails of scientists.[8]

Scientists who become bureau chiefs in the U.S. service are, of course, no longer practicing scientists; they are doing work that in the United Kingdom would be done by a member of the Administrative Class educated in history or the classics. Their training may not be ideally suited for their administrative duties, but neither was that of their English counterparts. Macaulay, after all, used to argue that he wanted to recruit university graduates in the classics not because they had been studying the classics but because the classics attracted the best minds which could adapt themselves to anything.[9] And the scientific training of many American administrators puts them on a level with their English humanist counterparts in at least one respect: their lack of interest in management as a science, or sometimes at all.

THE INDUCTIVE INITIATION OF POLICY

Though the scientists in top civil service posts have not been deeply interested in administration, they have been interested in policy. And this is the second major way in which the scientific civil servant in the United States differs from his British or European counterpart: he takes a direct role in initiating policies and publicly advocating them.

In their influence on policy, as in their advancement in the hierarchy, the scientists in American government have had a special opportunity because they have not had to work under a tightly organized corps of administrators, or a tightly knit political leadership. After the Civil War, there was no strong conservative tradition based on a landed interest, and no national party with a coherent ideology to take control of the programs of government. As a result, policy tended to develop separately in every field. There was no one with sufficient authority to tell the scientific experts that they belonged in a subordinate role.

Indeed they were listened to all the more readily because they were usually not thought of as bureaucrats. There was no one from whom Congress wanted advice less than from the regular career service. But each group of scientists had one foot in government, so to speak, and one outside, and the policy views that the insiders developed would come back to the Congress from the National Academy or the scientific societies.[10] In a government of limited constitutional powers, a research program could be justified in a given field when an action program could not. But the research ultimately seemed to lead to action, in spite of the lawyers' scruples and the party bosses' lack of interest in policy issues. Research was influential not merely because the politicians were persuaded by objective data; an even more important reason may have been that scientists (and in some fields, the economists) were the major organized communities of professional opinion with a continuous interest in specific public programs. This has been the pattern of the development of many new federal programs: you can trace it in agriculture, in natural resources, in the regulation of business, in labor and welfare, and we now see its beginnings in the support of education.

The most influential pattern was set in agriculture. Washington and Jefferson had been interested in fostering scientific improvements in agriculture, and in federal support of a national university. They were blocked by the lawyers' scruples about states' rights. But the agricultural scientists found a way to their goal by a different route—one that evaded constitutional barriers by merging federal and state interests through federal grants of either land or money to the states, and by building up a program on scientific and educational bases. The principal basis was, of course, the land-grant college; from it grew the experiment station, the extension program, and the whole interlocking system of institutions which has let the federal government play a more effective role in the agricultural economy than the government of any supposedly socialized state.

In all this development, the land-grant colleges and the associations of various kinds of agricultural scientists maintained an important influence on the Department of Agriculture, supplied most of its career personnel, and generally provided the intellectual leadership for national agricultural policy.[11] Thus in effect they greatly weakened the old constitutional distinction between state and federal functions, but without subjecting the field of agriculture to the control of a centralized bureaucracy.

The pattern of grants in aid, with its new set of administrative relationships, met two cardinal needs: (1) to provide money, as well as national policy direction, from Washington, and (2) to enlarge the operating responsibilities of the states, while preserving a large measure of their autonomy. It accordingly became the basis on which new programs were developed—highways, public health, social security, welfare, housing, and others. This was what political scientists came to call the "New Federalism," which has given the scientists and specialists in each field of policy a chance to work out programs without too much constraint by any party doctrine.

The classic theory of parliamentary government calls for something like a deductive method in the formulation of policy. That is to say, it suggests that policy originates in the doctrines or platforms of the political parties, and that it is then expressed in the enactments of the legislature. The role of administrators and their scientific and technical subordinates is merely to carry out the predetermined policy, to deduce specific actions from the statutory general principles.

It was of course not the scientists, but the lawyers, who saved us from this dogmatic belief. Some people still think that the function of judges is simply to interpret and apply the laws that legislatures enact, and the function of administrators merely to administer such laws. This was the conception of the extreme doctrinaires of both the American and French revolutions; sovereignty was in the people, and could be expressed only through their elected representatives in deliberative assembly. So for a time in France, during the Revolution, judges were required to go back to the legislature and ask for guidance whenever they found a case not covered explicitly enough by statute.[12] But the lawyers in the tradition of the common law never held with such nonsense. They knew that justice required a great deal of initiative and inventiveness from a profession with a corporate tradition. They knew that the political authority of a legislature would be destroyed, rather than enhanced, if the legal profession and the judiciary looked to it for all ideas and initiative, and failed to exercise their own.

In Great Britain the career administrators, for all their formal public deference to members of the cabinet, were soon accorded a powerful role in the initiation of policy, but the notion persisted rather strongly that the scientists were instruments for predetermined ends. In the United States, on the other hand, the politicians were rather more ready to accord to scientists than to general administrators the right to press their policy views.

The leaders of political parties or members of an elite administrative corps may like to look on scientists as properly subordinate, and science as a way of thinking that should deal with the means to support a policy, a tradition, or an ideology, rather than an end in itself. We can understand this relationship in other countries if we recall how, until recent years, our military services thought that civilian scientists in military laboratories should conduct their research only pursuant to "requirements" defined by military staff work. This notion was exploded as it became apparent that what scientists discovered by unrestricted research might be of greater military importance than the things the military officers thought they wanted—in short, that the means might determine the ends.

Weapons development provides the extreme (and almost the only conspicuous) example in American politics in which scientists have been faced with difficulties in getting a direct political hearing for their policy ideas. For members of Congress usually want their scientific advice on a specific problem undiluted by either party doctrine or the policy views of general administrators.

This attitude is something like an inductive approach to policy. It distrusts the deduction of specific decisions from general political principles, or from a party's ideology. It distrusts the presentation of facts by either bureaucrats or party managers who may distort them for their special purposes; it is afraid of the doctrine that the end determines the means, for it suspects that the politician does not really know in precise terms what is the chief end of man, and may be tempted to define it to suit purposes of his own. This approach may have been furthered, in American history, by the influence of scientific ideas along with rationalism during the Revolution. Later it may have been furthered by a dim realization that science, if not too much constrained by predetermined political ends (or, if you like, political teleology), could help develop a higher set of goals and purposes than had yet been dreamed of. But mainly, I suspect, it was given a chance because people were sick of the results of exaggerated party doctrine and of the Civil War to which it led.

So the President was not expected to run for office, or run his administration, according to a doctrinaire platform, or to coordinate his departments so closely as to suppress a certain amount of policy initiative from his technical subordinates. Similarly, the Congressional committees, which were fiercely partisan with respect to the spoils of office, became nearly nonpartisan, or at least weakly disciplined by their parties, in the consideration of new policies. And both the executive and the legislature developed the habit of turning for policy advice and assistance not only to the scientists in government, but to their colleagues in the universities and foundations. Both land-grant colleges and private universities were drawn into the processes of policy making, partly because they were, in the absence of a career bureaucracy, the main reservoir of expertise on which politicians could draw for advice, and partly in response to the influence of the philanthropic foundations.

By the 1920's, some of the major foundations had lost interest in the charitable alleviation of social problems, and had begun to hope that science might solve them. This idea led them to a strategy of supporting scientific research—and not only research but demonstration projects to test its application. After being tested, the research could be extended by the greater resources of government. The foundations' aid to scientific education and research is a familiar story in almost every branch of science. Equally important, they went on to help strengthen the professional organizations of scientists, to pay for the efforts of governmental agencies to reform their own systems of organization and administration, and to pay for research projects undertaken at the request of public officials who could not persuade legislatures to appropriate the necessary funds.[13]

By the time of the Second World War, the leading scientists knew that a grant-making agency like a foundation could initiate nationwide programs by making grants to independent universities and governmental agencies. Hookworm control, the foundation of public libraries, and the reform of medical education had amply proved the point. And political leaders were inclined to turn to private funds to help them explore future policy opportunities, or experiment with them, as when President Hoover sought foundation financing for his Committee on Social Trends and for a National Science Fund. The Public Administration Clearing House provided the initial administrative costs for President Roosevelt's Science Advisory Board.[14]

The process of responsible policy making is thus not something that begins with the definition of a political ideal according to some partisan doctrine, and concludes by using administrative and scientific means to attain that end. It is a process of interaction among the scientists, professional leaders, administrators, and politicians; ultimate authority is with the politicians but the initiative is quite likely to rest with others, including the scientists in or out of government.

POLITICAL DECENTRALIZATION OF THE EXECUTIVE

The presence of scientists and professionals in the civil service and their unusual degree of policy initiative are not the only differences that science has helped to bring about in the American constitutional system. The third difference is perhaps the most profound: the idea that the very organization of government itself is not something to be controlled by the insiders, but may be determined by the processes of open politics. Though the American scientific civil servant has policy initiative, and thus may seem to be tipping the balance of power against the politician, the politician more than makes up for it by assuming control over the internal structure of government organization and over its procedures.

The scientists were of course not the major influence in support of this tendency to open the inner workings of government to popular political control; that tendency came from many social and political sources. But it was encouraged by the early rationalism of the Jeffersonians, who believed that politics itself should be an experimental process. It was encouraged by the desire to give independent status within government to agencies with scientific functions, like the Smithsonian Institution, or agencies that were supposed to make their decisions more on technical than political grounds, like the regulatory commissions. And it was encouraged by the desire of scientific and professional services to have special status of their own apart from the general civil service, a desire which accounted for separate uniformed corps like those of the Coast and Geodetic Survey and the Public Health Service.

One of the classic principles of administration holds that with responsibility should go a corresponding degree of administrative authority. Within a limited managerial context, this is the proverbial wisdom, and sound enough. And at the political level, it is the key idea in the classic theory of parliamentary responsibility. The cabinet within the parliament, and the prime minister within the cabinet, were able to take control by saying, in effect, that they could not continue to carry the responsibilities of His Majesty's Government if not given full control over the means to their proposed ends. But in the United States the idea of authority commensurate with responsibility is contradicted by the history as well as the theory of our constitutional system.

For the Jacksonian revolution completed the efforts of the Jeffersonian rationalists to abolish all types of establishments. The Constitution had forbidden a national established church, and the Founding Fathers had moved rapidly to rely on the volunteer state militias rather than a national standing army. And the Jacksonians proceeded to root out the beginnings of a career administrative service, in order to prevent the democratic control of policy from being influenced by a vested interest within the government. In Great Britain, as A. V. Dicey was to point out, the civil servant (unlike his French counterpart) was kept subject to the same law and the same courts as the private citizen, in order to make sure that he did not exceed the authority granted him by law. The United States went one step further; the civil servant was kept, in effect, a part of the private labor market, rather than being made a part of a lifetime service with a corporate tradition. He worked for a bureau that was likely to be fairly independent of any general government policy, and rather more under the control of the particular Congressional committees to which it looked for legislative authority and for the appropriation of its funds. His Majesty's Civil Service was the embodiment of a national ideal; the U.S. Civil Service had only a nominal existence—it was only a set of rules and procedures that imposed negative restraints on a collection of nearly autonomous bureaus.

The President, in short, could not effectively demand control over the civil service or the form of organization of the executive departments, in order to control the means toward the ends legislated by Congress. For federal administration, like the process of policy making, was supposed to work on something like a parody of the inductive method. The existence of a general bureaucracy, committed to an integrated national purpose, was not to be taken for granted on general principles; each position in the civil service was supposed to be set up by law, or later by a formal proof of its necessity under a system of job classification, and the men recruited for their ability to fill these particular jobs were supposed somehow to constitute an organization capable of fulfilling a national purpose. The end did not determine the means; in Congressional procedure, the committee in charge of legislation defined the ends, and the appropriations subcommittee sometimes supplied the means.

This was the logical corollary of the peculiarly American assumption that it was just as appropriate for the voters and legislators to control the administrative organization and procedures of government as its policies, that is to say, to control the means as well as the ends. This was a radical departure from British or European assumptions. The parliamentary progression from conservatives to liberals to socialists never changed the fundamental European assumption that, although governments might be responsible to legislatures for the substance of their policies, it was better for politics and legislation not to meddle with internal administrative organization or the management of the bureaucracy. The socialist political leaders took the unity of the state and its bureaucracy for granted. If anything, they tended to make it all the more monolithic, and to push to its logical conclusion the tendency of Benthamite liberalism to abolish the privileges of guilds and public corporations.

But in the United States the current of radicalism ran in the opposite direction; after the age of Jackson, lobbyists and legislators were likely to concern themselves at least as much with the details of administrative organization as with major policies, generally with the purpose of creating centers of independence within government. Thus, in the nineteenth century, the states and cities adopted constitutions and charters that made them loose collections of independent agencies, with no responsible Executive.

This decentralizing tendency was pushed so far that it destroyed the unity of administration, and sometimes had disastrous effects on the competence and the political responsibility of government. But it also disproved the idea—often assumed both by those who admired and those who feared socialism—that an extension in the scope of governmental functions in the United States would automatically bring a corresponding centralization of power.

THE EXTENSION OF THE NEW FEDERALISM

Those three peculiarities of the American political system had made it possible, by the time of the New Deal, to bring the major programs of state and municipal government and the major programs affecting the agricultural economy within the scope of federal government policy, without destroying the operating autonomy of the states and cities or the land-grant colleges. The New Federalism, in short, had worked best in those aspects of public affairs in which the power of government and the power of the great industrial corporations were not in rivalry. Leaders of private universities and scientific institutions, partly with this example in mind and partly in view of their experience with the programs of private foundations, were beginning to wonder, a decade before the Second World War, whether they would have to accept some comparable relationship to the federal government.

The system of federal grants and contracts by which universities and industrial corporations now have been brought into a relation of dependence on federal policy and federal funds, but with a high degree of independence with respect to their internal affairs, was not the result of an immediate flash of wartime inspiration. Its essential idea can be traced back to the depths of the Great Depression. By that time the naive nineteenth-century faith in the contribution of science to democratic politics was less prevalent in the more important universities and the more advanced fields of science than in the agricultural colleges. Scientists in the major private universities were supported more by private corporations and foundations than by government, and leaders in the newer fields like nuclear physics and biochemistry had closer intellectual ties with their European counterparts than with the agronomists or engineers of the land-grant colleges. The scientists in institutions that derived their support from industrial wealth and were interested in problems of the industrial urban economy saw the constitutional model in a very different perspective. Among them, accordingly, were to be found both those conservative scientists who were most distrustful of government and those radicals who tended to take a Marxist view of the role of science in society.

It was from such institutions that the Science Advisory Board of 1934–35, set up by President Roosevelt to prepare a program to combat the depression, drew its rather conservative members. They came up with a report that shocked their colleagues, for they actually proposed government research grants to private institutions, citing as a precedent the previous programs of aid to the land-grant colleges. The federal government, however, or at any rate Public Works Administrator Harold L. Ickes, did not think it proper to give federal subsidies to private institutions, and rejected the proposal.[15]

But the reluctance of private institutions to accept government support, and the reluctance of the government to grant funds outside the framework of complete political responsibility, broke down under the pressure of the Second World War.

The scientists who were then put in charge of the most advanced weapons programs (including some of the same leaders who had served on the earlier Science Advisory Board) were ready to work out a thoroughly pragmatic set of arrangements for the conduct of weapons research, based on the same procedures that had worked in the foundation programs with which they were familiar. The approach that they adopted in the two great scientific programs of the war—the Office of Scientific Research and Development (OSRD) and the Manhattan District of the Army Engineers—was simply to enlist institutions rather than individuals.

To those who expect wartime crises and military authority to produce a centralization of authority, this approach must have been as surprising as if the Army had used the war as an excuse to increase, rather than decrease, its reliance on the state militias. But in the hands of Vannevar Bush, James B. Conant, and Karl T. Compton, the government contract brought private corporations within the scope of a still newer and more flexible type of federalism, one that was founded on the government contract rather than the grant-in-aid. Under the OSRD, the Massachusetts Institute of Technology took on the responsibility for developing radar, and the California Institute of Technology rockets. Under the Manhattan District, the University of Chicago set up the first sustained nuclear reaction and the University of California fabricated the first atomic bomb, while Du Pont, General Electric, Union Carbide, and other industrial giants built the facilities to produce the fissionable materials.[16]

The postwar extension of this system, already described, has brought private scientific institutions—universities as well as business corporations—into a connection with the federal government as intimate and active as that of any land-grant college. And in at least some parts of the industrial system it may now be bringing about a relation between government and business entirely different from the one that existed during the quarrels of the depression era, much as the grants-in-aid system transformed federal-state relations some decades after the Civil War. Indeed, it may now be breaking down the political opposition to federal programs even more effectively than did the system of grants to the states.

7 3 |

State and local governments and private corporations used to join in their jealousy of purely federal activities and to consider extension of them as socialistic. The federal grants to states in the field of agriculture, however, were no longer socialistic in the eyes of the governors and the farm bloc; they were a defense of the American way of life, even though they entailed government controls. And now that the atomic energy and space and military programs support such a large share of the nation's business, and so much of its enterprise and innovation spills over quite naturally and properly into related commercial fields, it is no wonder that private business corporations are less jealous of government. More accurately, their jealousy no longer takes the form of fighting socialism, but of haggling over the administrative provisions of contracts. A great deal of private enterprise is now secreted in the interstices of government contracts. In short, what the grant-in-aid programs did to the arguments for states' rights, the new contractual systems are doing to those for pure private enterprise.

The argument for a measure of independence from central authority still remains valid in either case, and so does the need to recognize that the fundamental responsibility of government cannot be delegated. Policy decisions remain the responsibility of government. But "policy" here means simply those aspects that government authorities believe ought to be controlled, either because they think them of major importance or because they realize that voters or Congressmen think so.

This means that they will consider as policy certain aspects of management (for example, fair employment practices or prevailing wage rates). But, so long as they retain ultimate control, they may act on the advice of contractors upon the most momentous new issues, or delegate major segments of the business whenever they can specify the purposes to be accomplished. The complex and costly nature of certain types of military studies, and the sophistication of the new techniques of operations research, make the possibility of such delegation very broad indeed. There is nothing in the nature of the contract itself (or the grant, which differs from it only symbolically and in technical detail) to determine whether a central bureaucracy will control every detail of the contractor's management or will leave him free to decide matters in secret that ought to be determined by the President and Congress.

But the general effect of this new system is clear: the fusion of economic and political power has been accompanied by a considerable *diffusion* of central authority. This has destroyed the notion that the future growth in the functions and expenditures of government, which seems to be made inevitable by the increase in the technological complexity of our civilization, would necessarily take the form of a vast bureaucracy, organized on Max Weber's hierarchical principles, and using the processes of science as Julian Huxley predicted to answer policy questions.[17] Where scientists have shaped this development, its political and administrative patterns have reflected the way scientists actually behave rather than the way science fiction or Marxist theory would have them behave; they have introduced into stodgy and responsible channels of bureaucracy the amiable disorder of a university faculty meeting.

Take, for example, our oldest and least scientific federal agency having a large operational mission—the Post Office— and compare it with the Air Force or the Space Administration. The Post Office is a relatively self-contained hierarchy. The Air Force develops its policies and runs its programs with the advice and cooperation of several dozen of the most influential universities and industrial corporations of the country, whose executives and faculty members consequently have independent bases from which to criticize any policies, strategic plans, or administrative arrangements they dislike—and they can always find a Congressional committee to listen to them.

The role of science in this difference does not seem to be merely accidental. For one thing, the pursuit of science itself is a non-hierarchical affair; the best scientists either personally prefer, or are taught by their guilds that they should prefer, the university's combination of research, teaching, and undisciplined administration—and to get the best scientists the government took them on their own terms. But more important is the long-range and indirect connection; when the revolution of the Enlightenment proposed that the organization and procedures of government as well as its policies should be open to scientific inquiry and independent criticism, it started a process which has had deep effects on the constitutional system. These effects showed first in the relation of scientific administrators to their executive superiors and to Congressional committees, and later in the new structure of federalism, and in the new contractual relationships between the federal government and private institutions.

The involvement of scientists in these contractual relationships since 1945 has extended their earlier influence on our system of political responsibility.

In the first place, scientists have acquired an even higher degree of initiative and independence in policy. Scientists who advise government or carry on research for government, but are not primarily on the government payroll, have an even greater freedom of enterprise than scientists in the civil service. A government department that gets its research or its advice from scientists on the staffs of private institutions, and pays for it through a contract or grant, is not going to be able to train such men in the disciplined habits of anonymous discretion. On the contrary, these scientists have plenty of opportunity to take the initiative in policy matters and to further the contribution that research can make to the opening up of new political alternatives. The stories of the most awesome decisions of recent years—such as the decision to make the H-bomb, or to establish a Distant Early Warning system, or to try to work out an agreement with the Russians for ending nuclear tests—reveal a great deal of political enterprise on the part of scientists. Many of them were men whose primary formal status was with private corporations or universities.[18]

In the second place, the developments since 1945 have given a new push to the decentralization of political responsibility. Already the American political concern with the means as well as the ends—the disposition to legislate (or even to establish by Constitutional provision) details of organization and procedure —had made it possible, within the framework of government, to decentralize administration even while centralizing our policies. What we did after the Second World War was to extend this process to a broader system that amalgamated public and private interests. For example, we have nationalized the support of research in the medical schools of the country through the grants of the National Institutes of Health. But administratively —which in this case means effectively—we have *denationalized* the process of controlling federal expenditures for this purpose. For Congress has by law provided that the principal control over medical research grants be exercised by a network of committees of scientists who are not primarily government officials.

If you think sovereignty is something real, this is not the way you will wish to run a government. You are more likely to deduce from the ideal of sovereignty the corollaries that the state is something like a person, and that its personality should be integrated and its ideas consistent with one another.

Since in the modern industrial world there is no way to keep government and business from being dependent on each other, this assumption of the reality of sovereignty, and the effort to find a system of legislative procedures and administrative institutions to translate its ideal purposes into actual practice, may lead to a continuous concentration of political and economic power. On what principles is that concentration to be controlled and held responsible?

Those who have abandoned the traditional value system of Western Europe, or who never held it, are likely to create a new ideology and a new elite to determine the ends of the state, and to control the entire society toward those ends. It may be argued (and this point will be considered later) that this is the way to let science control politics. But it is not a system of political responsibility, and need not be discussed now.

Those who hold to traditional values are likely to seek some new version of Plato's Guardians: the elite who are set apart from the rest of the citizens and trained and dedicated to the purposes of the state. The cruder way to do this, and the way that has been taken by a good many parliamentary democracies, is to rally round some military leader, or to give special responsibility to the career military corps. This is what has been done by those nations that lack the traditions and the skills of the nation that invented the parliamentary system. The United Kingdom can rely instead on its Administrative Class and its parliamentary leadership. The Administrative Class of its civil service is a corps that can continue to embody the purposes of the state as long as it is careful to avoid a role of authority or public responsibility. And the leadership of the House of Commons is a bipartisan group carefully self-schooled in the art of never letting the internal workings of Her Majesty's Government and Her Majesty's Services become objects of political or legislative determination. But under any type of Guardians—military, administrative, or parliamentary—the system of political responsibility is designed to test any new proposal in relation to the general purposes of the state, the ideal policies of the governing parties, or the effectiveness of the administrative establishment. It is not very much inclined to turn scientists loose to experiment with policy issues, or to license irresponsible private institutions to explore the inner workings of government, or to permit any of its parts to work at cross purposes with the rest.

In short, if you start by believing that sovereignty is something real, you are likely to design your constitutional system to focus political attention on the ends of the sovereign state, and to insist that the work of scientists supported by government be treated as a means toward the predetermined ends.

Politics in the United States has always seemed impossibly irresponsible to those who think from those premises. And this is perhaps because the United States started from a quite different premise. It not only abolished its allegiance to a particular sovereign, but abandoned the ideal of sovereignty, and treated it as only a word. Those who used the word most gave it the least reality. Those who talked most about the sovereignty of the several states were careful not to give the idea any administrative substance; if they had, they might have won the Civil War.[19]

In the period of the American Revolution, its theorists appealed against the idea of sovereignty to both the past and the future. They appealed to the past when they asserted, with the lawyers, that the king was under the law, and that even the parliament itself did not have unlimited power to make law; indeed they were just as eager to set up Constitutional safeguards against unlimited legislative power as against executive authority. But the Revolution appealed also to the future, as men like Franklin and Jefferson sought to free both politics and science from the monarchical and ecclesiastical institutions that defined traditional values.[20]

By consequence, democratic politics assumed the right to deal with the means of government as well as the ends, or even to put the means ahead of the ends. This meant that hardly anyone worried if neither the President nor the Congressional committees paid much attention to party doctrine in dealing with questions of policy, or to discipline and coordination in dealing with the administrative departments. This gave the scientists a chance to move back and forth between the government and private institutions, and from either base to take a lively initiative in matters of policy. And it made possible the development of more centers of dissent and criticism with respect to public policy even in those fields which government undertook to finance and direct.

This system makes it impossible to maintain an institutional distinction between ends and means, between policy decisions on the one hand and scientific research or administration on the other. Hence it makes party responsibility in the parliamentary sense impossible, and it greatly complicates the task of coordinating either policy or administration.

On the other hand, to blur the distinction between ends and

means is a part of the scientific approach: no scientist likes to feel that his basic values and objectives have been set by others so rigidly that he cannot follow where his research leads him. It may be even more necessary to blur the distinction between ends and means, in an institutional sense, in the twentieth century, when it is the requirements of new ideology, rather than old orthodoxy, that threaten freedom. For science itself, by introducing so many complexities into public policy, destroyed the comfortable nineteenth-century notion that public issues could really be determined by the parliamentary competition of two opposing doctrines. At the same time science, by developing new techniques of mass communication, made possible the means for producing disciplined support of authoritarian government. If the structure of political institutions does not specifically encourage some social experimentation based on scientific initiative, with some degree of deliberate freedom from the constraints of policy as determined by either partisan theorists or an administrative elite, it will narrow the range of free scientific and political development. Perhaps our eighteenth-century Constitution, with its implied distrust of party discipline, will yet prove to be more adaptable to our scientific era than the classic nineteenth-century parliamentary model of Walter Bagehot or Woodrow Wilson.[21]

American scientists, who have tended to be a little disillusioned about their relationship with politicians ever since the Jacksonian period, are now entitled to look with a little more satisfaction on the system of political responsibility that they have helped to establish. For it is a system that is congenial to the pragmatic and inductive approach that appeals to most scientists, especially those who profess no interest in philosophy. It puts a premium on their qualifications for promotion within the bureaucracy, and gives their policy views a respectful hearing. And it is based on principles quite different from either the classic parliamentary system or the single-party system that characterizes the new dictatorships.

But all this gives no grounds for self-satisfaction; it only helps us diagnose our troubles more accurately. It suggests that in the United States the main danger to political freedom and responsibility is not likely to come from the secrecy of scientific advice, or an excess of central executive authority, or a drift toward socialism. There is much less reason to worry that the great decisions of a scientific or technological nature will be secret than that they will be *popular;* the temptation of scientists to lobby for particular scientific programs, and to promise technological miracles in order to get funds for basic research may be a demoralizing one. There is much less reason to fear that the Executive will dominate the Congress than that the Congress as a whole will surrender its power to its own committees, and that they will be too obsessed with new technological toys to deal with broader issues of policy. And there is much less danger of a drift toward a socialist dictatorship than toward a system in which the government will pay all the costs of a series of expensive programs each of which will be contracted out to private corporations and managed in their private interests.

We do not need to believe in the traditional ideal of sovereignty to think that a modest measure of coherence in our national policies, and of discipline in our administrative system, may be desirable in the interest of political responsibility. Some argue that in order to attain those ends we need to strengthen the political influence of the traditional learning or religious values. Only by a return to traditional values, they argue, can party leaders be guided by moral and political theory, and career civil servants be trained in a philosophy of the public interest. Is this true? Or should we press ahead to a system in which science forms the basis for a new set of political dogmas, enforced by a new kind of establishment? Or do we have another and better choice?

The answers to these questions depend on the basic relation of the sciences to traditional values.

CHAPTER 4

The Established Dissenters

dual culture,

THE CELEBRATED CONFLICT between science and the humanities is real enough in that it takes up a lot of the time of those who prepare academic budgets or give out foundation grants. But in the American political system, it is a phony war.

The literary and the artistic branches of the humanities have never been in the thick of the political battle at all; they have never contended for the role of determining the values that guide policy decisions, or of supplying a systematic basis for political thought. The branch of the humanities that once undertook to do so was theology, the medieval "Queen of the Sciences." If science has had any rivals for the honor of providing the intellectual basis for government action, they have been law and moral philosophy, the branches of learning that were subordinate to theology, or closely allied to it, during the formative centuries of the European political tradition.

And if today there is hardly a real political battle between these rival fields of learning it is partly because, in academic politics, science has won a crushing victory; partly because, having won that fight, science seems to have no desire to occupy the political throne from which theology has been driven; and partly because theology shows no disposition whatever to regain its old uncomfortable seat of power, from which it once proclaimed the basic values by which government was to be guided.

Science, although it has become an establishment supported more or less on its own terms by society, is not moving toward the status of an Established Church, not becoming the citadel of a new orthodoxy. In the American (and generally, in the Western) political system, scientists behave more like Dissenters than like hierarchs. And this seems to be almost equally true whether a scientist in theory asserts the unlimited competence of science or whether he defers to traditional values.

In theory, indeed, there seems to be a wide range of opinion within the scientific community. The eminent scientists (and their professional allies among the engineers and physicians) who hold important positions of influence in government, and in the institutional structure by which government and science are now so closely connected, seem to retain rather conventional views. As Insiders, they are likely to accept the subordination of science to the value systems established by the nation's political tradition and interpreted by the authority of its government, and they can get along without much confidence that they are on the road to Utopia. The Outsiders, on the other hand—the scientists who prefer to appear as independent critics of present policy— are less willing to accept the validity of the traditional political ethos, or the necessity for science to be subordinated to a system of organized authority based on traditional values.

Obviously this is an impressionistic caricature of two wings of opinion, but it seems to me to identify roughly the difference of attitude between, say, the President's Science Advisory Committee and the members of the Council for a Livable World, and perhaps even many of the contributors to the *Bulletin of the Atomic Scientists*—even though the two attitudes are mixed in most scientists and in most of the rest of us.

The Insiders' view was typified by the Special Assistant to the President for Science and Technology when he told the National Academy of Sciences at its Centennial Celebration that 90 percent of the federal expenditures for research and development should be undertaken only after administrators and legislators had decided that the individual projects were needed. The role of the expert in such decisions was to give advice, and to pass on means, not ends.[1]

The Outsiders, on the other hand, are comparatively unwilling to fit into a system the ends of which were determined by a prescientific culture, and the institutions of which are still dominated by men trained in the legal or theological or philosophical assumptions of that culture. They are much more likely to believe that the methods of science, by their steady progress from the physical to the biological to the social sciences, are moving toward an ability to solve even our political problems, and that scientists as such have an obligation to take political action to that end.

But surprisingly few of them seem to be persuaded that such political action requires any fundamental change in our political institutions. In spite of their general distrust of the processes of politics and politicians, the Outsiders are still willing to put their faith in an oversimplified version of Jefferson's ideas about political machinery, even though they may have lost their confidence in applied science and its relation to Divine Purpose that was the basis of Jefferson's belief in progress. Their ideal would be an egalitarian democracy, with all issues decided by the votes of private citizens who have not been corrupted by service in the bureaucracy, and all of whom are earnestly studying science. The ideal has been depicted—with an admission of its lack of realism but still as an ideal—as a system of electronic communication in which every citizen could watch and listen to a Congressional debate and then register his vote instantaneously in a national referendum.[2]

In their different ways, both the Insiders and Outsiders are too deeply absorbed in current issues to think about the basic theory of their political status. To develop such a theory, besides, would call for a command of nearly all branches of scientific and humane knowledge. No professional scholar has any incentive to undertake such a formidable task; the specialized structure of the academic world makes the undertaking a disreputable one. But the scientist or administrator who is involved in the new relationship of politics and science is forced to worry about this problem and to have at least some tacit theory to guide him in dealing with it. As a beginning toward formulating such a theory, he might well recall the way in which science was freed from the domination of the traditional learning.

THE CONQUESTS OF SCIENCE

The political challenge of science was implicit in its seventeenth-century rivalry with theology and scholastic philosophy. Before that time, the scientists as well as the priests and poets were trying to understand the universe in terms of a set of analogies with man, and to understand man and the physical universe alike in terms of Divine Purpose. As the mystic, Jacob Boehme, wrote, *"man* is the great mystery of God, the *microcosm,* or the complete abridgement of the whole universe,"[3] and in his day this notion guided astronomers as well as poets and theologians. This was the point of view against which Boehme's contemporary, Francis Bacon, rebelled at the beginning of the seventeenth century. "It is incredible," he wrote, "what a number of idols have been introduced into science by the reduction of natural operations to a correspondence with human actions, that is, by imagining that nature acts as man does, which is not much better than the heresy of the anthropomorphists."[4]

Within the two centuries after Bacon, the tables were turned. When that period began, astronomers were just beginning to give up their belief, to which Copernicus had been fully committed, that they had to treat planetary orbits as perfect circles because only such perfection of form could embody Divine Purpose. When it ended, men were beginning to question the usefulness of Genesis as a textbook in biology and geology. When it began, philosophers and theologians were still insisting that nature could be understood by reducing its workings to correspond with the hopes and fears of men, and with what they liked to believe was the will of God. When it ended, nature was seen as a great piece of clockwork, with all of its movements obeying the same laws of mechanics, so that Laplace's ideal scientist, if he could know the position and motion of every atom in the universe at an instant, would be able to predict everything that would happen thereafter to eternity.

With this notion, it was not surprising that Bacon's "reduction of natural operations" would begin to work backward, and that men would begin to try to understand themselves and their society by *reducing themselves* to natural operations. Today Bacon might find it incredible to see what a number of models, if not idols, have been introduced into the social sciences, to reduce human actions to natural operations. The primary article of faith among the orthodox natural scientists (there are, of course, many skeptics and dissenters) is that rigorous scientific method is being gradually extended from the hard sciences to the soft sciences—from mathematics and physics, through chemistry and biology, to psychology and the social sciences. This is the spectrum of the sciences as described by August Comte, and his positivist followers ever since have expected the scientific method to make a progressive advance along this line: philosophy and theology were the enemies, and their defenses were to be steadily reduced as the rigorously impersonal method of the sciences conquered one field after another, occupying at last the practical field of government.

By the time of Thomas Jefferson, scientists were already assuming that this progressive advance of the sciences would revolutionize society and destroy the influence of the ecclesiastical establishments, the stronghold of authoritarian tradition. Jefferson was too much the practical politician to push his scientific theories to their abstract conclusions: he never agreed with the scientific doctrinaires of the French Revolution who would exclude Divine Purpose from their system of thinking about the future of man and society.[5] He was not interested in overthrowing one type of scholastic establishment and replacing it by another; he expressed great contempt for those charitable organizations that "spent themselves in founding schools to transfer to science the hardy sons of the plough."[6] This attitude, which held that science needed to justify itself to society by its practical applications, was superficially very similar to the attitudes expressed in England in the seventeenth century by the followers of Bacon.

The similarities show up most clearly if we compare the purposes of the Royal Society, founded by Bacon's followers in 1660, with those of the American Philosophical Society, founded in 1743 by Benjamin Franklin. The American society's purposes were expressed in Franklin's "A Proposal for Promoting Useful Knowledge," with an emphasis on "Experiments that let Light into the Nature of Things, tend to increase the Power of Man over Matter, and multiply the Conveniencies or Pleasures of Life." That Proposal was in the same spirit as the earlier purposes of the Royal Society, as Robert Hooke defined them in 1663: it proposed to avoid dogmatic philosophy, or "the explication of any phenomena whose recourse must be had to originall causes (as not being explicable by heat, cold, weight, figure, and the like, as effects produced thereby);" and to work on "Manufactures, Mechanick practices, Engynes, and Inventions by Experiments."[7]

And yet the political temper of the two groups of scientists, in their formative years, was quite different. One received a Royal charter; the other was finally chartered in 1780 by a statute signed by the clerk of the General Assembly of Pennsylvania, Thomas Paine. The leaders of the Royal Society proclaimed that they were "not meddling with Divinity, Metaphysics, Moralls, Politicks, Grammar, Rhetorick, or Logick."[8] The leaders who won control of the American Philosophical Society in 1769 were, in practice as well as in theory, revolutionaries.

The founders of the Royal Society had been associated with the Calvinist wing of religious thought that had been the active force in the Puritan rebellion and the execution of Charles I, so that their renunciation of politics may have been only the price to be paid for sponsorship by Charles II. But it was also in accord with the temper of the time: England was "satiated with

Religious Disputes" and civil war, and scientists, like others, were looking for a chance to cultivate their gardens and avoid useless quarrels.[9] By contrast, Franklin and Jefferson, who served as presidents of the American Philosophical Society for nine tenths of the period from 1769 to 1814, thought of science as the basis for world-wide political revolution and for continuous political progress thereafter. In the last letter Jefferson wrote, he attributed the beginnings of the rebellion against "monkish ignorance and superstition" and in favor of "the rights of man" to the "general spread of the light of science."[10] By his own role in politics, Jefferson set an example of political initiative on the part of a scientist; by the nature of the administrative institutions and legislative procedures that he helped to establish, he cleared the way for scientists to concern themselves with the ends of policy, as well as the technical means toward such ends. But all the while he assumed that science would not become a new establishment, and that it would justify its existence by the type of practical and applied work which it would undertake.

But it is striking to see how soon in the history of the American republic the scientist as such disappeared from political leadership. After Jefferson, the presidents of the American Philosophical Society were political nonentities, and American scientists seemed almost as eager to forget about republican egalitarianism, and to be accorded honors befitting their intellectual eminence, as the members of the academies of Paris or Berlin or St. Petersburg—which were the models for the scientists who, just before the Civil War, were advocating the creation of a National Academy of Sciences. The United States, like Great Britain, never managed during the nineteenth century to set up a strong set of institutions for the pursuit of advanced theoretical science, such as Napoleonic France developed in the *Ecole Polytechnique,* the *Ecole Normale,* and the revitalized *Academie des Sciences,* or such as the German renaissance after Napoleon produced in an impressive number of universities.

But even after the revolutionary ardor of American scientists cooled off and they seemed to become similar to the British in their concentration on practical rather than theoretical interests, there still remained a significant difference: the institutional and academic politics that hampered theoretical science in the two countries came from opposite motives.

In Great Britain, science (in spite of the political prudence of most British scientists) was quite correctly identified at the beginning of the nineteenth century as an intellectual force that had helped produce the American and French revolutions. During the reaction against republicanism in governmental politics, science suffered in academic politics. The ecclesiastical establishment that dominated the older universities had no sympathy for science; they were willing to tolerate mathematics and "pure" science, but nothing of an applied nature. This academic preference for pure over applied science did even theoretical science little practical good; it remained strictly a poor relation within the household of the unreformed academic establishments, dominated by the Church of England and the Tory party. It was no accident, then, that the principal leaders of science in Great Britain came from the Scottish universities, like Kelvin, or from obscure dissenting sects, like Faraday, or from among the Unitarians, like Priestley, or the Quakers, like Dalton. (It seems a little unfair to blame the slow development of basic science during this period on religion as such, for the dissenting sects were typically more earnest and puritanical and often more literal in their religious beliefs than the Church of England; the problem was not religion, but the politics of the ecclesiastical establishment.)[11] When more active support came for experimental science, it was in the dissenting academies, or in London and the newer universities founded on German models. The advancement of the sciences was thus left, in terms of the academic caste system, to the lower middle class.[12]

In the United States, on the other hand, theoretical science was handicapped not because Jefferson and Franklin, with their union of applied science and radical politics, were held back by an ecclesiastical establishment, but because they triumphed over it so completely.

In the eighteenth century, while science was still (under the name of natural philosophy) justified in American colleges as an offshoot and ally of theology, its international standing was higher than at any time during the next century. Curiously enough, in view of the conventional opinion that ecclesiasticism has been the great handicap to science, basic science seemed to flourish in the United States during the eighteenth century, when "natural philosophy was generally held to be the friend and not the enemy of revealed truth," and when the contemporary science was a part of the program of training for the ministry. By contrast, the nineteenth-century flowering of mechanical invention was comparatively barren of theoretical science.[13]

During this period, the great handicap was not the opposition of an upper-class establishment, but the popular acceptance of a vulgarization of Jefferson's philosophy: the notion that the practical ingenuity of the Yankee mechanic was better than theory for the advancement of science. Washington and most of our other early presidents might advocate the establishment of a national university, but Congress was quite content to do without such an extravagance. There is something symbolic in the fact that, when an Englishman offered the United States an endowment for a national scientific institution (being persuaded that only in the United States could science continue its liberating alliance with radical politics) Congress refused to accept the gift for many years, and when it finally did so, it invested the Smithsonian bequest in bonds of the State of Arkansas, which defaulted on them.[14] And when Congress did get around to providing national support for higher education, it was not for the diffusion of knowledge among men, but for the advancement of the agricultural and mechanic arts.

There was, indeed, a theological reaction in the United States against the scientific radicalism that Jefferson typified. For example, Transylvania College, the first college west of the mountains, had made a brave beginning in science under the leadership of Jeffersonian free-thinkers and Unitarians, but all that was stifled when it fell under the control of the Presbyterians during the great religious revivals of the early nineteenth century.[15] But in the metropolitan centers of the United States, from that day to this, theological obscurantism has been stronger in the lower than the upper classes. The elite universities were more independent of conservative theological pressures than were the backwoods denominational colleges or even the state land-grant colleges, which were formally quite apart from ecclesiastical influence. It was not theological prejudices that kept Harvard from throwing all its weight behind the theoretical sciences; when it founded the Lawrence Scientific School in 1847 it followed good Jeffersonian doctrine in putting its emphasis on the training of men who would serve "as engineers or chemists . . . applying their attainments to practical purposes."[16] The upper-class institutions of higher learning were simply becoming the technological servants of private industry, rather than of Jeffersonian democracy.

Jefferson had bet on the wrong horse. He had wanted to make sure that science would be applied to the purposes of an agrarian democracy. And so he proposed that in the universities of America agricultural science be recognized as "the crown of all other sciences." He was the first of our scientists to propose that his particular field, on account of its social utility, be given academic preferment with government aid. "The same artificial means which have been used to produce a competition in learning, may be equally successful in restoring agriculture to its primary dignity in the eyes of men . . . In every College and University, a professorship of agriculture, and the class of its students, might be honored as the first . . ."[17]

Hamilton, of course, had taken a quite different line. His *Report on Manufactures* had proposed government subsidies for the advancement of technology, but for the benefit of industry more than agriculture. All the forces of technology in the industrial revolution, and of science in the later scientific revolution, were to conspire to make twentieth-century America far more like his dream than like Jefferson's. And his victory was less the result of the conspiracy of corporate interests than of the failure of Jefferson's theory of the way in which man's moral and political purpose was to be advanced in practical politics. For that theory took for granted the essential goodness and harmony of men's purposes, provided that men were not constrained and oppressed by ecclesiastical and feudal establishments; it held that the accumulation of practical knowledge in a free and egalitarian society would automatically guarantee the advancement of both knowledge and human welfare, under the guidance of a "natural aristocracy" of talent.[18]

Within a few decades it was plain that popular politics in the United States would not be willing to support either a natural aristocracy in politics or the advancement of science. One half of Jefferson's theory defeated the other half. Jacksonian democrats were quite willing to follow Jefferson in opposing establishments and class privilege, and relying on applied rather than theoretical science. But they were not interested either in calling to office Jefferson's "natural aristoi," or in building up (as John Quincy Adams proposed) scientific institutions that would bring America up among the leaders of science. Hence, in spite of the unusual freedom of scientists to advance themselves and their interests in public affairs, and in spite of the widespread support of applied science for both agricultural and industrial purposes, basic science in America remained second-rate throughout the nineteenth and early twentieth century. It did so, not because it was held back by an upper-class establishment, allied with ecclesiastical politics, but because the scientists who had helped shape the politics of the Revolutionary period had come so close to getting just what they wanted. And this was a social and political system with no establishments, in which scientists would be given support on the basis of the practical utility of their research, and in which public affairs would be administered entirely by men who would hold office, or lose office, every time the electorate changed its mind.

But, as things turned out, the Jeffersonian hopes were disappointed. It was not enough to free science from the shackles of theological influence, and politics from the domination of the church and the bureaucracy or nobility. Once the academic and political worlds were freed of their subordination to such ideas and institutions, they were not content with the high thinking of pure science or the plain living of the small farmer. For the more that technology and science contributed to the material welfare and comfort of mankind, the more science seemed to be dependent on the patronage not of an egalitarian democracy, but of a new type of highly organized power, the industrial corporation and its philanthropic offshoots.

When support began to come for science as basic research, rather than in connection with specific applications, it came not from the influence of popular political leadership, but from a source that Jefferson would not have expected and might not have welcomed: a union of great wealth and religious motivation, now characteristically incorporated in an institution that is a legal descendant of the Established Church of England, namely the private foundation.[19]

The first major step, in frank imitation of the continental European institutions, came with the founding of Johns Hopkins, the first American university to put major emphasis on graduate research in the natural sciences. But the continuing push in that direction came from the general educational foundations that were established soon after the turn of the century. The several Carnegie and Rockefeller foundations had been established by industrialists who were motivated by strong religious beliefs, but the academic strategy that they followed was the opposite of support for an ecclesiastical establishment, or for classical theories of education. Andrew Carnegie, by making his pensions for professors available only to colleges that were not controlled by churches, led a great many academic institutions to separate

93

themselves from the control of Protestant denominations; Congress would not dream of attaching such a condition today to the federal funds pouring into American universities, in spite of the tradition of separation of church and state. And it was under the guidance of Frederick G. Gates and Wallace Buttrick, two Baptist ministers, and Wickliffe Rose, a philosopher, that John D. Rockefeller's fortune became dedicated first to the advancement of medicine and general education, and then to this proposition: "All important fields of activity from the breeding of bees to the administration of an empire, call for an understanding of the spirit and technique of modern science . . . Appreciation of its spirit and technique, moreover, determines the mental attitude of a people, affects the entire system of education, and carries with it the shaping of a civilization."[20]

This was the point of view that had come to dominate the academic and intellectual institutions of the United States, and the thinking of the business and political leaders who financed them. There was no important challenge to its influence; science was indeed ready to move on "from the breeding of bees to the administration of an empire." The ideas of objective techniques of inquiry, with notions of purpose and values rigorously eliminated, invaded the social sciences and then began to influence even the study of administration; universities undertook to teach that subject, foundations supported them in research as well as teaching, and government agencies began to recruit their graduates. As all this went on, the model most frequently held up for emulation was the Administrative Class of the British civil service. Yet after a half-century or so of effort, it is quite apparent that the United States has nothing in its governmental system like the established corps of general administrators, educated primarily in historical and classical subjects, whose influence is so great over the policies as well as the management of British government.

The reasons for this divergence are partly political, and some of them were dealt with in the previous chapter. But they are also partly academic and intellectual. Professors of political science assumed that the basic values and purposes of man were determined by his religious beliefs, his philosophical ideas, or other irrational notions, and that science did not deal with such matters at all. They tended, next, to assume that in government the major issues of policy properly depended on value judgments, and that these matters should therefore be reserved to politicians; administrators would be subordinate, and *their* work should be made as objective and scientific as possible.

This theory was supported by Woodrow Wilson's essay, "The Study of Administration,"[21] which held that administrative science was the same no matter what the policy or the purpose to be served: "If I see a murderous fellow sharpening a knife cleverly, I can borrow his way of sharpening the knife without borrowing his probable intention to commit murder with it . . ." Accordingly, in imitation of the way that scientists renounced any interest in purpose and values, administrators were supposed to renounce any interest not only in the election of their political superiors, but also in the decisions which politicians would make on policies. The theory that science has nothing to do with values and purpose has its practical political corollaries: the Hatch Act forbids civil servants to take part in political campaigns, and the Internal Revenue Code denies tax exemption to scientific institutions that use their funds to influence legislation.

This approach, it was generally assumed, was an imitation of the British civil service with its impartial administration, but it was quite different in theory as well as in practice. For it asked the administrator not merely to abstain from public participation in contests for power, but to avoid an interest in the substance of governmental programs. This approach, when followed in university programs of training for government service, turned out experts in managerial techniques—such as specialists in budgeting or personnel administration—far more successfully than it produced general administrators. A little later, in imitation of industrial management, the application of science to training for public administration came to include the use of psychology and sociology and cybernetics to deal with the morale of the workers, the effectiveness of their interpersonal relations and communications, and the technical aspects of the decision-making process. But this approach, though it took a broader view of the concept of efficiency, still refused to deal with the policy objectives of the organization. Consequently, the label "administrative," which in the British civil service means the top career men concerned with policy issues, came in the U.S. service to apply to jobs and to men charged with the means rather than the ends of a program, and therefore properly to be subordinated to the "executives" responsible for the substance of policy.

The substance of policy, on the other hand, was generally assumed to include the scientific and technological aspects of the program. Scientists, however rigorously they may think they keep ideas of purpose out of their research, are not so inhibited on questions of policy. They are likely to assume, in the best Jeffersonian tradition, that the pursuit of science is not only a good end in itself, but a means toward political ends that are so obviously desirable that others ought to accept them automatically, or at least permit the scientists to propagandize for them while holding public office on a nonpartisan career basis. This is not merely the way scientists think; it is sanctified by public acceptance. If a career official in the Internal Revenue Service or the Post Office or the Commerce Department were to campaign publicly and conspicuously for higher income taxes or the public ownership of the telegraph system or more government regulation of business, it would be considered at least mildly improper, and perhaps even grounds for dismissal. If a rocket expert or a nuclear engineer or a psychiatrist in government service advocates vast appropriations for his field of interest, or major shifts in the relationship of the federal government to private institutions, he may be thought of as zealous to a tiresome degree, but he is only doing his duty.

"Establishment" has come to be a fashionable term for purposes of political ridicule, as young English authors deride the upper classes. But it is a pity to let the dramatists spoil a useful political term by making it mean any type of clique or class with a powerful influence. It is useful for a more precise purpose, to define a social institution that is given permanent public support and status apart from current shifts in political power. Thus the Church of England is established, and so are the dons at Oxford and the permanent parts of the British Civil Service. The intellectual disciplines that dominate this interlocking establishment are those on which the traditional values were founded; those whom this system has promoted to high rank are licensed to counsel the government on its most important policies, as long as they do so privately and discreetly, and do not get involved publicly in partisan disputes.

In the United States, the intellectual and academic tradition was different, and it produced a quite different institutional system, even though it had some of the features of an establishment. In the Jeffersonian tradition, the system was founded partly on the land-grant colleges, whose scientists created the unique American agricultural system; then Jeffersonian theory mixed with Hamiltonian practice established the great foundations, and made the principal private universities, once thought of as centers of pure scholarship, into decentralized systems for furthering not merely the advancement of science, but its application to public policy.[22] And if the mark of an establishment within the government is the ability to maintain a continuous access to the ear of the chief executive, the scientists have gained this status. The change in party control of the White House in 1961 brought in a new Council of Economic Advisers, and a new Budget Director, but the President's Science Advisory Committee was hardly affected. Both of the men who had served as chairman under Eisenhower remained on the committee under President Kennedy, and he chose as his new chairman a scientist who had been on the Eisenhower committee.

G. K. Chesterton once remarked that Great Britain could take pride in the fact that the sailors in the Royal Navy had never—well, hardly ever—mutinied, except for more pay. A social system is stable as long as its disputes are not over fundamentals. On this principle, the present scientific establishment in the United States is healthy enough; its internal arguments are mainly over the ways in which its grants and contracts are distributed, and from the outside it is challenged mainly with respect to the amount of money it gets, or the specific uses to which the money is put. With one exception, there has never been in American politics a serious effort to present the arguments, from the point of view of a conservative philosophy, against the intellectual approach of the scientific establishment whose theories have so profoundly influenced our national policies.

That exception was not altogether serious; it had some tragic elements, but they were mixed with low comedy. It was the effort made by a special committee of the House of Representatives, under the chairmanship of Congressman B. Carroll Reece (Republican of Tennessee) to investigate the work of the tax-exempt foundations. And the intellectual core of the investigation was an attack on the "growing movement to apply the methods used in the natural sciences to research in the social sciences."

This movement, the committee report argued in 1954, had led the social scientist to believe that the main purpose of his discipline was to catch up with the rigorous and value-free methods of the natural sciences. The effects of this belief were "an excess of empirical research," based on "inductive reasoning from observed data," and this in turn led to " 'moral relativity,' to the detriment of our basic moral, religious, and governmental principles."

It was, of course, the final political result of this methodological influence of the natural sciences that the writers of the report were interested in. They said of the scientific method: "Its natural outcome is an approach to Marxism—it is not surprising that so many of the social scientists tend to collectivism." This is dangerous both because "public opinion is greatly determined, in the long run, by the influence of intellectuals," and more specifically because "the government has come to rely upon foundations and foundation-supported organizations to provide 'social scientists' for research and in advisory capacities," with the effect of "infiltrating government with subversives."[23]

Except for the point about subversives, the argument was one that might have gained considerable support from any of the several conservative schools of thought that were becoming fashionable in American academic life, and that were undertaking to defend the traditional against the scientific culture. For there were many respectable scholars who had been arguing that the structure of American society had been so shapeless, and its tradition so deficient in firm theological or philosophical principles, that it had no inner defenses against the domination of public affairs by a technology devoid of purpose or spiritual values. Science, this line of argument ran, had had its modern origins in Western Europe in the intellectual movement that was associated with the rise of Protestantism, and perhaps even earlier with the heretical ideas of the nominalists. Its radical implications were kept in some check in Western Europe by the traditional structure of society, but in the United States—with no aristocratic tradition, and no established church or bureaucracy —the scientists and their intellectual allies had no real opposition in imposing their ideas on public policy. Worst of all, they seemed to have an edge in the competition for foundation grants.

This was a legitimate though highly debatable point of view, and something like it had become current in various centers of academic and governmental thought. For examples, one might cite among the professional scholars the ideas of the neo-Thomists gathered at the University of Chicago under the leadership of President Robert M. Hutchins and Mortimer Adler,[24] and among public officials, the quite different ideas of George F. Kennan, who had never been persuaded by liberal scientists that the atomic bomb had made us into One World, or that technical assistance was rapidly turning all the underdeveloped countries into democracies.

But intellectuals of the genuinely conservative tradition were not the allies that Mr. Reece was seeking: he listed Messrs. Hutchins, Adler, and Kennan in his report among those whose names were in the files of the House Committee on Un-American Activities, and used their association to help document the subversive guilt of the foundations. And Mr. Reece's purpose was certainly not to establish a conservative political authority in the United States; it was only to prove the charge that he announced as he started his inquiry: "Here lies the story of how communism and socialism are financed in the United States."[25] The success of his effort depended on his ability to persuade the country that the main ideas in American intellectual life had been invented by a big-money conspiracy, a feat so obviously beyond the competence of "big money" that it was hard for politicians to take the charges seriously, even in the era of McCarthyism. The investigation collapsed shortly after a minority member of the committee read aloud (without identifying) excerpts from Papal encyclicals, and a member of the committee staff said that they were "closely comparable to Communist literature," and that their objectives "parallel very closely communistic ideals."[26]

The Reece report was a good example of the empirical research that it denounced: it amassed a great deal of detail to prove what every academic administrator in the United States knew—that the major foundations, the major universities, the major scholarly associations and their federations, and the major government agencies all kept in touch with each other and exchanged ideas and personnel, and that science was the main source of the ideas they respected most. But it was tragically deficient in the theoretical interpretation of its data. It did not recognize that the main source of the intellectual tradition that it was attacking was not Marxist, but Jeffersonian—just as its own attack was based on a Jeffersonian dislike of concentrated economic influence, rather than on a conservative philosophy drawn from the prescientific theological tradition.

For better or for worse, science escaped from the institutional domination of the older culture very early in the history of the United States, and in its relation to the administrators of academic and public affairs it has been in a position of predominant influence ever since. The traditional culture, derived from theology and the old philosophy, has had comparatively little organized influence on politics; there is simply no conservative political faction of any consequence that has its intellectual roots in the old tradition, to counterbalance the newer and more radical influence of science. This is perhaps a weakness in American politics; the most ardent conservatives are, like the late Congressman Reece, not conservatives at all in the historical and philosophical sense of that term; they are radicals committed to a particular set of economic and technological interests.[27]

Science in the United States might as well quit rebelling against the older culture from which it sprang. It has become independent of its father long since; its more dangerous rival is its technological offspring. If science wishes to continue to guard its freedom and emphasize its purpose of knowledge and understanding for their own sakes, it might well begin to worry about the prospect of a society dominated entirely by technological purpose. Science might well wonder whether it might not have fared better in a society in which the theological and political traditions of free institutions remained powerful. But if that is so, science cannot count on being protected by the older tradition, which unaided is much too feeble in the United States to set limits on the purposes of technology.

THE SELF-RESTRAINT OF SCIENCE

Out of its own methods and its own approach, science will have to make some contribution to a new theory about its proper relation to politics. We can best judge what that contribution may be, not by listening to what scientists say specifically on political subjects, but to what they say about their own work as scientists.

The average citizen who reads Sunday supplements or the

political scientist who reads Congressional hearings may get the impression that scientists now think that science may some day, even if it cannot now, provide the answer to any question of policy. Many scientists feel obliged to assert their potential jurisdiction in this way; they believe that science, for more than three centuries, has been winning its intellectual battle against theology and traditionalism, and do not see why it should accept any limits on its victory except as a temporary tactic. At times, this point of view—which is characteristically expressed more often by the Outsiders, who are most conspicuous as critics of public policy, than by the Insiders, who have to help administer it—seems to represent nearly a consensus in the scientific community. Many scientists, even when they support the Insiders as a practical necessity, seem to think that they are making unworthy compromises with politicians and administrators, much as pious vestrymen feel guilty if they support local politicians who tolerate a certain amount of commercial vice in order not to hurt business.

On the other hand, if the layman takes even a brief excursion into the writings of leading scientists, and takes note of what they say about their own business, he is not persuaded that science is a form of knowledge whose practitioners are growing in confidence about their ability to understand and interpret reality, especially with respect to problems that are related to human purposes. Still less is he persuaded that scientists themselves are inclined to unite in an organization that could help to persuade the general citizenry to accept science as an authoritative guide to policy decisions.

For example, the revolution in physics over the past half-century left many of the more philosophical physicists, especially the leaders of the older generation, with much less confidence that physics can ever reach a complete understanding of concrete reality. The majority of the younger generation may not accept this philosophical pessimism, and may hold to a faith that science can in principle answer any question that is scientifically meaningful, but they set such limits on the kinds of questions that they consider to have real meaning that they exclude many of the philosophical or political questions that most interest the layman. During the same period, scientists in other disciplines have come to be much less inclined to think that it will ever be possible to develop a single mechanical and deterministic science, to which all other sciences can be reduced in a grand and unified system.[28]

I am not concerned here with the issue whether in theory physics (or any other science) may some day actually provide a complete understanding of nature, or solve any concrete political problem. That is a metaphysical issue that has no operational meaning to a student of politics. I am concerned rather with what scientists themselves think about that issue, for it is hard to imagine that science could provide the intellectual basis for a new theory of politics unless scientists generally believed that their methods contained some promise of dealing comprehensively with major political issues—as the materialist dialectic proposes to deal with problems of history and politics as well as problems of physics. And the most pertinent fact is that most American scientists seem to think that such an idea is either irrelevant to their interests, or merely silly.

Their attitude comes in the main not from any loss of self-confidence on the part of the scientist in his particular discipline. Few doubt, moreover, that there is in some sense a fundamental unity of science, and that over the past half-century the several sciences have greatly enlarged their common stock of general principles, and of their conceptual tools of inquiry. Many hold more firmly than ever to their belief that scientific concepts will be progressively unified in principles of increasing generality. Nevertheless, all this is quite different from the much simpler scientific faith of the nineteenth century, which showed more confidence in the complete adequacy of science as a means of understanding reality, and in the possibility of extending the principles of mechanics so as completely to understand and then to predict and control human and social affairs. That was the kind of intellectual faith on which a genuinely authoritative political philosophy could be based.

Physicists began to lose that kind of confidence in the nineteenth century as they went beyond the solid and predictable matter that seemed to correspond to the ordinary man's notion of what was real. The electromagnetic theory of Faraday and Maxwell, for example, made Kelvin uncomfortable because he could not devise a mechanical model of it.[29] And as the physicist got inside the atom, he entered a universe to which some of the older generation never became reconciled; to them it seemed to contain phenomena that were for the first time, even in principle, unknowable and unmeasurable; and individual bits of inanimate matter seemed to behave without obeying the classical laws of cause and effect.

The younger generation of physicists apparently got used to all this quite promptly. They did not even expect to think in terms of the mechanical models, or the aesthetic analogies, that had been the foundations of the scientific faith of their elders. Einstein tried to convey to the layman some notion of the mathematical and abstract nature of modern physics by saying that the scientist "certainly believes that, as his knowledge increases, his picture of reality will become simpler and simpler and will explain a wider and wider range of his sensuous impressions." At the same time, he warned, the scientist has to understand reality in the way a man might if he had to study a watch without opening it. "He will never be able to compare his picture with the real mechanism and he cannot even imagine the possibility or the meaning of such a comparison."[30] The younger physicists characteristically did not even care whether there was a watch there in the first place; if they could identify the things they could observe, and measure and predict their relationships, they were not interested in the kind of "reality" that was beyond their observation, and were not sure that it made sense to assume that it existed.

The great advances in the physicists' understanding of the material world have apparently come from this kind of selective interest. Science has achieved its great power by insisting on defining for itself the problems it proposes to solve, and by refusing to take on problems merely because some outside authority considers them important. But that power, and the precision of thought on which it depends, is purchased by a refusal to deal with many aspects of such problems. Some of those aspects are those that always appeal to the child and the poet, and that used to concern the philosopher—notions of ultimate cause and of human purpose. Thus Newton refused in the *Principia* to try to answer the question how one celestial body could move another without touching it; by setting aside the question that Aristotle and Descartes had considered important, he made it possible not only to predict the movements of the planets, but to relate them to the general laws of mechanics on earth. The demand of each scientific discipline for the right to choose its own problems, and fit them to its concepts and techniques and instruments, suggests that science is not eager to undertake to solve the problems of society as society would define them—especially since politicians so often insist on defining such problems in terms of purpose.

A generation ago, a number of physicists were so impressed by the new quantum mechanics, and especially the new uncertainty principle—resulting from the discovery that it was impossible at the same time to determine with precision the position and the velocity of an electron—that their confidence was shaken in the regularity of natural phenomena, and the operation of cause and effect. As a result, a few of them took to mystical speculation, and most of them concentrated on their specific research interests and ignored the philosophical implications, but those with the broadest interests undertook to grapple with the problem in a scientific spirit. In recent years, for example, the less mystical and more positivistic among the physicists—for example, the late Percy W. Bridgman—have been likely to worry about the limits on the ability of science to know and to predict.

Even if the physicist retains full confidence, in principle, in the regular sequence of cause and effect, in practice he acknowledges that it is impossible to predict the future from the present position and motion of the atoms without having a limited number to observe under controlled conditions, which means without letting anything come in from outside to upset the experiment. The idea of determinism, in short, has meaning only within a controlled experiment of reasonable size; to talk of determinism throughout the universe, Bridgman argued, becomes meaningless for any but metaphysical or religious purposes.[31] Moreover, there is the limit that is set on the exactness of science by the need to take into account, in any observation, the instruments which give you the knowledge of the things you are studying, as well as the things themselves. As Bridgman noted, this problem comes up not only in dealing with the very small-scale phenomena— as when it becomes impossible to determine simultaneously the position and velocity of an electron precisely—but in dealing with very large systems. For you cannot understand and control your data unless you understand and control your instruments as well, and once your data reach a certain quantity the control of those instruments will require other instruments, and so on "in infinite regress."

Bridgman summed up these limitations—in a bit of fanciful speculation—by considering the problem of studying the functioning of the human brain by looking at its individual atoms. In addition to the time required to observe all their vast number, and to consider their interrelationships, there would be the time needed to put the observations into words, and then argue about those words. This would lead, he gloomily observed, to another infinite regression.

The biological or social scientist is not nearly so frightened by the quantity and complexity and (in practice if not in theory) the unpredictability of the data he has to work with. He is used to dealing with statistical models and probabilities, and inclined to scoff at the timidity of the professor of the supposedly more rigorous discipline who considers it impossible to think at all scientifically about a subject unless it is subject to completely deterministic rules. But the "harder" sciences seem less eager than they once were to extend their jurisdiction, or to assert their readiness to solve all problems. They are inclined to avoid many questions that the layman would wish to ask, because they consider them either too difficult or meaningless, and they seem to take pride in the discovery that they have reached limits on what can be known about certain physical phenomena.

The main purpose of science as such can no longer be defined in terms of "useful knowledge"; it is less a matter of providing answers than of opening up new questions. James B. Conant defined science as a series of concepts arising from experiment and observation, and fruitful of further experiments.[32] This emphasis, as Gerald Holton has pointed out, has led in its extreme form to an interest in highly specialized and sharply defined problems, and simultaneously a complete suspension of curiosity in all other directions; and in its less extreme form, to an "existential acceptance of the known and unknown."[33]

Thus the logical affinity of modern science, in its most rigorous and positivistic forms, does not seem to be with nineteenth-century idealism, the philosophy which was allied with a belief in the unity of all knowledge and which was taken to serve as the basis for powerful authoritarian systems of politics. Instead it seems to be with existentialism. Science does not seem to expect to establish a body of set truths that can serve as a dogmatic basis for political action. The main philosophical threat to our freedom is not that science will tempt us to invent a new materialist dialectic, or establish a "1984" style dictatorship. It is rather that if we rely on science alone we will be left with no sense of the purpose of existence, and thus no basis for determining our political goals to guide the blind forces of applied technology.

Let us leave the physicists for the moment, move along the line from the hard toward the soft sciences, and look at biology.

Here we find a number of leading biologists worrying about the relevance to science of the idea of purpose, and openly in rebellion against the "reductionist" philosophy, which proposed not only to make biology more scientific by eliminating notions of purpose, but also by reducing it to the analytical approaches of physics and chemistry. Niels Bohr once noted the limitation on the methods of physics in studying a living organism: to make a complete analysis would destroy it and ruin the observation. But the point made by biologists is even more fundamental: as René Dubos argued, even if you could carry on such an analysis, the analytical process inherently ignores the fact that "the traits, properties, and activities associated with the living process are the expressions of the interplay between the constituent parts, rather than of their individual characteristics." The analytical techniques associated with physics and chemistry cannot account for the phenomena most characteristic of life, especially "a continuous interplay with the environment involving 'purposiveness' or at least 'directiveness.' "[34]

If Dubos shows a little unwillingness to commit himself altogether to the word "purposiveness," he may well be trying to distinguish his position carefully from those who, like Teilhard de Chardin or E. W. Sinnott, are considered by some of their colleagues to be guilty of sympathy with the scientific heresy of vitalism, which skirts close to the edge of mysticism.[35] Even those biologists who dislike to use the term "purpose" in connection with the evolution or development of biological systems are likely to be just as insistent as Dubos on the limitations which science must acknowledge when it undertakes to deal with living organisms. Ernst Mayr, for example, will have nothing to do with any teleology (in the sense of anything that smacks of the notion of evolution guided by a final goal or purpose) but insists that biology, unlike most physics, has to admit a high degree of unpredictability or indeterminacy in its subject matter. Individual events take place essentially at random, particularly in heredity; each animal is truly unique; each is so complex that a complete description of it is quite impossible; and in the interaction of living beings new qualities emerge that are not logically predictable from their previous properties. For all these reasons, though statements in biology can have scientific validity, it is a statistical validity, and the future of an individual organism is not predictable.[36]

As we move along Auguste Comte's spectrum from physics to biology, and on to the social sciences, we find all these same difficulties intensified. Social scientists generally have hoped that, by making their disciplines more exact, and by imitating the quantitative and rigorous methods of the natural sciences, they could (a) provide more reliable guides to those who have to make policy decisions, and might even (b) provide the answers to the main policy problems. These two hopes, at first thought, seem very much the same. But they are fundamentally different, and the difference turns on some of the points I have been discussing.

The critics of the social sciences have been inclined to say that they will neither provide reliable guides to the policy maker nor provide the answers to policy problems, for two reasons: first, their subject matter is too complex, and second, they mix up their scientific approach with value judgments. There is no doubt that these two limitations, as a matter of degree, have been severe. In the same way that biology is more complex than physics, and therefore involves less certainty and predictability, so the various social sciences are more complex and difficult than biology. Moreover, as in physics, problems arise not only from the magnitude and complexity of the data, but from the unreliability of the instruments of observation. Man in society is hard to study scientifically less because he is a complicated object of observation than because he is the instrument of observation, and a refractory one indeed. If modern psychology has taught man anything, it is just how irrational and perverse and unreliable an instrument he is for scientific purposes. It is certainly much harder for him to purge his mind of prejudices and value judgments when he is dealing with human and social problems than with the data of the physical sciences.

Yet these two limitations can be overcome to a very considerable degree, and are being overcome, by those aspects of the social sciences that rely on quantitative techniques, such as econometrics, or that are developing more reliable methods that are linked with biology and psychology, such as the behavioral sciences.[37] Every advance in the precision of our understanding of facts can also contribute to the sharpening of our value judgments. As a result, these disciplines are beginning to furnish the politician or administrator who must decide policy questions with an increasing quantity of data and of methods that can be useful to him. There is every reason to believe that, as they become more exact and reliable, they will continue to do so.

But that is fundamentally different from the question with which we are concerned: namely, whether scientists believe that science can solve major policy problems, and thus provide the basis for a new system of political decision. And on that question, as the social scientists succeed in pushing rigorous and exact methods of research toward the "soft" end of Comte's scientific spectrum, they are less inclined to try to relieve political and legal authority of its burden of making decisions in which unscientific value judgments will play a major part.

I will go into the practical aspects of this problem in more detail in the next chapter, but one illustration may be useful here. The most widely discussed use of the social sciences in a major governmental decision in the United States was probably the use by the Supreme Court of sociological evidence in its decision forbidding racial segregation in public schools. A good many social scientists were at first eager to take as much credit as possible for this decision, and to argue that it proved what objective scientific method could accomplish if freed from irrational beliefs and prejudices. Then came a tangled public argument between those anthropologists and psychologists who held that science proved that the races were intellectually equal, and hence should not be segregated, and those who argued that they were not, and hence should be. And so the Committee on Science in the Promotion of Human Welfare of the American Association for the Advancement of Science concluded in a public report that the question of intellectual equality was too complicated to be proved one way or the other, and in any case was not really germane; the main question turned on a political and legal principle that was at bottom a matter of ethical belief.[38]

This suggests that the social sciences may now be following the earlier examples of the physical and the biological sciences not merely in trying to achieve greater precision and reliability in their methods, but also in understanding that such precision is purchased by an abstraction, and an exclusion of concern for purposes and values, that make it impossible to deal simultaneously with all the aspects of any concrete problem. The maturity of a science may be measured not only by its power, but by its discrimination in knowing the limits of its power. And if this is so, the layman does not need to worry lest the social sciences, as they become more scientific, will be more likely to usurp political authority. On the contrary, they will stop short of trying to solve completely our major political problems not because they are unlike the natural sciences, but to the extent that they are like them. And the more they get to be like them, the more they will be of specific service to the policy maker, and the less they will pretend that their methods can measure all relevant aspects of any concrete problem and supply its final answer.

The scientist at work in his laboratory has not, during the twentieth century, been pursuing the ideal of a single scientific method that is gradually giving a single comprehensive view of reality. He has been developing the particular method of a particular discipline, the one that works well and produces results with respect to a special aspect of reality. And when he undertakes to join with his fellow scientists to advance his discipline, he finds it most useful to associate not with a continuously broadening group, but a narrower and more specialized one.

The first scientific organizations in the United States were comprehensive, like the American Philosophical Society, which in the eighteenth century included all the sciences together with all other branches of learning, or, in the next century, like the American Association for the Advancement of Science, which united at least all the natural sciences. But the more advanced the science, the less it seemed to be interested in building up a comprehensive organization; the physicists and chemists concentrated their attention so much on their respective specialized societies that they were much weaker in the American Association for the Advancement of Science than the biologists and geologists.

Even when new scientific concepts and techniques began to integrate the methods of certain sciences, the result was not to unite their organizations but to split them further. As the techniques of chemistry began to be more useful in biology, the result was not to unify the associations of chemists and biologists, but to add a new American Society of Biological Chemists. The scholarly and professional motives of the scientist led toward ever-increasing specialization; the 1960 catalogue of scientific and technical societies in the United States and Canada listed 1,836 organizations.[39] Scientists have indeed managed to maintain comprehensive organizations. But they have done so only when they have been interested in some purpose beyond science itself. For example, they established the Federation of American Scientists, and in recent years built up the American Association for the Advancement of Science, out of an interest not only in science but also in its social and political implications. Similarly, they have set up organizations to represent them in doing business with the government—the purpose that led to the creation of the National Academy of Sciences in the nineteenth century, and the American Institute of Biological Sciences in the twentieth.

THE RETREAT TOWARD ABSTRACTION

So it seems obvious that science is not moving toward the development of a unified system of knowledge that can solve political problems. And it seems equally obvious that scientists are not developing a unified and disciplined organization through which the scientific community will become a powerful political force.

One might then ask whether the intellectual world is moving in the opposite direction. From the point of view of the scientist, are we on the road to reaction? If the methods of the natural sciences have not proved adequate to deal with the complexities of social problems, are we about to give up the effort of the Enlightenment to introduce rationality into politics, and surrender to a revival of theological authority over moral and political purpose?

This possibility might seem a plausible one but for one curious fact: it was not the conservative but the liberal wing of theology that tried to take advantage of the uncertainty that developed in the self-confidence of science. When a few of the twentieth-century physicists began to note that certain things were in principle unknowable and others did not seem to follow the classical laws of cause and effect, it was mainly the theological liberals who thought that we might smuggle back into our philosophical system some notion of Divine Providence intervening occasionally in the affairs of the world. If the biologists, they went on to suggest, find that the study of living matter requires us to think in terms of its purpose, may not Evolution be seen as the working of a Divine Plan? Some of the more liberal theologians thus undertook to reconcile science and religion, to the great relief of many of their followers who had been made uncomfortable by finding the old unity of faith and learning disrupted. So they were reassured to think that, in Henry Drummond's words, "science has supplied theology with a theory which the intellect can accept and which for the devout mind leaves everything more worthy of worship than before."[40] Some of the scientists, too, were willing to take on the mantle of prophets, and to draw religious or mystical consequences from the new uncertainties of their science. Thus Sir James Jeans argued that the mysteries of Nature could be understood only as phenomena of Mind or Spirit—or, as he said in his presidential address to the British Association for the Advancement of Science in 1934, the compulsion of determinism may originate in our own minds.[41]

Now it is quite clear that the leaders of scientific and those of religious thought do not waste as much time quarreling with each other as they did a half-century ago. But this cessation of hostilities did not come about through a real reunion, with more scientists discovering grounds for faith through their science and more theologians relying on science for evidence of their beliefs. On the contrary, during the past quarter-century the most important leaders in both fields have been inclined simply to pull their troops back from the battle and to respect the territory of the other camp.

Thus the Catholic philosopher Jacques Maritain, while welcoming the spiritual effects on certain scientists of the "troubled and divided state of mind" resulting from the crisis of modern physics, goes on to argue that "most of the great contemporary physicists who turn to philosophical problems"—he had mentioned Jeans, Sir Arthur Eddington, Arthur Compton, and Erwin Schrödinger—get into all sorts of logical weaknesses and confusion by trying to extend their scientific methods into another field. By contrast, he praises the scrupulous logic, within fields which have meaning for the scientist as such, of the logical positivists, who are interested only in things which can be observed, measured, and dealt with by mathematical symbols. The concepts of modern science like physical indeterminism may in the end help establish true faith, but only if science and theology are seen as distinct fields of knowledge.[42]

In this point of view, Maritain is at one with the most influential leaders of the new Protestant theology. In different ways, Karl Barth, Paul Tillich, and Reinhold Niebuhr neither try to fight against science nor make use of it; they are concerned with things that operate on another plane altogether. There is clearly, among such theologians, much less of a disposition today than a quarter-century ago to buttress theology by finding uncertainties or mysticism within the ranks of the scientists, or analogies between theological and scientific concepts.[43]

It may be significant that this reaction against the earlier type of theological liberalism has not led theologians to try to develop more precise moral codes on the basis of their theoretical doctrines, or in practice to argue that organized religion should have greater political authority. The new leaders of Protestant theology not only seem to have no ambition to re-establish the controls over public morals in which their Calvinist ancestors took such pride, but they have given up the interest of their immediate liberal predecessors, the advocates of the Social Gospel, in striking up an alliance with applied science to solve specific social problems. This is true, obviously, of the theologians like Tillich[44] who represent the existential wing of contemporary religious thought, but it is even more true, perhaps, of the neo-orthodox, like Barth, whose God is abstracted nearly as effectively as the space-time continuum from the practical moral and political issues of the world today.[45] And those neo-orthodox theologians who are most interested in practical politics, like Reinhold Niebuhr, are as eager to avoid the belief that man can translate Divine Purpose into political decisions as they are to base their faith on something other than the evidences of science.[46]

If science and theology are less in conflict today, it is only partly because science is now less inclined to insist that its method is the only way to think about man and the universe. It is more because theology—or at any rate, leading theologians—make much less confident claims today than a century ago that their form of knowledge can be related with certainty to material and political affairs. Academic theologians may indeed have gone too far in this direction for the taste of the average scientist and engineer, as well as the average man. If one straw can show which way the wind is blowing, it may be significant that the main strength of the more fundamentalist Christian association in American colleges and universities, the organization created by those who considered the World Council of Churches and its student affiliate too modernist and not literal enough in their beliefs, has been drawn from faculty members and students in the natural sciences and engineering.[47]

Some philosophers of science may look forward to the day when science will displace the traditional values of morals or politics. But the working natural scientist usually seems to be bored by the idea. Typically, the notion appeals more to certain types of social scientist or political theorist; it was Thomas Hobbes, after all, who anticipated the physical scientist's taste for reducing human actions to physical phenomena, by building his political theory on the assumption that all change is nothing but motion.[48] The recent skepticism of the natural scientists about their ability to attain ultimate and certain knowledge, and their growing unwillingness to reduce the sciences themselves to a single operational or philosophical system, do not offer much intellectual basis for the development of a new ideology or a new ruling priesthood. Scientists, in the way they think, are still dissenters, even after they have gotten themselves established.

As individuals, scientists have no great trouble in reconciling either their skepticism, or their confidence in determinism, with moral purposes and values. Some of the physicists and mathematicians, when reality seemed to dissolve into meaningless symbols, took refuge in the sane realities of ordinary personal relationships. Hermann Weyl, for example, described the "ridiculous circle" of meaninglessness into which he had been led by the formalism of modern mathematics and physics, and said, "We escape it only when we understand the manner in which we deal in daily life with things and people to be an unreducible foundation."[49] And thus Bridgman was able to say, on the level of personal knowledge, "In the end, when . . . human weariness and the shortness of life forces us to stop analyzing our operations, we are pretty much driven to accept . . . a feeling in our bones that we know what we are doing." "We disregard determinism when dealing with ourselves; we have to disregard it also, within reason, in our everyday contacts with our fellows."[50]

If the scientist makes something like a leap of agnostic faith in his personal life, the sciences do something of the same sort when they deal with public issues. By eliminating the bias of human purpose from their methods, and by concentrating on material causes, they do not seem to destroy the political independence or sense of commitment of scientists, who as citizens seem no more inclined than laymen to be either determinists or skeptics. Perhaps they know better than anyone else that science does less to provide final answers to political issues than to open up new ones, and that men in authority will always have to make responsible choices without the assurance of absolute certainty. Far from despising moral and political values, or doubting their existence, they seem to think them so important that science ought to be concerned with helping to test and refine and clarify them—and to refuse to be used as a mere instrument of any political authority that is based on values that are not able to stand up to such testing.

But in undertaking to relate knowledge to the responsible use of political authority, the scientist runs into complications that do not confront him as he adjusts his personal philosophy to his individual behavior. Here is where the great power of the natural sciences does not do away with the need for a political or constitutional theory, but makes it all the more necessary.

This problem cannot be solved by encouraging science to extend its progress in a single dimension, along Comte's spectrum from the hard to the soft sciences, with the expectation that at the end it will conquer and occupy the old stronghold of theology and philosophy in the determination of the values that form the basis of our political decisions. For the fortress of politics has long since been deserted by the theologians and philosophers, at least by the more scholarly among them. And the value system of politics, like that of most individuals, is not a code of rules discovered in advance by abstract study, but is a less precise set of attitudes developed in a series of concrete actions. In politics those actions take place in a continuous process of cooperation and compromise between those who work to discover or develop abstract and precise systems of knowledge and those who make use of such knowledge to further human purposes.

This system of relationships runs along a spectrum in a quite different dimension from Comte's; it runs from the abstract and theoretical knowledge of science, which is by its nature free of human purposes and passions, first to the types of skills and knowledge organized and applied by the professions (like engineering and medicine) that are based on science, and then to those of administrators, and finally of politicians. These several types of skills and knowledge are in turn progressively less concerned with precise abstractions, and more with the responsible use of power in the application of value judgments to questions which science is never quite able to answer completely.

Along this spectrum, science is not in conflict with the disciplines of the older tradition of humane learning. On the contrary, it shares with them a common set of problems. It is impossible for either kind of scholarly knowledge, in a free constitutional system, to be translated directly into political decisions. In Western nations, the theologians have long since been forced to learn how to let lawyers and administrators serve as the intermediaries between their abstract truth and the politicians who exercise supreme authority. The scientists are newcomers to the status of being established with public support, and are not yet altogether persuaded that they need to develop a clear constitutional theory of their relation to political authority.

The scientists have one advantage: in theory it has been rather more clear to them than to most of the theologians that they can develop their kind of knowledge only by freeing themselves from assumptions about human purposes and values. Thus they have protected themselves, to some extent, from the temptations of power and the dangers of political control. By the very nature of their discipline, they remain dissenters, with no interest in founding a new political dogma. But they need a great deal of money from the government, and what they do with it has an obvious impact on public policy. Even as dissenters, they must be established, and the future status of their estate must be developed with care if we are to adjust our constitutional system to modern technology without losing our freedom.

CHAPTER 5

The Spectrum from
Truth to Power

EDDINGTON, AS A POPULARIZER of the new science, used to startle the layman by pointing out that the table in front of him was really two tables. One was the table of everyday experience, firm and solid. The other was the real table, the table that was known to the hard sciences, and it was made up of insubstantial atomic particles and a lot of empty space. The mere housewife, after listening to such a lecture, was a little inclined to be afraid that the dinner she set on the table might fall through it. At this level of experience, of course, not many people are unduly confused by the problem how to relate the abstractions of science to their concrete policy problems; Eddington's lay listeners went on eating substantial dinners, and took no more practical notice of his abstractions than his scientific students took of his religious views.

The ordinary citizen, in his everyday personal experience, does not need to worry about the abstractions of modern science. He can ignore Eddington's other table. The real table, for him, is the one he sees and feels; his test of the relevance of the new physics is the same as the one that Dr. Samuel Johnson applied to Bishop Berkeley's metaphysics when he kicked the stone in the street and proved to his own satisfaction that it was real. But the ordinary citizen today must be more discriminating in his thinking about abstractions and their relation to reality. For some practical purposes, the concepts of the new science are as irrelevant as were Eddington's theories to the housewife's dinner table; for others, they are the key to the future. So the ordinary

abstractions

citizen, with respect to the larger issues that face the nation and the world, cannot afford to dismiss the abstractions of modern science as ideas that are irrelevant to practical concerns; when properly applied they are obviously the source of tremendous power that can determine the success or failure of human purposes. How they are applied to those purposes may determine the future of humanity, or whether it is to have any future. This is a question that the ordinary citizen is interested in, no matter how ignorant he may be of science. So his problem is how he, or his representatives, can control the purposes to which science is applied, especially when he cannot understand science, and is not in the habit of electing representatives who know any more about it than he does.

To cope with this problem, it is tempting to turn to one of two alternatives, both of which try to preserve the ideal that an electorate, or its elected representatives, should make policy decisions by public discussion of the key issues, including their scientific aspects.

The first of these alternatives proposes to rely on giving the average citizen a deeper understanding of science. This is the classic formula of Jeffersonian democracy, and there is no doubt that if the electorate can have a better comprehension of science, the processes of politics can deal more rationally with the issues of a technological age. But this is a less plausible prescription for a complete cure than it once seemed. It is less plausible because, as we have seen, science has not only become so abstruse and so specialized that the great majority of men and women (including scientists) cannot be expected to understand very much of it, but it has also become so abstract that it is hard for the expert, let alone the layman, to tell just how it may be relevant to any given problem. While the physical sciences have for several decades been making themselves less comprehensible to the layman, the social sciences have been casting doubt on the concept of the rational voter, and on the idea that the rational debate of issues in a legislature is the main balance wheel of a democratic system.

As a result, many are persuaded not merely that we cannot build a nuclear-age society on a Jeffersonian model, but also that government must be entrusted to those who are expert.

As a result, some are inclined to turn to the second idealistic alternative: to advocate the advancement of scientists to positions of high authority, and to urge the scientific community to organize itself more adequately to accept its social responsibilities. This too is desirable, but like the proposal to educate the average citizen in science it is subject to considerable limitations. For a basic approach of modern science has been to purge itself of a concern for purposes and values, in order to deal more reliably with the study of material phenomena and their causes and effects. Men and institutions dedicated to this approach may find it hard to convert themselves to an interest in the purposes of politics, and when they do, they are as likely to disagree about them as any other citizens.

These two ideas are not exclusive alternatives; both are desirable, and (within limits) feasible. But they are not required by the political theory on which the American (or British) constitutional system was based, and we fortunately do not in practice rely mainly on them. For even if we had an electorate and a Congress made up entirely of scientists, we should still have to face the difficult part of the problem: how, after we know the scientific aspects of an issue, we may proceed to agree on what we wish to do about it and then to apply science to effect that purpose. And scientists as such prefer to have no more to do with the idea of purpose in the practical affairs of government than in their own scientific methods. That part of the problem they leave to the professions and to administration.

THE PROFESSIONALS

Enginering, medicine, and law, in different ways, have the function of taking the abstractions of science (or other systematic knowledge) and applying them to the concrete and practical affairs of men. That is not only their function; it is their purpose.

Science can insist on ignoring questions of purpose in order to be objective and precise; the professions cannot. So they sometimes take their purposes from generally accepted traditional values, which as professions they have to convert into working codes, as the physicians do when they start with the assumption that people generally wish to be healthy, and use to that end anything they can learn from biology. Or the professions take their purposes from the demands of their customers or employers, as an engineer does when he designs a bridge or an automobile, or from the decisions of duly constituted public authority. And that, of course, brings us to the kind of problem with which we are here concerned: the way in which a profession like engineering or medicine can serve as a bridge between the sciences and politics.

This function of the professions is not new: it has been of vital interest for a long time. When an engineer, following the safety regulations of the Coast Guard or the Federal Aviation Agency, translates the laws of physics into the specifications of a steamboat boiler or the design of a jet airliner, he is mixing science with a great many other considerations all relating to the purposes to be served. And it is always purposes in the plural— a series of compromises of various considerations, such as speed, safety, economy, and so on. Similarly, when a public health doctor or sanitarian translates the laws of biology into a system for the prevention or control of disease and epidemics, he is doing the same thing. With a little less precision, a budget officer or central banker does the same thing with respect to the science of economics.

Scientists who made the jump all at once from exploring the nucleus of the atom to thinking about the international control of atomic weapons—the long leap from science to politics— were tempted to transmute knowledge directly into political decisions without thinking much about the normal intervening stages, the stages of engineering and administration. To them, it seemed intolerable that decisions affecting the lives and welfare of themselves and their families should be made without full public understanding and debate of the issues, and especially of their scientific aspects. It is a safe guess that not many of them had the slightest interest in the technical procedures that governments were taking to safeguard the purity of the water that they drank every day, or to enforce building standards to make sure that their homes would not collapse or burn over their heads, or to make sure that the commercial airliners would carry them safely on their way to Los Alamos or Washington.

Each of these functions of government is carried on by engineering or medical professionals, applying scientific knowledge in the light of administrative and political considerations, and each is shot through with compromises (or, as weapons engineers like to say, trade-offs) among various purposes. We accept these compromises as a matter of course. It would be possible to eliminate nearly all cases of any particular epidemic disease, or nearly all transportation casualties, or for that matter nearly all professional crime, if we were willing to pay the price, in money or freedom or both. How far we go in any given case depends in part on scientific and technical considerations and in part on the opinion of the average citizen. But it depends, too, on the degree to which scientific and professional people are permitted to act on their own, and the degree to which they are subject to administrative and political control. And as the new science and new technology are now producing forces so powerful that they are matters of world-wide, rather than merely municipal, concern, the relation of the professions that are based on science—especially the engineering and medical professions—to the scientific community on the one hand, and to the world of administration and politics on the other, becomes a problem of some political and constitutional importance.

The role of these professions as intermediaries between abstract knowledge and political action is very like that of the profession of law (including the courts), which had to be created as an intermediary between church and government. Many of the great constitutional issues from the Middle Ages to the nineteenth century, in England and the United States, grew out of the relation of religion and politics. Religion was accepted as the source of truth, but laymen had the right to ask by what institutional arrangements, and what procedures, was that truth to be applied to human affairs? The solution was to take away from the churches the power to enforce their ideas, or even to define the laws that were to regulate personal and public affairs; this led to the growth of the legal profession, the independent judiciary, and legislatures that were conceded the power to enact new law as well as define traditional law. The Constitution of the United States was not merely an abstract invention, creating a mechanical system of checks and balances among masses of undifferentiated voters. It was also an attempt to find a workable balance in society among institutions and types of people—among the churches, which were to be established or disestablished according to the tastes of the several states, and the judiciary, which would of course be dominated by the legal profession, and the various types of military and civil officials and politicians.

Now that science is accepted as a source of truth at least equal in practical significance to theology, the institutions that proclaim its truths and apply them to public affairs have to work out with administrative and political authority their constitutional relationships. And the constitutional history of the twentieth century will have to be as preoccupied with the university laboratory and security clearances and the status of systems-engineering corporations, as that of an earlier era was with episcopacy and the test oaths and the independence of the judiciary. The analogy is by no means perfect, if only for the reason that there is no way out of our difficulties by means of disestablishing science; without government money you can worship but you cannot run cyclotrons and radio telescopes. More important, science has wrought changes in our society—in its urbanization, its standards of living, and its increase of population—that can be dealt with only with the help of science and the professions.

In another way, however, the analogy is helpful. The effort to disestablish the churches, and thus to reduce the direct control of ecclesiastical authority over secular affairs, was not the work of scientists, and perhaps not mainly of men with skeptical temperaments, but of men with strong religious convictions. The dissenters, wishing to restrict the political power of churches in order to keep them free of political control, had as much to do with their disestablishment as did the skeptics. Similarly, scientists themselves are generally not eager to have scientific institutions identified too closely with political power and political responsibility.

In the previous chapter, I considered the limitations—in practice and perhaps in theory—that science sets on its own ability to provide a complete knowledge of reality and to answer policy questions. The professionals who make it their business to relate scientific knowledge to political purpose are keenly aware of an analogous set of limitations on the competence of their professional skills.

THE LIMITS OF PROFESSIONAL COMPETENCE

In recent years, the most systematic professional experience that bears on this problem has been that in the field of operations research. In this very practical field, which has undertaken to apply the techniques of the exact sciences to the problems of almost all kinds of large organizations, public and private, the professional practitioners have been discovering limits on their techniques that are analogous to the limits that scientists have been discovering on their ability to acquire deterministic knowledge and to predict phenomena. Operations analysts, in manufacturing corporations as well as in government service, repeatedly observe that their scientific techniques work with greater power and precision on the problems encountered at lower levels of the administrative hierarchy. They observe that the higher the rank of the official needing answers to policy questions, the less exact and less reliable are the answers that scientific techniques can provide.[1] And these common observations correspond in some ways to the limitations—already discussed—on the ability of science to give a complete and predictable picture of the real world.

The first of those limitations comes from the very quality that has been responsible for science's great power: its high degree of abstraction, which has ruled out of consideration the biases and prejudices of human purposes, and rescued it from a confusion of ends and means. Because the sciences have moved ahead fastest in the most abstract fields, we as citizens (and our administrators and political leaders) have at our disposal precise techniques for answering questions before we know the questions we wish to ask. We like to make use of the skills about which we are sure, without always being willing to wait to consider with equal depth of study the more complex aspects of issues which are not susceptible to quantitative techniques. We prefer to leave those aspects to be decided by snap judgment or the prejudices of politicians.

As one operations analyst has put it, we have too many "studies which try to determine the exact best way to perform an operation which shouldn't be performed at all."[2] We ask our scientists and engineers to tell us the best way to design a high-altitude high-speed bomber to attack Moscow, when we may need instead a low-speed low-altitude observation plane to help get the guerrillas out of the jungles of Laos, or vice versa. It is clear that the aeronautical engineers can develop either kind of plane for us; it is also clear that we cannot decide what kind of strategy to adopt until the engineers tell us what kinds of planes they can develop, and just what those planes can do, and about what they will cost; but it is, unfortunately, equally clear that aeronautical engineering cannot solve the strategic and political question what kind of planes we ought to have.

This is a painfully obvious point, perhaps, but at times it seems that we are determined to ignore it. Our columnists and

Congressmen are not much interested in talking about whether we should put a man on the moon; it is much more interesting to argue about the various techniques of getting him there. You can readily invent chemicals to kill a pest like a fire ant, but it is harder to visualize the damage you may do to other animal and plant life if you use that chemical, and very much harder to decide how to staff the Department of Agriculture so as to get the right mixture of chemical and biological and political judgment involved in the decision whether to use it or not.[3] Chemistry is a more exact science than biology, and biology than administration, but the order of exactness may turn out to be the opposite of the order of importance for political decisions. For the importance and usefulness of a science may turn not on giving exact answers to the question that has been asked (or taken for granted) but on suggesting new or alternative questions. In public affairs as in physics, the problem never holds still; it is always being redefined.

This is in general the lesson learned by the social scientists, statisticians, and mathematicians who have worked on the theory of decisions. Science can contribute to the making of a decision only if someone has first specified a consistent set of objectives or values which he seeks to reach with maximum efficiency. And it is much easier to be consistent in thinking about small things that are closely related to each other, or in making a small additional improvement in a device or a procedure that is already well understood, than it is in thinking about a major problem of policy.[4]

Another limit on scientific precision that I discussed was the limit of size and complexity. In any major issue of policy or strategy, you cannot isolate and control all the things you are dealing with. And so in problems of military tactics and strategy, even though the weapons systems have been developed by engineers on physical principles, it has often been observed that some of the most effective operations research has been carried out not by the physical scientists, but by biologists or economists.

The head of an Air Force operations research unit at the time of the Korean War had been trained as an ichthyologist. This surprised some of his colleagues who had not read what P. M. S. Blackett had written in 1943. Blackett had pointed out that military forces were not willing to operate under the controlled conditions that please the physicist, who likes to have a "great deal of numerical data about relatively simple phenomena," so that the problems of analyzing war operations are "rather nearer, in general, to many problems, say of biology or of economics, than to most problems of physics."[5] Here again, the range from the more exact to the less exact sciences runs in inverse proportion to their suitability for solving problems that seem important to the average citizen or the administrator.

In administration as in physics, velocity can alter mass. The faster a situation is moving, the more it is affected by the problem of the quantity of data available. When a decision has to be made in a short time, you cannot wait to gather all the data that are relevant and determine your course of action according to the results of objective research. So the responsible official and his scientific adviser have to treat some parts of the problem as matters of pure chance, and others as value judgments, even though both might be determined by exact study if they had world enough and time.[6]

This is illustrated by the negotiation of the agreement between the United States and Russia for the prohibition of nuclear tests in the atmosphere. Throughout the talks, some political leaders seemed to be looking for ways to push their difficult policy problems off on the scientists, while some scientists were eager to make clear the limits on the ways in which science could contribute to the problem. As Dr. Wolfgang Panofsky, one of the technical consultants, pointed out later, the balance of risks in the proposed agreement turned only in part on the technical and scientific data—although these data provided the essential foundation and starting point for the discussion. They depended also on such other factors as the relative military posture of the two nations, and the effects on that relationship of various degrees of compliance or evasion of an agreement; on the capacity of intelligence agencies, by traditional espionage as well as technical means, to detect violations; on the effect of an agreement on world opinion and on the prospects for further arms limitations; and on the effect that control measures might have on international secrecy.[7]

It was the inherent uncertainty of such factors that caused the scientific witnesses before several committees of the Senate either to disagree with one another in their policy recommendations or to refuse to express any opinion at all on any questions but limited technical ones. This inability to give a scientific answer to a complex question was commented on with either cynical pleasure or despair by Senators of varying shades of opinion.[8]

Still another limit that physical scientists see on their ability to achieve precision and make predictions comes from the inadequacy of the instruments of observation. Bridgman despaired of getting a complete picture of the configuration of the atoms in any material system. How much greater is the problem of knowing the total picture in detail on any major political or administrative issue! Even before you get to the problem of human error and human motivation, you run up against the sheer cost of information in any operating system. The amount of time and effort spent in producing the data for the guidance of the executive and the legislature—the accounts, the personnel forms, the organization surveys, and the statistics—all this puts obvious limits on the use of a scientific method to govern large-scale economic or political systems.

But if the limits on predictability and control in the physical sciences have their analogies in public affairs, the limits of biology are even more relevant. The utterly random occurrence of significant events in biology, the uniqueness of every issue, the incalculable complexity of every system, and the way in which new issues and problems emerge when old ones are combined—

all these points have their obvious parallels in the world of public affairs. Such factors put limits on the precision and the predictive capacity of the sciences but, it is necessary to emphasize, they do not by any means make them powerless. There are many ways in which the scientific method can operate in situations of uncertainty. The statistical approach, and the modern techniques of cybernetics and control theory, can provide essential guides to action in fields in which the individual case cannot be observed or predicted. Even so, the essential decisions regarding the purposes which are to be served by such techniques, and the cases to which it will be useful to apply them, and how much to rely on their findings, generally remain matters of judgment which the techniques themselves cannot supply.[9] When statistical models fail to provide an accurate forecast of the future, it may be because of scientific or statistical uncertainty, or it may be because the statistician has deceived himself about the essential nature of his problem.

In the professions that make use of the sciences, there is plenty of controversy regarding the extent to which science can guide professional judgment. The profession of medicine has obviously made tremendous advances as a result of scientific research; yet even among professors of medicine warnings are raised against excessive faith in science. As one senior statesman of the profession put it, "The dogmatic assumption of determinism in human behavior, fostered in large part by the sophomoric expectation of certainty in knowledge," has a pernicious effect on the practice of medicine, by leading the young doctor to "try compulsively by the unwise and neurotic multiplication of tests and superfluous instrumentation to achieve the illusion of certainty . . . —a modernistic and expensive superstition."[10]

A similar distaste for excessive reliance on scientific methods is often shown by military officers, especially those who dislike the way in which the political executives of the Department of Defense use the findings of civilian operations analysts to refute recommendations from professional military men. As one military planner wrote, "Today's planning is inadequate because of its almost complete dependence on scientific methodology, which cannot reckon with those acts of will that have always determined the conduct of wars."[11] But in general, such critics have not been nearly as systematic and clear in explaining the limitations on scientific methods, and the necessity of subordinating them to a system of administrative judgment and political responsibility, as the leading operations analysts themselves have been.

Those analysts have a lively appreciation of the tremendous contributions science has made and is sure to make in the future to military affairs, but they also have a thoroughly professional understanding of the limits on the competence of scientific techniques to solve administrative and political problems. These limits do not derive from any traditional or mystical values, about which scientists are skeptical. Nor do they derive from any romantic conception of the importance of practical experience in actual combat, which they are inclined to resent—as one Pentagon scientist showed when, having been taunted by a noted general with his lack of battle experience, asked "How many thermonuclear wars have you fought?" They derive instead from the limitations, equally clear in scientific theory and in professional practice, on the possibility of applying abstract and systematic knowledge to the confused world of partial perception, in which the important problems are usually those that arise in unique and unpredictable situations.

THE FOUR ESTATES

So it is abundantly clear that some types of decisions have to be made, not by professionals using scientific techniques, but by other kinds of individual thought and collective deliberation. The members of the professions based on the sciences thus have a role in public affairs that is different from the role of the scientists on the one hand and from the roles of administrators and politicians on the other. Though the distinctions among these roles are not fully defined in legal terms, they are clear enough so that the several types of thought and action can be related to one another in an ordered system of authority and responsibility—in short, in a constitutional system.

The professions (for example, engineering and medicine) make tremendous use of the findings of the sciences, but they add something more: a purpose. Science has advanced by getting rid of the idea of purpose, except the abstract purpose of advancing truth and knowledge. But the profession puts it back again; basic science could not cure a patient or build a bridge or an airplane, but the medical and engineering professions are organized to do so. Each is organized around a combination of a social purpose and a body of knowledge, much of it drawn from science. Each is organized as an almost corporate entity, with some control over its standards of admission. Its responsibility to an individual client, or to a corporate or governmental employer, is to serve within a defined and limited field; within that field, the professional has an obligation to standards of ethics and competence that his profession, and not his employer, dictates. The engineer has a sense of responsibility to build structures or systems that will work, and this responsibility is not merely to his employer. The doctor feels an obligation to the patient that goes beyond any contractual relation with an individual client, or any administrative instructions from the clinic or hospital that may pay him.

The general administrator is, in these senses, not a professional: his responsibility is not restricted to some special aspect of an organization's affairs that is related to a special body of knowledge or a special type of training, and it is more difficult for him to define a sense of obligation to a professional purpose that to some degree transcends the purposes of his employer. He is obliged to deal with all aspects of the concrete problems that his organization faces, and for that reason his education—no matter how thorough and useful it may be—cannot be reduced to a specific discipline or a restricted field. On the contrary, he must be prepared to understand and to use a wide variety of professional expertise and scholarly disciplines, as he helps his political superiors (or the directors of a business corporation) attain their general purposes. Administrators may organize themselves into associations of a quasi-professional type, but they cannot, like the true professions, undertake to determine the standards for entrance into their vocation, since it is too much subordinated to the unpredictable purposes of politics or business. They are obliged to maintain standards of objectivity and competence; without their enforcement of these standards the politicians would be powerless to control the machinery of government. But administrators cannot base their standards on precise scientific knowledge.

Still further away from the precision and abstraction of the sciences, and from the self-discipline and body of established principles of the true profession, are the politicians. The men who exercise legislative or executive power may make use of the skills of administrators and engineers and scientists, but in the end they make their most important decisions on the basis of value judgments or hunch or compromise or power interests. There can be no common discipline or body of established principles to guide them, for their business is to deal with problems in which either the inadequacy of scientific and professional data, or the conflict of expert opinion, makes it necessary or possible to come to decisions that are based on judgment and must be sustained by persuasion or authority. In government, the politician is apt to make every decision both to accomplish its ostensible purpose and to maintain or increase his power—just as in private business, the principal executive or owner is apt to make every decision both to produce some product or service and to make a profit.

These distinctions exist within any large institution whether it is public or private. In a business organization the owners, or the board of directors and the principal executives, have the function of making the general and ultimate decisions that correspond to political decisions in government. The larger the corporation, the more the function will be political in the sense of being related to the politics of the local or national government, as well as in the sense of being concerned with such incalculable elements as public and employee relations.

The four broad functions in government and public affairs —the scientific, the professional, the administrative, and the political—are by no means sharply distinguished from one another even in theory, but fall along a gradation or spectrum within our political system. At one end of the spectrum, pure science is concerned with knowledge and truth; at the other end, pure politics is concerned with power and action. But neither ever exists in its pure form. Every person, in his actual work, is concerned to some extent with all four functions. The laboratory scientist is probably interested in some professional association with his colleagues, in the administration of his laboratory, and in the support for his work that comes only from money or influence. At the other extreme, the Congressman or the President must be interested in the ways in which new knowledge affects his status and his purposes, and in which professional skills and administrative competence can support them.

Yet men and institutions tend to associate themselves with one function or another, and many of the more interesting problems of politics arise from the ways in which these four types cooperate or conflict with one another. Their relationships have not made obsolete the classic concern of political science with the relations among branches or levels of government, and between them and competing political parties and economic or ideological interests. But they have added a significant and interesting complication to the study of contemporary politics, and one that will be of growing importance as long as science continues to increase its influence on public affairs.

In one sense, this is the revival of an old topic, and not the invention of a new one. The existence of political groups of institutions and individuals that are distinguished not by formal public office, nor by economic or class interest, but by the differences in the nature of their training and their skills, is no new phenomenon. To remind myself and the reader that this is not an altogether new phenomenon, but only an old one in new form, I am calling these groups by the old term "estates"—hoping that no one will imagine that I intend to suggest anything more than a very loose analogy indeed between these modern estates and their medieval counterparts.

The differences in function among the several estates are not merely based on tradition; they correspond in a measure to the nature of knowledge, and are found in every modern country. If a government is to act as an organized whole, it must make decisions on problems for which neither the sciences, nor the professions that are based on them, are prepared to give the complete answers. But although science can never provide a complete solution for any major political problem, no major problem can be dealt with today without its help, and its help can be effective only if it is given generous support, and a large measure of freedom, by government.

The scientific estate, of course, is merely a subdivision, although perhaps the most influential one, of the broader scholarly estate. Historically, the philosophers and the theologians, being concerned with another variety of pure knowledge, have played an analogous role in society. And the lawyers and the clergy, in taking over their basic ideas and applying them, with modifications, to human purposes, play important roles in the professional estate along with the engineers and the physicians. The difference between the older and the newer wings of each estate is that the Western world has had several centuries more experience in working out a satisfactory constitutional position for the lawyers and the clergy, while the scientists and engineers and physicians have risen so rapidly in influence as a result of the advancement of science that the politicians have not had time to develop a new set of relationships with them.

THE TWOFOLD PRINCIPLE OF FREEDOM AND RESPONSIBILITY

But the United States is clearly working out some crude principles as a basis for these relationships, or adapting some old ones, and these principles may help to establish a new set of checks and balances within the constitutional system. That system will be the subject of the next chapter, but it will be useful here to anticipate a general point. The most important principle seems to be a twofold one: (1) the closer the estate is to the end of the spectrum that is concerned solely with truth, the more it is entitled to freedom and self-government; and (2) the closer it gets to the exercise of power, the less it is permitted to organize itself as a corporate entity, and the more it is required to submit to the test of political responsibility, in the sense of submitting to the ultimate decision of the electorate.

It is true that in the United States the college or university is not organized in legal form as a self-governing community of scholars; it is either under the legal direction of a private board of lay trustees, or of a board of state officials. But in actuality, the American university, with respect to its academic affairs, is a community to which society concedes the right of self-government; the full members of the academic fellowship—the tenure professors—consider that they are entitled to control the admission of new members, and to protect them in their freedom. Similarly, the government concedes completely the right of scientists and scholars to organize any self-governing societies for scientific purposes that they please.

When it comes to the professions, whose work mixes a commitment of service to the public with its scientific interests, the government is usually content to leave the control of standards to the professional society as a matter of practice, but in theory (and sometimes in practice) it insists on maintaining the right to exercise control.

The administrators, who can rely less on systematic and testable knowledge and are closer to ultimate power, are not permitted to exercise, through their quasi-professional societies, any influence on the terms of their admission to their vocations. They are appointed, on terms regulated by law, by procedures controlled by politicians.

And as for the politicians who exercise ultimate power, but can never be certain that their major decisions are justified by scientific knowledge or provable truth, they are permitted to hold office only by periodic re-election by the people.

This twofold principle about the spectrum between power and truth is not generally accepted in all other parts of the world, even though the practice is reasonably similar in other English-speaking countries and in some countries of Western Europe. The existence of the four estates seems to be common to all countries with advanced science and technology: the respective functions of the estates seem to derive from the way in which any large-scale institution has to be organized in order to translate abstract scientific knowledge into purposeful action. But the mutual independence of the several estates seems to be a quite different matter, that is, one that is not determined by the nature of science and technology (or if you like, by the mode of production) but by the way men think about political power in relation to truth.

For the twofold principle that seems to be accepted in the United States is by no means axiomatic. The idea that an institution concerned only with truth should be permitted to govern itself, and the idea that those who hold political power should be accountable to the people, are plausible only on the basis of certain historic political assumptions. If you think of a nation primarily as an organization that must have a coherent purpose, and think of its inner institutional relationships as a problem in communications and control, you will come out with a quite different approach. The logic of that approach is quite simple: If we have a reliable method for discovering the truth, namely, science, should we not use it to solve all our most important problems? If we propose to do so, should not those who make our most important decisions be selected for their understanding of the most relevant science? How can such a process of selection be carried on except by the judgment of their peers (as any university department chooses its professors) rather than by a popularity contest among ignorant and apathetic voters? And if they are controlling society on scientific principles, should they not direct scientific institutions to carry forward their research along lines that will be of the greatest service to society?

The logic of these questions forces us to admit that, although the way in which scientific knowledge is related to political purpose seems to require the existence of something like our four estates, it by no means requires the relationship among them that is conventional in the Western constitutional tradition. "The real brains at the bottom," as our science fiction hero put it, is an accurate observation if not a justified complaint. Is it really right that supreme authority should be vested in the Congress and the top political offices in the executive branch, which are filled with men who by any conventional test of abstract and theoretical intelligence are not the match of the scientists and professionals who work several layers down in the hierarchy? Even if the government must make decisions that cannot be determined completely by the rigorous processes of the natural sciences, many new techniques exist for dealing in a scientific way with situations of uncertainty and incomplete knowledge. Since science is producing the dynamic changes in our society, why should not our government be headed by men who will bring to its administrative and political functions the greatest possible ability to use science to the maximum?

The answer to these questions turns not on what you think about the nature of knowledge, but on what you believe about the nature of man and politics.

The Western, and particularly the American, point of view is determined by two traditional fears. The first is the fear that the scientist or the professional will never be guided completely by his desire for scientific truth and his professional ethics; the second is the fear that he will. In logic, these fears are contradictory; politically, they lead to the same end.

As for the first fear, neither the politician nor the administrator is prepared to accept any institutional arrangements that depend on the detachment, the unselfishness, and the purely scientific motives of the scientist. His distrust is warranted by what the scientists themselves have told him. For if limits to objective knowledge are set by the nature of things and the imperfections of the instruments that science can use for observing them, the limits are even more severe when men are serving as those instruments, and making deductions from the observations. For it is not merely that there are finite limits to what man can observe and understand, but that he has a capacity that is nearly infinite for reading the evidence in the light of his own interests and passions.

To say this is not at all to deny that the sciences, within their own fields, provide a remarkably effective training in the virtues of objectivity and honesty. Even more important, they have the world's most effective policing system. Since the main prize in the game is the esteem of one's scientific colleagues for the results of one's research, and that esteem is based on the publication of the results of experiments which can be tested, the scientist has a most powerful incentive for objectivity and honesty. But the system works only when it deals with scientific data and logical patterns—abstractions from reality which can be dealt with uniformly in laboratories and studies all over the world. And to keep the system pure, scientists tend to frown on any colleague who mixes with such data irrelevant considerations like purposes or values that cannot be tested according to uniform standards by everyone else.

When scientists and engineers undertake to apply science to practical problems, however, they find it impossible to stick to quantitative data and rules of logic. The problems include too many other aspects, and in dealing with them they naturally behave like human beings. And so weary cynics like lawyers and political scientists take a certain malicious pleasure in showing that the natural scientists are led by confidence in their special scientific techniques to try to make judgments on political values or policy decisions, without realizing all the other components of a nonscientific nature that go into those decisions. The lesson is a valid and important one, and needs to be driven home to the general public much more than to the scientists, most of whom know it already even if they do not like for nonscientists to remind them of it.

If you feel obliged to document the lesson, the illustrations are plentifully available. Read the hearings published by the Atomic Energy Commission in the case of J. Robert Oppenheimer, and see how two groups of eminent scientists and engineers, differing very little indeed at any given time on specific scientific matters, mistrusted each others' political intentions to such a point that we had the closest thing to a heresy trial that modern American politics has provided. Or read the history of the disputes over nuclear fall-out, or the civil defense shelter program, or the use of insecticides, in each of which both sides used much the same statistics and drew widely different conclusions. Or the story of the Geneva disarmament negotiations with the Soviets, in which the scientists themselves must have found it difficult to tell when they were trying to sort out the technical evidence and when they were making judgments about foreign-policy priorities or estimating the intentions and good faith of the Russians.[12]

You can explain these difficulties in professional and scientific terms, if you like, by saying that the physicists and chemists all ought to realize that issues of this kind need to be worked on by social as well as natural scientists. This is obviously true, although the social scientists are at least as guilty as physicists of mistaking the abstractions of their respective disciplines for the sum total of all wisdom. Or you can add an extra bit of rational explanation by noting that the physical scientist is used to working with data that may be difficult but not malevolent—that is, the data have no will of their own to exercise against the experimenter—whereas in politics the data not only have wills of their own, but sometimes oppose the experimenter not because they dislike what he is doing but because they dislike him. Thus

Einstein remarked, as an encouragement to those scientists who seek to find order in the complex universe, that "God is subtle, but He is not malicious."[13] But in an international negotiation on, for example, arms control, no matter how high a scientific content the subject matter may have, the contribution that science can make is a limited one because the Russians may be malicious. In the eyes of the Democrats, so are the Republicans, and vice versa. Maybe in the eyes of the Russians, so are the Americans.

And this type of conflict creates in politics, domestic or international, a problem quite different from those problems on which the scientific observer can take a detached and superior point of view, and ignore the elements of conflict. It sets up a system of relationships on any major political issue in which it is hard to judge the capabilities and intentions of your adversary, and to determine the exact degree to which he means exactly what he says, or is discounting your own reaction in advance, or is deliberately using conflict with you for other irrelevant purposes or out of irrational ill will—and equally hard to judge your own motives.

If we understand that the scientist and the engineer cannot be guided in their political actions entirely by what science teaches them, and that even when they think they are doing so they may be deceiving themselves and others, we are led to a realization that the fruit of the tree of knowledge is not always peace. Maybe this is the reason that, among professional political scientists, we read a great deal more today than we did a generation ago about the dogma—or to moderns, the myth—of original sin. Perhaps the fear that scientists and professionals will not be guided entirely by their scientific knowledge and professional ethics in public affairs, and hence cannot be trusted with political power, is a political attitude derived directly from an old Puritanical prejudice. The Reformers began by observing the immorality of the higher clergy and therefore distrusting hierarchy in an ecclesiastical establishment, and ended by dividing and weakening the role of the church in political affairs. An analogous attack has begun in recent years on the ethics of scientists who use government funds, and on their conflicts of interest.

But the old dogma had a more subtle side to it: it recognized that it was not only the base or material side of man's nature that caused him the greatest trouble, but his spiritual pride. Men are more likely to fight with each other for noble than for base motives. The most powerful personal motive is not the gratification of the senses, or the acquisition of mere wealth or power, but the conviction that one's own skills and knowledge have a special contribution to make to the salvation of humanity, or that they have provided an insight which the rest of the world must be induced to accept.[14] The most tyrannical political systems are those built not on corruption, but on self-righteous fanaticism.

That is why, in regulating the constitutional relationships among the estates of our society, we should be less concerned that the scientists and professionals will yield to material interests or sensual temptations, than that they will be utterly and unselfishly devoted to their respective disciplines or professions. The two types of temptation of course can be related; the more importance society attaches to chemistry, the more income it will let individual chemists earn; the more it is persuaded that doctors can cure its ills, the more likely it is to concede to the American Medical Association the right to prescribe the terms of public insurance for medical care. At any rate, so the chemists and doctors are tempted to believe. But if we tend to think of the problem as one in which the main incentive is material gain, we not only fail to do justice to the motives of the contending parties, but we fail to understand the more difficult part of the problem.

Because of the rapid advance of the sciences, and because of the contribution that they are making continuously to engineering and medicine, there can clearly be no set limit on the contribution they may be asked or permitted to make to our social problems. They do not merely produce things that the public asks for; what they discover determines the range of new possibilities that are open to us. Invention is the mother of necessity, as a British observer recently remarked.[15] Since scientists and mathematicians and engineers are extending their ability to solve problems in which there is a high degree of uncertainty, the administrators and politicians would be stupid not to encourage them to go as far as they can. But the administrators and politicians would be even more stupid if they failed to note the aspects of those problems on which the scientists and professionals are making judgments not required by the nature of their subject matter—judgments that have the effect, and perhaps the purpose, of extending the power of their particular estates.

THE CASE OF "COMMAND AND CONTROL"

This problem may be illuminated, perhaps, if we take as an illustration the field in which the most fateful social consequences are mixed with the most advanced scientific techniques. This is the current problem that has become the subject of countless sermons, novels, and speeches: the problem that the engineers call "command and control." It has to do, of course, with the way in which the nation prepares to control its intercontinental missiles and aircraft, armed with nuclear and thermonuclear weapons. This is the most threatening problem with which science and technology have confronted society. The nature of the relation of political to military power has always been one of the most difficult constitutional problems, and here it has been complicated by the vast increase in the power and velocity of the weapons at hand. The problems of command and control have been thoroughly studied from the point of view of their effect on international politics and diplomacy; somewhat less attention has been paid to the way in which they affect the relationship, within our own constitutional system, of the several estates. If we can identify the main outlines of the problem it may help us to deal with other problems in which scientific advances may alter the balance of power within our system of government.

Command and control is the problem of dealing with intricate, lethal, and nearly instantaneous weapons systems through the exercise of fallible human faculties, and even more fallible systems of organization.[16] When the British air defense forces, in the Second World War, found that the old system of airplane spotters telephoning reports to a command center was sure to break down under mass attack, they began to develop something that evolved into a highly automated system, in which radar and the most elaborate electronic computers were used for spotting and tracking the attacking planes (or missiles), cataloging the weapons at the disposal of the defense, and directing them against the attackers. All this now goes on over distances that stretch across seas and continents, and it involves most massive calculations, at speeds made possible only by electronics, of the velocity and distance and altitude of each of a myriad of weapons. The general type of system has now, of course, been developed not only for defense against air attack, but for control of the long-range bombers and intercontinental ballistic missiles—the ICBM's, in military jargon—that would be used in retaliation.

So we have a lot of ICBM's scattered around our deserts and mountains, each one subject to command from an electronic system that identifies an enemy attack by means of long-range radar observation, and that can technically be made to respond either absolutely automatically or by waiting for orders from authorities at any level you choose. It is possible to have each ICBM aimed at a single predetermined target, or (at greater cost) made ready to be ordered to alternative targets.

Now observe the effect on our constitutional system of this particular bit of technology. A generation ago, the outbreak of war abroad gave the United States, with its ocean shelters, a year or so to start making its weapons and training its troops. A decade ago, the time scale had shortened, but it still would take a good many hours for a bomber plane to travel from Russia to America or vice versa, and this left some leeway for decisions;

after the alarm, planes could be moved from vulnerable bases, and retaliatory planes could be started off, and recalled at will after some hours of flight. But today, an ICBM could travel in either direction between the U.S.S.R. and the U.S.A. in half an hour, and a ballistic missile (though it may be blown up in flight) cannot be recalled. If you add to the problems caused by this compression of time the possibility that most or all of the top political executives of the government might be killed by a single unexpected attack, you can readily visualize the difficulty of making plans to decide who will be entitled (and by what procedure) to give the ICBM's the command when to attack, and what to attack. The simple Constitutional principle of the supremacy of civil over military authority is meaningless unless all this can be worked out in technological and administrative detail.

Since no system can be infallible, people have worried about the danger that this kind of intricate and sensitive system will get out of hand. Can we start a nuclear war that nobody intended, because someone mistakes a radar signal, or some piece of equipment fails, or someone in authority is drunk or crazy? Such a disaster is not inconceivable, but we should worry much more about a less spectacular type of threat. For this kind of worry before the fact is the equivalent of the typical clamor for an investigation that goes on after an event: everyone seeks to pin on some unhappy culprit the responsibility for a disaster that was caused not by the criminal intent or delinquency of an individual, but by the negligence or inadequacy or lack of responsibility built into a system, sometimes as the result of the misguided zeal of the most honorable and patriotic men.[17] The system itself is what we should worry most about. The professional engineers and military officers have as urgent a motive as any professional pacifist for preventing the obvious potential failures of men or equipment.[18] But they do not have the motivation to inquire into the limits imposed by their own professional biases.

The United States, shortly after the bungling victory in the Spanish-American War proved its military incompetence, undertook to create a professionalized system of top military command. In order to reconcile this with the traditional distrust of a standing army, Congress did not set up an independent command headquarters, but based the system on staff advice to a civilian Secretary. True, the Chief of Staff has always been in some senses a commanding general; nevertheless the distinction has been an important and significant one,[19] because it made it clear that in constitutional theory military operations were under civilian command, a theory that could be translated into reality by any strong Secretary. But the whole theory of advice depended on the premise that it was in fact possible for the civilian authority to refuse military advice.

It has long been true that the President and the Secretary of Defense (or War) were almost powerless if they waited until a crisis and then were presented with advice in the form of a proposed operational order; if they wished to have influence, they had to have a hand in ordering the assumptions on which were based the war plans and the research and development plans. The quicker the reaction time involved in the potential military operations, the slower the process of translating policy decisions into effective policy. As technology requires us to be prepared to take in a very few minutes decisions affecting the survival of the nation and perhaps the world, it also requires the Secretary of Defense and the President to make decisions five or ten years ahead of the possible event if they wish to influence it. The problem that the nation should be worrying about is not the dramatic possibility of a war caused by the insanity or malevolence of an individual, but the much more difficult problem of building an organized system to make the engineers and the military officers as responsible in fact, as they are in law, to political authority.

If we look at the broad outlines of the command and control problem in this context, they suggest to us three lessons about the relation of science and the professions to administrative and political authority.

First, the scientists and professionals, in order to do their own jobs, must be involved in the formulation of policy, and must be granted wide discretion in their own work.

Second, politicians and administrators must control the key aspects of technological plans if they are to protect their own ability to make responsible decisions.

Third, the ability of a free society to make effective use of science and technology depends on some workable (though probably informal) system of checks and balances among the four estates.

1. *The professional role in the formulation of policy.*

The surest way for the top administrator (in this case, a general or a general staff) to lose control over his essential purposes is to try to tell his professional subordinates exactly what to do, and make them stick to it. His problem is not to control things that he fully understands, but to control the development of new possibilities that he cannot understand. As Brockway McMillan, Assistant Secretary of the Air Force, put it in a speech in 1962, the function of engineering is to start with a problem, which is of course a statement of purpose, or an expression of political values that the top administrator and his political superiors must define. But then the engineer must translate that purpose into specific objectives, requirements, and criteria of performance. This is not a matter of pure science; that term, Secretary McMillan pointed out, is too precise and rigid. It is a matter of engineering doctrine, which must be developed on the basis of scientific concepts, but it must also govern the allocation of resources—in short, a kind of budget—to make the system work. You cannot state the requirements for a moon rocket, he pointed out, without using the concepts of physics, such as the laws of conservation of energy and momentum, but you cannot do so either without deciding what you want to do, and what various parts of the job are worth in terms of money and scientific effort.[20] In this process, the best way for the top administrator to ensure failure is to prescribe a specific plan of action in advance.

In an age of slow technological development this fact was not so clearly apparent; the engineer moved to novel systems slowly enough so that his boss could keep up with him. But the more abstract sciences, by greatly speeding up the velocity of development, have changed all that. And this is why the more scientific engineers have been so stubborn about insisting that they not be asked merely to make improvements that the administrator can foresee and state in a set of prescribed requirements, but that they be permitted to play a role in the interaction between ends and means, between strategic purpose and scientific possibility. This kind of stubbornness showed up in the process of developing the first radar for immediate use in combat. Sir Robert Watson-Watt quoted with pleasure the exasperated military comment that the radar engineers "won't tighten a nut on a bolt until they have had the whole strategic plan . . . explained to them." And this attitude is what led the Royal Air Force to become the first military service in which scientists became an integral part of the military planning process.[21]

The process of planning, insofar as it involves the use by politics of the sciences, is not a one-way street. In the case of the command and control system, the engineer cannot know what kind of help he can use from the scientist until he knows what the military officer needs. But the military officer cannot know what he needs unless the engineer, with the benefit of new knowledge from the scientist, can tell him what is becoming possible. No military officer in 1939 could have written an official requirement for the atomic bomb, or a little earlier for radar. In the politics and administration of large-scale engineering enterprises, as in the basic sciences, it is necessary to guard against a kind of teleology—the desire to make what we can learn conform to the way we think things ought to be.

2. *The role of the politician and administrator in technological planning.*

As Secretary McMillan warned in the speech already quoted, "a command and control system exists to support the commander, not to supplant him." What reason is there for concern on that score?

Science makes it possible, of course, to develop gadgets that are so effective in doing specific things that they outrun the possibilities of human control. A fighter airplane or a communications system can operate too rapidly for the human nervous system to follow. If your problem is to do exactly the same thing over and over again—to handle larger quantities of standardized operations, or even to vary the job according to conditions and rules you can foresee, you might as well put a computer on the job and make it thoroughly automatic. But the limit on the usefulness of this approach is that the machine does not care what it does; it has no sense of values or purpose.[22] (By values or purpose in this context we do not *need* to mean ideas coming from supernatural sources; it is enough to refer to those of the responsible political authorities—including those aspects of a decision on which adequate knowledge is lacking, either because they relate to things that are unpredictable by the present methods of science, or about which it would take too long or be too costly to get the information.)

So the man for whom the machine has been designed may find that he has invested resources in an elaborate system that cannot be changed to do the new job required by new conditions or new discoveries. Or he may find that it is a system that commits him to do things he never wanted to do, and that the engineer who built it failed to warn him that he was putting all his eggs into one electronic basket. Accordingly the better computer experts are now warning the customers that if the purposes of an organization are to be best served, in the light of future uncertainties, it is often better to resist the temptation to install the biggest and fanciest computer and the most complete system of automation based on the most elaborate concepts. The purpose of the organization has to be protected against the desire for technical elegance, and a simpler and slower system may make it possible to attain the desired ends of the organization more effectively in a changing environment. It helps, in determining that purpose, to look at the problem from the perspective of various scientific disciplines and various professions, but no one of them can define that purpose, and each one may be tempted to try to do so for its own professional interests.

The administrator's need for flexibility is least in some types of business operations where the product is standardized and nearly sure to remain so. But it becomes much greater in military matters for the reason that a commander is dealing with an adversary whose responses he cannot know in advance. He may not want, after all, to fire at the targets he had first picked; the enemy may have moved them. Or there may be a different enemy. Or he may need to change the rate of his fire to hold a missile supply in reserve, or to make negotiations with allies or enemies possible. This is why the experts warn us that "strategies should not be inadvertently built into the command and control system."[23]

Any reader with an interest in politics, of course, should ask just what this warning means. It is stated in the passive voice, and therefore covers up the issue. *Who* might be tempted to build an undesirable strategy into a system? Is anyone likely to do so entirely by inadvertence? The real danger is probably that the top political authorities of the government might find themselves in charge of a system which gave them too little flexibility, and too little range of choice in difficult diplomatic or strategic situations, because it had been based on decisions by engineers and military officers which the politicians did not fully understand. If this should happen, it might be very hard indeed to tell whether the engineers or the generals had caused the trouble, and for what motives. The engineers might be tempted to do so, either for the purpose of developing the most advanced technology possible in the interest of national security, or so as to help their companies sell something fancier and more costly to the government. Or the generals might be tempted to do so, either in order to get the quickest and most reliable response to an enemy threat, or in order to put their political superiors in a position where they would have to leave the conduct of a war more exclusively to military commanders and would be unable to compromise the chances of all-out victory by diplomatic and political bargaining.

If we choose to make use of the techniques of automation to accomplish things we are sure we wish to do, it is important to recognize two things. First, although an elaborate system of command and control may let you get a particular thing done much more rapidly and more cheaply and more reliably, it will very probably force you to do it in one particular way, and cut off other choices. Second, unless you are very careful to understand the whole business before you start, your lack of understanding may conceal a number of ways in which other people, with quite different biases and preferences, have committed you to do things you never meant to do. Or, in more technical language, "A machine has the advantage of making its synthesis without personal bias . . . But it also tends to eliminate any allowance for the personal biases of the inputs which it uses."[24]

3. *Checks and balances among the four estates.*

We have to look at this problem of automation—or any problem involving the large-scale use of new technology by society—not merely as one of providing information to make possible the unified action of a lot of people with a common purpose. Instead it is the problem of providing a system of authority that can reconcile widely different purposes—and with the differences resulting not merely from conflicting material interests or general ideology, but from the differences in intellectual discipline or professional background that distinguish the several estates in modern society. Consequently, as the government has developed the system of command and control of air defense and intercontinental missiles, it has in practice shown an awareness that the relationship among the several estates is one that must be handled on the basis of constitutional principle, even though it may be a principle unknown to the courts and the Constitutional lawyers.

One might have thought that air defense and missiles offered the greatest potential scope to the unbridled development of technology and automation. The military nature of the programs meant that legal restraints on discretionary power were weak. The purpose was comparatively clear, and had almost unquestioning public support. The scientific techniques were advanced and complex, and well beyond the full comprehension of the layman.

Yet it is obvious that there has been a lively system of checks and balances at work. The conflicts of interest have been identified and fought over at length; the most important issues have been debated by competing scientific and professional groups, and brought urgently to the attention of administrative officers (both military and civilian) and political authority (both executive and legislative). If the competing interests of the four estates have been able to bring a measure of responsibility and restraint into the command and control of guided missiles, it seems probable that there is nothing in the nature of advanced technology and automation that will inevitably bring about a highly centralized system of political authority.

We have been establishing new kinds of checks and balances within the governmental system that depend not on formal legal provisions, but on a respect for scientific truth and for professional expertise. This respect is stronger, no doubt, among the scientists and the experts—including the engineers, the generals, and even the administrators—than among the general public. But even the general public has come to distrust political authority and to support those who defend the scientists and experts against political interference. As a result, it is possible to defend pure knowledge, even though it is legally powerless, at each step along the gradation from science through professional work and administration into politics.

At each step, one estate distrusts the next for compromising objective truth in the interest of political purpose. Thus, in a problem like command and control, the scientists are likely to distrust the engineers for not being alert to the great discoveries that could be made if basic research were not restricted for pragmatic or economic (or other irrational) reasons, and to resent the limitations that are put on the laboratories for reasons of short-run expediency. The engineers distrust the generals and admirals and budget officers for restricting their full development of technological possibilities on account of operational or traditional—usually reactionary—reasons. The generals distrust their political superiors for wishing to interfere in strategic matters on nonmilitary, and presumably immoral, grounds; they suspect politicians of putting a concern for dollars ahead of the lives of soldiers, or of being soft on Communism, or of being unreliable when life-and-death issues are at stake, or even of trying to make decisions that military men know more about.

There can be no completely hierarchical relationship among the four estates. Even within government itself, the collective pride and ethical beliefs of a profession and the firm faith of the scientist in intellectual freedom are by no means overridden easily by political authority. An organization chart is conventionally drawn in terms of a pyramid of power, with the chief political officer on top, his administrators just below, and his professional or scientific subordinates lower still. But if that chart were drawn in the order of scientific precision, or demonstrable truth, it would have to be turned upside down.

This point of view, which sees the spectrum from science to politics as one involving a steady decline in demonstrable truth, is naturally held most often by the scientists. But if they were alone in that view, it would not have much weight in practical affairs. It has weight because it is shared quite generally, at least at various times and for different purposes. Even politicians themselves will appeal to it in cases in which the apparent majority of scientific testimony supports their side of a policy debate, or in the perhaps less frequent cases when it genuinely persuades them to accept a new policy.

But this general view of the moral superiority of science and the professions is counterbalanced by another way of looking at the spectrum from science to politics. For it is possible to see it as ranging not from pure truth to naked power, but from inhuman abstraction to moral responsibility. And this is the way the spectrum looks as the chain of distrust runs in the opposite direction to the one we noted above. The political executive distrusts the generals and admirals for wishing to have such tight control over their weapons systems that statesmen and diplomats are given no room to maneuver, and for using the argument of military necessity to demand so large a share of the nation's resources that its total strength is actually weakened. The generals and admirals are impatient with weapons engineers for developing endless technical refinements, rather than being willing to supply the combat units with simple and reliable weapons when they need them. The weapons engineers are even more impatient with the basic scientists, who are too much interested in fundamental knowledge to think very much about the feasibility of their ideas, or their practical and economic development.

There is hardly any social problem on which science cannot make some contribution. Science may help not only in the development of particular techniques for reaching the goals that others have determined; it may help refine our value judgments, and determine the nature of the goals themselves. For this reason, the infusion of science, as a way of thinking, should be welcomed in the professions, in administration, and in politics. On the other hand, the motives of the scientist (and of anyone else who may seek to apply science to any given problem) may be tainted by various forms of self-interest, and he may be defining the problem, and making assumptions about the relevance of his science to it, in ways that are unjustified from various points of view—from the point of view of other sciences, or of perfectly valid value judgments of the layman. For this reason, there is no major public problem that does not have its political aspects, and none that should be left entirely to the judgment of the experts.

But if this is true, one might say, we have a set of conflicts of interest built into every issue, with the four estates involved in perpetual civil war. Quite obviously that does not happen; in some way, in every society, a realization of common purposes and values transcends these differences of approach, and unites the estates at least partially in a common effort. The extent to which there must be union, and the circumstances under which division and disagreement are tolerated or encouraged, are crucial questions in the development of any constitutional system. No matter what common purposes unite us, we must still work out a number of practical questions about the relationship of the four estates. We must ask, for example, just how government should decide to have a particular issue (or a part of a particular issue) decided by one estate or another; how each estate selects its leaders and is governed; how much interchange there is among them, and on what terms; and how the checks and balances in this system are related to those of our formal Constitution.

Even if all Americans agree on the twofold principle suggested above—that the more a function or institution is concerned with truth, the more it has a right to freedom, and the more it is concerned with power, the more it should be subjected to the test of political responsibility—those practical questions must be faced. I will take up such questions in the next chapter, but first I will try to be clear about the general approach that in the end will probably determine the answers to them. This general approach is summed up in the twofold principle, and it is quite different from that of the Marxist dialecticians.

THE WESTERN TRADITION

In our domestic politics, we have gradually been getting accustomed to the necessity of working toward common ends with people whose theoretical philosophic views or religious beliefs we disapprove, but whose human qualities we respect, and whose practical purposes we share. In international politics, the power of modern weapons now may be forcing us to recognize similar elements of common purpose with those we consider our adversaries—if only a common interest in survival as separate nations. On this subject, it may be even more dangerous for us to be cynical than to be naive.

Some therefore are tempted to imagine that the scientific-technological revolution (a term that Communist Party theoreticians are beginning to use more frequently) has been making the social systems of the advanced industrial nations more compatible with one another. Advanced science and technology, so the argument runs, require higher education and critical minds, and thus lead toward a more liberal and open kind of political system. On the other hand, industrial technology has been centralizing economic power in the United States, and unintentionally bringing it more and more under political control. As the two systems come more nearly to resemble each other, why should they not get along better? Quintin Hogg, British Minister for Science, illustrates this train of thought. In 1964 he told the Second Parliamentary and Scientific Conference of the Organisation for Economic Cooperation and Development and the Council of Europe he believed that current technical developments would drive the economic systems of all developed nations closer together. Speaking of Soviet Communism, he remarked, "I fancy that it may not turn out to be so different from the American way of life as the inhabitants of the Kremlin or the White House may expect."[25]

The same view has often been expressed, though usually in private, in the United States, in conservative as well as liberal circles. Many scientists are tempted to share that view by the old utopian dream of a future in which technical and industrial progress would let political authority wither away, or at least greatly reduce its influence. This still seems to be the hope, in spite of recent evidence, of many conservative businessmen.[26]

There is no doubt, too, that the common requirements of technology have brought about great similarities in the organization of factories or laboratories or military forces, regardless of the nature of the political system. This leads not only scientists, but even administrators and politicians, to develop a certain amount of international sympathy on the basis of common problems, and may soften the harsh outlines of ideological conflict. Thus Khrushchev, in a major speech to the Communist Party Central Committee in 1962, reviewed his economic and technological problems, and admitted that, "having destroyed class and social barriers in October, 1917, we later, in the course of economic construction, in many cases erected departmental and local-interest barriers that, intentionally or unintentionally, restrict the possibilities of our development."[27] Americans may well take a sympathetic pleasure in such a bit of realism, with its general theoretical implications, and in other comments on technical policy in Khrushchev's speech. For example, he admitted that the Soviet Union, for all its central party authority, finds it hard to centralize science for civilian purposes as it has managed to do for military purposes. He warned that capitalism has the advantage of competition to spur the adoption of new technology. And he summed up some of the common human problems of technological innovation in all societies as he described his visit to an old blacksmith who told him directly to get that girl efficiency expert with her stop watch away from his forge and cut out those time-and-motion studies.[28]

The official Communist Party doctrine, of course, has painted a quite different picture of the way in which science and technology contribute to the planning of a new society. A party theoretician put the argument thus in an article in *Kommunist,* the theoretical journal of the Bolshevik Party: "The present scientific-technological revolution is unfolding at a time when there exist two opposite social systems in the world. Its most important elements are as a rule not a secret of this or that industrially highly developed country. The struggle for the fullest, fastest, and most economic utilization of the possibilities offered by this revolution is one of the most important aspects of the economic competition of the two systems . . . The general realization of the fruits of the scientific-technological revolution requires a level of socialization, and of a planned coordination of science, technology, and production, that are unthinkable under the capitalist system."[29]

As the Secretary of the Central Committee of the Communist Party of the Soviet Union put it, "The Party has restored a Leninist and profoundly scientific approach to the *solution of economic problems.* Just as Lenin put forward the task of establishing the material and technical foundation for socialism through industrialization of the country, so the Party has worked out, at this new stage, a plan for the creation of the material and technical basis of communism. One of the distinctive features of the past decade has been the fact that the Party initiated and led the scientific and technical revolution and thus placed the Soviet Union in the forefront of world scientific and technical progress, making socialism its standard bearer."[30]

This doctrinaire argument has been immensely persuasive to many underdeveloped nations, which wish to shape their political institutions so as to take full advantage of technological progress. Considerable doubt, to say the least, has been cast on the argument, not only by Khrushchev's earthy and practical comments, but by many intellectual leaders in the Communist countries who have discovered, with Milovan Djilas, that conflicts of interest can arise among the estates in society without having any basis in private property. This discovery, and the parallel discovery that in the United States a new mixture of governmental and private enterprise has been invented (partly as a result of scientific and technological programs) to modify or replace the classical form of capitalism, have reduced the apparent difference between the two systems with respect to the national planning of technological progress. In that respect, the two systems are now close enough for most people to be willing to have them judged on the basis of peaceful competition.

But there is a fundamental aspect of Communist theory regarding the relation of science to politics that makes it more difficult for the rest of the world to confront the Communist world on terms of friendly rivalry. One party theoretician put the issue in the form of a question: "Is it really possible to call scientific the concepts of contemporary bourgeois sociology . . . if all of them question the existence of objective laws of social development, and the possibility of predicting the paths of this development?"[31] Although this quotation pertains to a rather academic issue, it seems to me of much greater importance. It sums up the demand of Communist theory not only that the social sciences and history be included with the natural sciences in a single philosophical system, but that this system predict the future development of society.[32] Is this a scientific approach to the problems of society?

Half a century ago there may have been some reason for the ordinary citizen to think so, and to fear that the progress of science would bring about a drift toward some form of dogmatic materialism as the basis for a dictatorship. But this does not seem to be in accord with the way science itself has been working, in either its theoretical or practical developments. The "scientific prediction" of the future development of society is not really a prediction; it is an assertion of purpose. The several sciences can combine to make such a prediction only if they are asked to conform to a predetermined theory, and if the request is supported by the authority of a small and disciplined and indoctrinated party. To combine in such a corporate body control over both ends of the spectrum from political authority to scientific knowledge is not a decision that is encouraged by science. It comes instead from a very old and uncritical faith: the belief that an organization of human beings can know the ultimate purpose of the world, bring a select group of its members to a state of superior knowledge and power, and provide the doctrine to guide an authoritarian government to rule the rest.

The Marxists have not been the first to fasten such a notion on Eastern politics. Their belief has its ancient analogy in the belief of the Orthodox church that it could make perfect the faithful; a vision of perfection can justify the use of any ruthless means. The Roman church never shared this belief in the possibility of human perfection, and the Reformed churches, of course, were at the opposite extreme with their dogma of total depravity. And no matter how self-righteously and rigorously Calvinists may have tried to rule their cities and countries, it was pretty hard to set up a permanent authoritarian rule, or even to maintain a unified church, when their basic doctrine put rulers and ruled at a common level of imperfection.[33]

If the inner logic of the sciences themselves does not bring all of them—including the social sciences—together in a uniform methodological system, there is no reason to think that anything in the political habits or traditions of the West will force them to do so. The several sciences may indeed acknowledge allegiance to a common set of very general principles; they all believe in truth and objectivity, in the publication and verification of a scholar's findings, and so on. But this is like the agreement by the dissenting Christian sects on a number of basic doctrines. Agreement on organization or action is a different matter. The countries in which theologians have long insisted on organizing themselves in separate sects, and on not letting the government set up an orderly and unified establishment for them, seem to be the ones in which scientists do the same.

We may well have faith that there is, in some ideal sense, one system of truth comprehending the approaches of all the sciences—physical, biological, and social—but they cannot be unified to produce a governing ideology or social plan without closing off a tremendous variety of possible future choices, and without being used as an instrument by which a new governing class may maintain a monopoly on power. Like an excessively automated system, this may produce impressive results for a time in a predetermined direction. But there is no logical reason to suppose that it is more efficient as a general political system, whether you prefer to think of the main purpose of such a system as keeping open the opportunities of technological and economic progress, or of protecting the human freedoms that are fundamentally based on even more important values.

The most fundamental disagreement between the nations of

the Western political tradition and those of the Communist world does not turn on their attitudes toward private property. The greatest mistake in Western political strategy consists in committing itself to the defense of property as the main basis for the preservation of freedom. Private property is indeed a useful and important means to that end, but it is not an absolute end in itself, and the effect of scientific advance on a technological civilization has made property less and less important as a source of power, and as a way of limiting political power. Far more fundamental is the way men think about the desirability of organizing truth in the service of power, and using power to determine truth. Whether truth is conceived in the old terms of religion, or the new terms of science, the greatest source of tyranny is the conviction that there is a single way of determining truth, and that it should be interpreted by a single disciplined organization.

Having rejected this conviction, Americans need to base their constitutional system on a division of power that will take fully into account the newer institutional forms of power as well as the old—the new estates of the scientific era, as well as branches of government and business corporations. And as we do so, a clear understanding that science alone cannot solve political problems will be the surest safeguard for the protection of the sciences and professions in a proper degree of independence from political authority.

CHAPTER 6

Constitutional Relativity

SCIENCE, BY HELPING technology to increase prosperity, has weakened the kind of radicalism that comes from a lack of economic security. But science has helped to produce other kinds of insecurity: the fear of the new kind of war that science has made possible, the fear of rapid social and economic change, and the fear that we no longer have a fixed and stable constitutional system by which to cope with our political problems. And these fears are breeding a new type of radicalism.

The new radicalism is ostensibly conservative. It springs in part from the resentment men feel when their basic view of life is unsettled—as medieval man must have felt when he was asked to think of a universe that did not revolve around the earth, or as some physicists felt a generation or two ago when their colleagues began to talk about relativity and indeterminacy. The new conservative radicalism had a fundamentalist faith in the written Constitution, and the high priests of that faith seem to have desecrated it. The Supreme Court has applied relative policy standards in place of fixed rules of precedent; but worse still it has admitted into its system of thinking not only the moral law as revealed in tradition, but arguments from the sciences, even the behavioral sciences.

CHANGES IN THE UNWRITTEN CONSTITUTION

Science seemed a radical influence very early in American history. The dominant ideas in the Constitutional Convention came from Madison and Adams and Hamilton, who were, in varying degrees, skeptical about democracy, and eager to give representation to different economic interests and different orders of men. But Jefferson and those who joined him in his rationalistic and scientific opinions were eager to abolish the special electoral and legal privileges of various classes and interests; their views were rather closer to the simple doctrine of "one man, one vote." It was Jefferson's democratic doctrine that over the next half-century destroyed—and not by formal amendment—some of the principal safeguards that had been built into the Constitution to protect the conservative interest, especially the independence of the Executive. The President, it was originally intended, was to be protected against too much democracy by being selected by an aristocratic Electoral College, and the unity of the executive branch was to be protected by his authority to appoint and super-vise its principal officers. But the Jeffersonian party system de-stroyed both safeguards, reducing the Electors to party tools and organizing Congressional committees so as to give members of Congress substantial control over executive appointments and executive actions.

These changes, however, were minor compared to those wrought a little later by the industrialization of the country and the accompanying advances in technology and science. Now property is no longer a stable separate mass by which political power may be balanced. Since the weakening of the judicial de-fenses of the private corporation, the federal government has acquired, through the income tax, the grant-in-aid, and the gov-ernment contract, ample powers by which to control national economic as well as political affairs, and indeed to treat the two as merely different aspects of the same thing.

In formal Constitutional terms, the results might seem to justify all the gloomy predictions of the conservatives among the Founding Fathers. There no longer seems to be any fixed Con-stitutional barrier at which the courts will protect the absolute independence of the states, or of private corporations, against the power of the federal government on any major issue of policy, or protect the Congress against the influence of the President and executive branch, or vice versa. Indeed, these results might justify the fears of a thoroughgoing conservative like Edmund Burke, who thought he saw clearly where the doctrinaire radicalism of the scientists would lead if the traditional organic nature of the state, with its many vested political interests, were destroyed: toward a mass democracy that would then turn toward tyranny.[1] If Burke could take a look at the twentieth century, he might think that his foresight had been vindicated by the story of a considerable number of nations; the centralization of power in a single governing assembly, responsible only to a mass electorate, has too easily and too often been turned into the means to let a dictator and a single party indoctrinate and control the electorate.[2]

But how could Burke explain what has happened in the United States, or for that matter in the United Kingdom? To the extent that the unwritten portion of the American constitutional system responds to new changes in science and technology, it seems to be no stable constitution at all, but a system of constitutional relativity, virtually Einsteinian in its lack of fixed standards. Yet, Burke might remark with surprise, this first among the revolutionary republics has been the most resistant of all major nations to the centralization of power, or to the conversion of its mass democracy to totalitarian ideas; indeed, the United States seems actually to be strengthening the independence of its private institutions, and increasing their role in public affairs. It is hard to reconcile with the actual State of the Nation the fears of those who think that American freedom has been subverted by relativism in moral or political beliefs.

But they may have been misinterpreting relativism. They may be tempted to attribute today's lack of fixed moral standards, or fixed constitutional standards, to Einstein's relativity. But they should perhaps have greeted Einstein's theory with a totally different reaction. What should have surprised mankind was to be told that the speed of light was absolute—not that everything else was relative. After decades of growing disbelief in fixed standards or values, someone at last had come up with a single absolute one: here was a unique standard, a single truth to which everything else could be related. It nevertheless seemed inconvenient to a great many laymen to have their household idols—their clocks and yardsticks—discredited in favor of this monotheistic abstraction, especially since no one could say just what light was. It looked in some ways like waves, and in others, like particles; and there seemed no final way of ever understanding the ultimate mystery.

Perhaps the only political lesson laymen should draw from this scientific theory is that it is always a great mistake to put one's confidence too completely in concrete practical standards that are suitable only to a system of a certain size, or to a particular time and place. If there is to be an absolute, it has to be considerably more abstract. If we are to measure the political values of our constitutional system, our standard today cannot be the right of Massachusetts or Virginia to defend its sovereignty against the federal union, or even that of General Motors to protect its property, as important as all those rights are in limited and relative ways. If there is an absolute political standard in our tradition—if our system of constitutional relativity has any constant—it seems to me to be the idea of freedom.

One must admit immediately that freedom is no easier to define than light. Philosophers have debated for centuries whether it is, at one extreme, the unrestrained assertion of individual will, or, at the other extreme, perfect submission to truth, whether truth is expressed as the laws of nature or as the will of God. These two aspects of freedom are both real. They complement each other, and need to be balanced in a constitutional system.

If Burke's gloomy prediction held true for many countries, it was at least partly because their revolutions, while sweeping away institutions like absolute monarchies and ecclesiastical establishments that were anachronisms in a modern age, put all their emphasis on the first aspect of freedom, and established no institutions to counterbalance the exercise of pure political will.

Equality of voting rights proved no guarantee of freedom at all in countries that established no institutions to defend the second aspect of freedom—to maintain a systematic pursuit of truth and incidentally to criticize and check the exercise of power.

It was perhaps on this basis that Burke distinguished between his violent dislike of the French Revolution and his comparative sympathy with the American. He feared the doctrinaire rationalism of French republican theory, and quite correctly attributed the impetus of American revolutionary thought not to egalitarian theorists, but to the lawyers, who, he remarked, "augur misgovernment at a distance, and snuff the approach of tyranny in every tainted breeze."[3] He might well have added the dissenting clergy, whose churches were among centers of antimonarchical influence. The stability of the American political system owes an incalculable debt to the lawyers, who have played a role of political leadership and constitutional guidance that is without parallel in any other country. Political doctrinaires like Tom Paine did not lead democracy in the United States into too great a concentration of power in unchecked legislative assemblies, and for this the lawyers deserve most of the credit.[4]

Jefferson's theory of politics was, of course, much closer than Burke's or Madison's to that of the French revolutionaries; he was much more willing than his legalistic and orthodox colleagues to put his faith in political equality. But he stopped well short of the doctrinaire theory of the French ideologues: in science, he never held with complete materialistic determinism, and maintained a belief in Divine Purpose; in religion, he remained Deist rather than atheist; and in politics he was positively contemptuous of turning over all power to a single elected assembly and putting executive functions in a committee. So it is not surprising that his conception of freedom retained a substantial element of its second aspect; after all, his Declaration may have asserted Independence and universal equality, but it justified that assertion by an appeal to the laws of Nature and of Nature's God.

A few scientists of that period had a disproportionate influence on its political ideas,[5] but they were negligible in number. Jefferson and his followers may accordingly have been inclined to assume that it was only professions like the clergy and the lawyers that were apt to have any organized influence on politics. They were suspicious of those professions' conservatism and therefore may have wanted to give them as little established status, and as little influence, as possible. In this respect, scientists today continue to share his prejudices. When they make speeches on political subjects, especially if they are Outsiders (with respect to administrative responsibilities) they tend to define freedom and democracy largely in terms of absence of restraint and equality in voting power.

But if this first aspect of freedom is what the Outsider preaches, it is not the one the Insider practices. The administrators of scientific institutions today and the leading scientists within government are busy defending their version of the counterbalancing aspect of freedom, which is respect for the laws of nature. That respect leads them to try to protect the institutional arrangements that give science a measure of influence and independence within our constitutional system. Just as the scientists have not been inclined in theory to insist that only their version of truth has any validity, in practice they have not let their old rivalry with the clergy and the lawyers become all-out warfare. They have instead become numerous enough, and sufficiently established, to join those older professions in a status of influence which those who hold political power must take into account.

If scientists in public affairs today talk more like Jefferson, but act more on the theories of Edmund Burke or John Adams, they may in this too be following Jefferson's example. For Jefferson as an Outsider preached what sounded rather like Rousseau or Condorcet. But Jefferson as an Insider founded institutions that set science on its way to becoming an influential estate in public affairs.

Jefferson on paper was not much interested in giving representation in the processes of government to different orders of men. His main theory looked toward a more mathematically equal distribution of political influence through the destruction of the older estates of special privilege—through the disestablishment of the church, the substitution of a militia for a standing army, attacks on the lawmaking power of the courts, and the abolition of the primogeniture and entail that would have perpetuated the landed gentry.

But what Jefferson actually did may in the long run do more to establish the second aspect of freedom, as a proper counterbalance to the first, than all the efforts of his more pessimistic and conservative colleagues. The constitutional checks that they designed to protect the aristocratic and property interests did not work for very long. But Jefferson helped lay the foundation of new estates that would in the long run begin to counterbalance the simple and uninformed will of the voters. He founded a state university and presided with great energy and distinction over the elite scientific society of his time, the American Philosophical Society. And his predecessor in that position, Benjamin Franklin, had a similar role in our history. Though he may have influenced the ideologues in France by his democratic ideas, he put his enduring stamp on American politics by founding the Society, the original scientific association in the United States, and by establishing a university and endowing an educational foundation.

As science and the more scientific professions have joined the clergy and the lawyers in acquiring substantial influence in public affairs, they have learned how to strengthen their roles as members of estates whose influence in the constitutional system does not derive from electoral support at all. The ways in which they maintain their institutional autonomy and influence are not usually defined systematically by law, or enforced by the courts. The same changes in the nature of governmental activity that decreased the autonomy and influence of business corporations enhanced those of scientific institutions. When the main emphasis in government turned from the enforcement of law by coercive measures to large-scale spending for positive measures of welfare and defense, the legal defenses of private business against government control were greatly weakened. But the influence of the scientific and professional estates was actually increased: their capital was intellectual, not material, and their influence was exercised as a matter of advice, not legal right. Their status in the constitutional system became stronger, but it can be described only as a part of the unwritten constitution.

This is not to say that the unwritten constitution has displaced the written Constitution, any more than the competition and cooperation among the estates has made obsolete the conflict of interest among economic classes. In the United States, at least, the unwritten constitution functions only within the framework of the written Constitution. Though many of the procedural checks of the written Constitution have become obsolete, its fundamental structure is enduring, and more important than ever, especially in the way in which it protects the existence of the estates and sets limits to their influence. This point I will come back to later, but first it is necessary to consider how the roles of the several estates in the unwritten constitution are determined.

The main reason why private property was once considered the best safeguard against centralized political power was that it was so different. When Washington and Jefferson were in public office, they were always, in the best Cincinnatus tradition, looking forward to giving up their authority and retiring to their farms. Property on the land called for the exercise of individual virtues, not power over others; it committed its owners to a sense of public responsibility, but also to the defense of personal rights against impersonal power. This tradition leads some people to "see in the sanctity of private property the only durable foundation for constitutional government in a free society."[6]

Many people share the traditional sentiment, but then in practice find it hard to identify the tradition of the small farmer with the kind of private property that is politically most influential today. The manufacturer of an intercontinental missile, or the director of a national bank, or the operator of a subsidized shipping fleet or a regulated railroad, has seen private property merge with political power to such an extent that it is hardly a separate and balancing force.

Science, on the contrary, has become more important as a basis of pluralism in our constitutional system because while it has been growing more influential it has remained just as distinct from politics in the nature of its interests and the basis of its organization. Many who are eager to keep science and democratic politics compatible are tempted to argue that they are alike in many ways, especially in their common reliance on freedom, and that ideally they should be even more like each other. Obviously, the argument runs, scientists should work in a democratic way toward democratic goals, and politicians should be guided by the methods of science. It seems to me, on the contrary, that we will do more to protect the freedom of our constitutional system by recognizing how fundamentally different politics and science are, and must remain; each is concerned primarily with one of the two complementary aspects of freedom—free will and truth.

The union of the political and scientific estates is not like a partnership, but a marriage; it will not be improved if the two become like each other, but only if they respect each other's quite different needs and purposes. No great harm is done if, in the meantime, they quarrel a bit. Scientists are always likely to complain that politics is based neither on knowledge nor principle. Politicians are apt to retort that science is neither democratic nor responsible. These charges are resented on both sides more because of their emotional overtones than their essential meaning. For, stripped of their overtones, they state the fundamental distinctions that enable these two estates to help maintain a balance between the two aspects of freedom in our constitutional system.

Let us see, then, how these distinctions put science and politics on a different footing with respect to the basis of their authority, or the ways in which they govern themselves, and the basis of their responsibility, or the ways in which they are accountable to others.

THE BASIS OF SCIENTIFIC AUTHORITY AND RESPONSIBILITY

Science is neither democratic nor responsible, in the political senses of those two terms.

It is not democratic, nor is it undemocratic. The notion of democracy, or ultimate rule by votes of the people, is simply irrelevant to science. For science is mainly concerned with the discovery of truths that are not affected by what the scientist thinks or hopes; its issues cannot be decided by votes. The average citizen cannot help decide its crucial issues, or even understand their significance; the apprentice scientist, and some journeymen, are only a little better off. In a fundamental sense, science is not ruled by authority at all; quite obviously, an experiment by the lowliest research assistant may discover truths that will be accepted by his fellow scientists against all the earlier opinions of the most eminent academicians.

But most scientists are prepared to work most of the time within the framework of ideas developed by their acknowledged leaders. In that sense, within any discipline, science is ruled by oligarchs who hold influence as long as their concepts and systems are accepted as the most successful strategy. Although they may reinforce their rule by control over the various types of academic patronage, the essential basis of their influence is the success of their system of ideas. Once in a great while, a rival system is proposed; then there can usually be no compromise between the two ways of viewing reality, and no settlement of the issue by majority opinion. The metaphor of "scientific revolution" suggests the way in which the losing party is displaced from authority, discredited, and its doctrines eliminated from the textbooks.[7] Even though such a change usually takes place slowly, and without affecting the security or income of the losing oligarchs, the intellectual battle for dominance is sometimes a bitter one.

The vulgar view of science is still based on Bacon's description: science is a matter of finding a great many facts, and out of those facts developing a theory to explain them; its essence is a painstaking and objective approach. This is the popular view of science as an inductive process. But the greatest influence is exercised by those leaders who supply a new theoretical view which comes to seem more adequate as a guide to the choice of experiments and as an explanation of a great many formerly unrelated ideas.

And while those leaders retain their influence, the system by which they dominate their respective fields is (from the point of view of a politician or administrator) a most authoritarian one. They control admission to the various grades of status within the estate. The Ph.D. degree and the several academic ranks, and the subtle but powerful distinctions in status among the various universities and research institutes, show an even greater respect for hierarchical order among scientists than soldiers. And the concentration of authority is enhanced by the system of combining research and advanced education in the universities. The young scientist is likely to be under the influence of the same older scientists while he takes his advanced training and later moves on into his postgraduate research.[8]

The system is loosened up considerably in American institutions by the possibilities of secession, which is sometimes easier than revolution. In science, unlike politics, you can secede by creating a new field, without taking any territory away from anyone else. The creation of a new discipline or subdiscipline often makes it possible to bring about progress without complete revolution. In science, as C. P. Swanson has observed, the "elements of conservatism are most clearly seen in curricular stagnation; lack of innovation in university departments and in entrenched personnel; societies and journals which . . . still cling to life . . . Dynamism, on the other hand, finds its public expression in splinter groups operating outside the framework of traditional societies, in an occasional department or institute created around a frontier subject, and an occasional publishing house . . . willing to gamble on the future."[9]

The ability of the scientist to create new scholarly societies, or to find possibilities of advancement through the creation of new professorships or new research institutes within universities, provides pluralism in the self-government of science. The contrast with the old system of academic administration in some Western European countries, in which the pattern of university departments is fixed and each is typically ruled by a single professor, is one that gives much greater possibilities of freedom and initiative to American science.[10] This is important within science as such; it is even more important to the extent that scientists become the source of innovations in policy and become the critics of political decisions. The move of some of the new African states to control the creation of their scientific and professional societies is perhaps as dangerous for the future of free society as the creation of a single-party political system.[11]

Which laws of science are true cannot be decided by majority vote, any more than faith can be imposed by the sword. Nobody outside a particular scientific society needs to worry how it runs its business; the notion of democracy is irrelevant, except to the extent that the competition for honor and prestige leads to a minor-league brand of politics within any association. For the real protection of the political system against the usurpation of power by scientists is the same as the basic protection of the scientists against domination by the politicians: the institutional structure of science is too fragmented, and too divided against itself, to make it a political force worth building up by its leaders, or corrupting by its rivals.

To be responsible, politically speaking, is to be accountable to some higher authority for work done toward a purpose that it has defined. In this sense, science is not responsible and should not be. To the typical scientist, it makes little difference for this purpose whether the higher authority is a business, or a government, or God; basic science as an organized activity cannot work well toward ends defined by others.

If indeed it does make any difference who the others may be, science has looked on a mere employer as the least of the dangers, and someone who presumes to speak for God as the greatest. This is true even of scientists who believe in God. For one can either bamboozle an employer, or find an accommodation with him, since he may be willing to gamble that undirected research in a particular field might pay off in terms of his interests. But a commitment to relate one's research to Divine Revelation permeates the way a man thinks about his problem, and makes him fail to respect material evidence; by a sort of reverse Gresham's Law, the higher or spiritual concern drives out the lower.

In this respect, one must admit, science and politics have something in common. For politics, too, can be free to solve its problems only if it does not pretend it is solving them according to Divine Revelation. It learned this lesson about the same time that science did, between the Puritan Revolution in England and the American Revolution. Nothing annoys most Congressmen so much, I suspect, as to hear a colleague introduce God into a debate as a fellow partisan. He knows that this is merely a way of avoiding the substance of a reasonable argument, and usually a hypocritical way, and that it is dangerous to use a religious appeal as the test of an issue between parties and factions. The politicians and the scientists probably learned the lesson from the reforming theologians: that religious or political or scientific discussions are often corrupted when one type of purpose is made the test of the other.

But, religious beliefs aside, basic science is quite unlike politics in the way in which it refuses to be responsible for following a purpose. This is not an issue which university presidents invent to justify their institutional independence from government; it is a principle that operates against their authority within the universities as well.

For the fundamental principle of organization of a university or an institution devoted to basic research is not the economic or political or social purpose that science is to serve, but the discipline.[12] That is to say, universities generally do not set up one scientific department to serve heavy industry, and another to serve transportation, and another to serve medicine or agriculture; instead they have departments of physics and chemistry and biology. Special professional schools of engineering or medicine or agriculture are of course not bound by this rule; they may set up departments rather more on the basis of purpose, but the departments of applied engineering and clinical medicine are not those that are expected to make the fundamental advances in science.

From the point of view of the lay observer, the most convincing proof that this peculiarity of science is not an outworn tradition is that it constitutes the basis on which—within each department—the universities with the highest reputations make their decisions on money and on appointments, the two keys to the strength of any organization. It is reasonably obvious that each scientific department in the universities of the highest rank neither apportions its budget, nor makes its principal permanent-tenure appointments, mainly by calculating the social and economic benefits to be gained from the decision. It makes such decisions by judging how much the work of a particular scientist, or a particular group of scientists, is going to advance knowledge or understanding.

The incidental effect of this approach is to put the issue on a basis that strengthens the case for the independence and self-government of science. If a department of chemistry, for example, were to be judged on its contribution to the chemical industry, the selection of professors of chemistry might logically be taken over by the board of trustees of the university, which might include (or consult) executives of the chemical industry. As long, however, as the most respected faculty positions are awarded on the basis of the candidates' contributions to the discipline, the permanent tenure appointments—the key actions that determine the whole structure of influence within the field—are bound to be made by the scientists themselves. And they are made on the basis of considerations that are hardly related at all to the interests of the layman or the general citizen.[13]

But the essential purpose of this approach is not hostility to those interests. On the contrary the approach is related to the intellectual structure of science and its system of motivation. Science, in setting its goals and measuring its progress in ways that do not correspond to the layman's purposes, does not do so in order to escape political responsibility; it seeks to escape such responsibility in order to be free to discover the most fruitful ways to advance knowledge. The body of accepted theory within a discipline, and the system of assumptions and tools with which it works, set the standards to which the scientist must conform in order to advance in reputation and influence. Modern science makes rapid progress because in this way each discipline chooses the problems which it encourages its members to undertake. It rejects many problems as belonging to other disciplines, or too difficult, or as metaphysical and unscientific, that is, not defined in a way that enables them to be studied productively. This is a way of protecting the scientist from being asked to do things that are socially important—important in the sense that a layman would like to see them done, even if a miracle were needed to accomplish them—but that do not seem currently within the potential scope of scientific techniques.[14]

From the point of view of a politician, this arrangement seems slightly unfair; it is like letting a batter call his own balls and strikes, a rule which would surely send his batting average up. Nevertheless, since the politicians and scientists of a country are playing on the same team, the politicians like to see the scientists get as many hits as possible. And on the recent historical record, the politicians have been persuaded that the science that is not held responsible (at least in the short run) for the attainment of predetermined purposes has the highest batting average. Science had already freed itself philosophically from the idea of *ultimate* purpose; American scientists at the end of the Second World War undertook to free the financing of basic research from subservience to political and economic purpose.

The most powerful tool for the enforcement of responsibility in any large organization is control of the budget. Responsible government, in particular, evolved as representatives of the British taxpayers insisted that their taxes be used for purposes that they approved. To take public institutions off endowments, and to subject them to the control of annual appropriations, was the historic strategy for destroying establishments and for enforcing political responsibility. Basic science, however, has largely escaped this fate; politicians have been persuaded to give it the money without the responsibility, and in this sense have made it an establishment, although a highly pluralistic one.

The universities do almost half of the basic research in the United States, and their influence within the scientific estate is much larger than that figure suggests. Of the $695,000,000 that they spent in 1961–62 on basic research, $442,000,000 came from Congressional appropriations; $73,000,000 came from industry and foundations, mostly in short-term gifts; and a substantial proportion of the remainder was spent by state universities from state appropriations.[15] A very small proportion of the money available to university scientists, then, comes as income from fixed endowments. How, then, can basic science be said to be established and freed of political responsibility?

The answer is obvious to most of those who serve on university faculties; it is not so easy to explain to anyone who thinks in terms of governmental or business organization. It can be given in summary form in four points:

1. The leading private universities, although legally under lay trustees, long ago came to follow the old European ecclesiastical tradition that the academic affairs of a university were to be governed mainly by its faculty, and that its senior faculty members were to enjoy permanent tenure—that is to say, were not to be completely responsible to administrative superiors.

2. The leading state universities, in order to compete for the best talent and to become academically respectable, followed

suit; in some states this was accomplished merely by practice and tradition, and others wrote it into laws or constitutions.[16]

3. The practice which the best-endowed universities follow (and all others wish that they could) is generally to safeguard the permanent tenure of senior professors by paying their salaries out of the income that is most certain (whether endowment income, or regular recurrent appropriations), and to accept short-term funds from private donors or from government agencies only for temporary purposes, such as special projects. Such projects are normally under the supervision of a tenure professor, but pay the salaries only of junior and other temporary staff members. This protection of the independence of the senior scientists, in a system in which most of the money comes from short-term grants, gives the university the maximum bargaining power and independence as against the donor. And within the university it gives the maximum control to the scientist as against the dean and the president (the trustees are normally not in the picture at all). The professors are, so to speak, the holders of the intellectual stock that carries voting rights; the foundations and government agencies are only the bankers. (The favorite metaphor of philanthropy is that foundations supply risk capital; it would be more accurate to say that the universities risk their capital on every tenure appointment, and lose on most; the foundations then bank on the winners.)

4. The previous three safeguards were adequate as long as short-term funds came from many sources in relatively small amounts, so that no single donor would have too much financial influence over a university, just as no single advertiser can dictate the editorial policy of a large newspaper. Those safeguards would not have been adequate, once the federal government became the predominant patron of science, but for an additional safeguard: the arrangements for the distribution of funds for *basic* research were contrived so as to make it impossible for federal administrators to require that they be spent toward applied purposes, and so as to put the essential decisions in the hands of university scientists themselves. These arrangements turn on several points:

(a) The granting of basic research funds is not centralized in a single federal agency; there are five agencies each of which spends more than one hundred million dollars per year in grants or contracts with universities for basic research.[17]

(b) Each of these agencies is free, of course, to define the fields of science which it is willing to support. But each not only believes in the virtue of basic research, but also wishes to do business with institutions and individuals of the first quality in the scientific world. Each agency therefore has a powerful incentive to offer grants of the type that appeals most to the best scientists, namely, grants with the fewest possible restrictions on basic research.

(c) These agencies distribute their research funds largely according to the part-time advice of scientists most of whom are employed by universities and research institutions. In the National Institutes of Health, now the biggest contributor to basic research in universities proper (omitting special research centers), their advice is given statutory status; the Institutes cannot make a grant which the advisers have not specifically endorsed. In other agencies, the role of the advisers rests on custom, and on the fact that their expertise is respected; their influence differs in the several agencies but usually is substantial.[18] Panels of advisers are organized, like university departments, by scientific disciplines, with the same effect of strengthening the influence and independence of the scientist. (In the Institutes of Health, each statutory advisory council is organized to deal with a type of disease; the implicit pressure that this system exerts toward responsibility for particular applied purposes is offset by the existence of subordinate panels of advisers which screen the projects and make all but final choices among them—and these panels are organized by discipline.)

The sum of these four safeguards is that the leading scientists in the leading universities are self-governing with respect to their scientific ideas or decisions. In that sense they are not responsible to administrative superiors or to those who grant them financial support. They are responsible, of course, in a fiscal sense, and accountable for compliance with the regulations of their universities as well as the public laws. This can lead to plenty of difficulties. But the issues are those of red tape, not of the essential control of scientific strategy. It seems clearly established that the principles of academic self-government, which were first extended from the private universities to state universities to guarantee the autonomy of science, have now been extended to the relation of the federal government to the university scientists who control the expenditure of their funds.

Most scientists once feared that if they had to depend on subsidies from federal agencies, they would be committed to work toward those agencies' purposes, and thus lose their freedom. On the contrary, it is now clear that the university scientist of reasonably high status in his field realizes that he has more freedom by virtue of his ability to seek funds from a wide variety of federal and other sources than if he were entirely dependent on the decisions of his university administration. Many academic critics dislike the project system because it keeps the scientists busy begging government agencies for funds. But the scientists themselves are typically cool to the idea of some university administrators that the government should give research funds to the universities and let their officers decide how to distribute them within their respective faculties.[19] Not even the university presidents are very eager to have such authority; the scientific estate is too difficult to govern from outside.

The result of this system is that science, in the constitutional system, is in no sense merely concerned with the means toward ends defined by politicians or administrators. Though it considers knowledge an end in itself, its leaders are always willing to invade other estates to translate their new knowledge into new policy. They are tempted to define the freedom of scientific institutions not merely in negative terms. They are interested not only in protecting the autonomy of their disciplines, but in protecting their ability to recommend new programs and policies to society as a whole, on the basis of new scientific discoveries.

As a result, the more eminent scientists have an opportunity for influence that extends far beyond the strict boundaries of their science. Those who are in universities on permanent tenure are their own masters, to a degree that is true of no other vocation. They do not let their scientific inquiries become dominated by purposes that are irrelevant to science itself, whether those purposes are philosophical or political. And if they are interested in applying their scientific knowledge to business or governmental purposes, they can find within the limits of academic tolerance a substantial minor fraction of time—and sometimes a major fraction—to assume roles in the administrative or political estate.

Perhaps no other major group in society, except members of law firms, is in a position to put its expert knowledge to use in issues of public policy and at the same time maintain a safe avenue of retreat. Responsibility is a good thing in politics, but only within limits. The most tolerant and free systems have usually been in those countries where members of the governing groups were not required to pay too heavily for their mistakes. In the nineteenth-century House of Commons, the rival parties could be relatively tolerant of each other because members were unpaid, and lived off their estates or their investments; to lose power was a minor deprivation. Not many lawyers in the American Congress would suffer financially if defeated for re-election. A system in which those who lose a policy contest lose their heads as well, or even their incomes, makes compromise impossible; it is likely to be tyrannical and unstable, or to base its stability on total oppression. The United States does well, it seems to me, to include scientists (and other professors) with lawyers and millionaires among the classes which can afford to take part in public life without making it an exclusive career.

THE BASIS OF POLITICAL AUTHORITY AND RESPONSIBILITY

By contrast with the scientific estate, the political estate is concerned with the use of power in ways that affect the ordinary citizen, and it must therefore gain his support. It may do so by persuasion and consent, or by the compulsion of superstition, indoctrination, or terror. In a free constitutional system, the political estate must be democratic and responsible. But, again by contrast with the scientific estate, it does not base its authority or responsibility on knowledge or principle, as a scientist would define those terms.

This difference comes not from its concern with power, for power may be manipulated effectively with systematic knowledge and on fixed principles. It comes rather from a concern that distinguishes the political estate even more clearly from science: a primary concern for purpose. The scientist has found it necessary to exclude the idea of purpose from his basic research, but it is the central concern of the politician, especially the most successful ones at the highest levels. The lesser politicians, and their lesser agents, may be concerned with power for its own sake, and preoccupied with the techniques of attaining it. The great leader is the one who, while prudent enough to make sure of his base of power, is able to persuade the people that he best expresses their essential purposes.

Science, of course, helps change those purposes from time to time, by enlarging the range of possible choices; man cannot know what he wants until he knows what it is possible for him to get. But science cannot determine those purposes, and the scientist has neither a better right nor more competence to make such decisions than anyone else. In a free constitutional system, the problem then is to order affairs so that the major issues of purpose come up from time to time for consideration by the voters, as a means of consenting to the authority of government and holding it responsible.

The key to the problem is to organize the government according to its purposes, and not, as in a university, by fields of science.

Purpose as the basis of organization is usually thought of in connection with administration and efficiency: you must organize the executive departments by purpose so as to bring together, at any given level in a hierarchical system, problems that are of a comparable nature, and that pertain to related interests. This lets you make the best use of the several types of skills in your organization; it lets you decide how much money to spend on various things that can reasonably be compared with each other; and it lets you make equitable awards to competing claims, and assess equitable punishments against comparable offenses.

But this way of organizing a government is based not only on administrative principle, which is valid enough, but also on the principle of political responsibility, which is even more important. The best way for a politician to be held responsible by a political superior, or by the electorate, is by the definition of the purposes he is expected to accomplish, and the measurement of his accomplishment against them. To organize a government into departments and bureaus according to their purposes is more responsible than to distinguish them according to scientific or professional skills or processes. There are two reasons for this. The first is one that has little or nothing to do with the kind of political system involved; the second depends on it entirely.

Whether or not the government as a whole is responsible to the people, its cabinet or dictator or president probably wants it to be internally responsible. So he is interested in the first of these reasons, which follows from the fact that each of the main purposes of government—the major ends for which men are willing to subject themselves to authority and be taxed—requires the use of several or many scientific disciplines and professional skills. No one of these sciences or professions contains within its body of systematic knowledge an understanding of the way in which it should be related to other special fields. An organization that is organized around a particular body of technology or professional skill is likely to be very bad at judging its effectiveness, by comparison with other special skills, in accomplishing a political purpose. Moreover, the most common fault of any organization is to fail to adapt to change, and this failure most often takes the form of worrying more and more about the technical processes that it uses, and caring less and less about its essential purposes. In a governmental system, the major defense against this tendency is for its chief executive to pin responsibility on each of his principal subordinates in terms of a major purpose, and not a professional skill or scientific specialty. This makes it much harder for an official to dodge the big new issues, and to take refuge in routine.

The second reason is one that has force only in a free system. Political responsibility can be effective in a democracy only if the government is organized so as to fix public attention on issues the average voter—or at least, the leaders in every community and every institution—can understand. To organize by technical or scientific process—to set up a department of chemistry, for example—would bring up for the attention of the political estate the kinds of issues that the electorate is not capable of considering. On the other hand, it is perfectly capable of considering the main issues that are raised by the existence of departments of agriculture and of health, in both of which chemists serve important roles. For the heads of such departments will be obliged to make decisions regarding their general purposes that are of interest to everyone.

Government organization cannot be tidied up and then left alone, but is a continuously changing problem. And this is true at least partly because new scientific and technical developments change the relation of particular fields of knowledge to political purposes. It then sometimes follows that the appropriate political action is not to try to legislate a definition of the scientific process to be employed, or even the general policy, but to make a change in organization that would put the technique to work for a different purpose. For example, the support of research and development in aerodynamics was drastically changed when it was transferred from an agency whose purpose was to serve aviation, into an agency whose purpose was to take man into outer space. The engineering of air traffic control was changed when it was transferred from the Civil Aeronautics Administration, a purely civilian regulatory agency, to the Federal Aviation Agency, whose purposes were defined to serve military aviation as well, and whose organization and personnel system were adjusted accordingly.

The use of pesticides has stirred up a lively debate among the chemists, biologists, agricultural extension workers, chemical manufacturers, and public health doctors. Their varying views will be debated for many years in the press, the Congress, and the executive councils. But the key to the problem will probably be found not in a policy formula, but in a decision either to increase the authority of the Public Health Service or to leave control of the matter in the Agriculture Department—for one agency is dominated by the purpose of preventing disease and the other is more concerned with the increase of crops. Or, to take two older examples, certain work began in the Department of Agriculture in 1862 when the Bureau of Chemistry was set up with the purpose of helping the farmer. Another program began in the Treasury Department in 1798 with respect to the quarantine and medical care of merchant seamen, for the purpose of furthering the commerce from which our customs revenues were derived. The Agriculture Department program made it possible to define the standards for the purity of food. The Treasury program opened up possibilities for the broader protection of the public health. Both programs are now in the Department of Health, Education and Welfare (as the Food and Drug Administration and the Public Health Service) where the purposes to which their science is put are judged in a different context from that of their original departments.

These examples do not argue either that considerations of purpose are superior in merit or ultimate influence to those of science, or that they ought to be. They suggest, on the contrary, that the main lines of our policy, over the long run, are likely to be determined by scientific developments that we cannot foresee, rather more than by political doctrines that we can now state. For none of these programs came about simply because politicians deter-

mined in advance that they should. There was no political requirement for a general public health program, or a pure food
and drug program, until advances in medical science gave the
politicians the opportunity to establish one, any more than there
was a political requirement for air traffic control before the
Wright Brothers.

But these examples do indeed argue that for establishing
responsibility the government should be organized, and the issues
stated, in terms of purpose rather than of scientific or any other
specialized knowledge. The key to a major purpose today may
be one scientific discipline; tomorrow it may be another. How to
relate the several sciences and professions to one another, and to
judge what they are worth in terms of money and administrative
organization and political effort, is not a question that can be
answered in terms of any systematic scholarly discipline. It is an
intellectual process that requires putting together too many of
those sciences to become one itself. This type of intellectual
process, if we may judge it by the complexity of its subject
matter, may be a kind of wisdom that is superior to any science.
If scientists despise it (and social scientists seem at least as guilty
as natural scientists of this offense) it is because the politician's
judgment (at its best) is too subtle and varied to be judged by
the artificial standards that they set up as guides within their self-
limited and abstract fields of inquiry.[20]

So the politician must judge himself and his political colleagues, and be judged by the voters, not on an estimate of what
a man knows, but on the desirability of his purposes—and also
on two other questions: (1) Can the man acquire the power to
make his purpose effective? (2) Does he want the power in order
to accomplish the purpose, or is he mainly pleading the purpose
only as an excuse to get the power? These questions have their
relevance in other estates as well; even scientists are sometimes
favored for appointment because of their qualities of personal
leadership. But they are least relevant in science, and progressively more relevant along the spectrum to politics, where they

become the paramount consideration in a system of enforcing responsibility.

The same questions become even more important to a politician when his interests are related not only to the scientific wing of the scholarly and professional estates, but also to the wings representing the older and more traditional culture. Policy questions are only part of the concern of a politician; they usually relate to the positive aspect of government, on which it can do something or change something, and in this aspect science and technology have great weight. But this is a peculiarly modern view of government; the older functions of government were to dispense justice, to maintain authority, and to symbolize and encourage the desirable virtues. Until science discovers how to make all men both immortal and unselfish, they will have to be interested not only in solving problems, but in living in a civilized manner with those problems they cannot solve. On problems that no one can do anything about, as well as in the encouragement of the arts and the maintenance of justice, the politician's interests are related especially to the interests of the legal profession, the clergy, and the arts and humanities generally.

This does not mean that in these matters only the theologians and philosophers and lawyers have anything to contribute. The biologists and social scientists have done much to change our ideas of the principles of justice and of aesthetics. On the other hand, the theologians and philosophers and lawyers still have a lot to say about the ways in which politicians make use of the work of the natural and social scientists. The political estate, without systematically understanding any of these schools of thought, has to represent the rest of humanity in trying to reunite them in action. It has to incorporate the various aspects of knowledge in the purposes of man as a whole.

As it tries to do so, the political estate is not based on principle, any more than on systematic knowledge. This is not to suggest that a politician should not respect truth and principles. It is not meant to imply that politics is merely a matter of "who gets what, when, where, and how," or that there is no such thing as a public interest, which the politician ought to be expected to defend against private and partial interests, even if neither he nor any philosopher can ever define it. It is only meant to argue that politicians should not (and in the United States ordinarily do not) join together for the exercise of responsible authority on the basis of a set of principles that distinguishes them from their rivals, and from which they deduce their practical policy decisions.

The country finds it highly useful to have political parties, to hold them responsible for the guidance of public policy, and even to demand that they tell us in advance by their platforms what they propose to do. But a party platform is not a systematic doctrine, or a statement of principle, and much of our cynicism about politics comes from the mistake of expecting it to be.

A science can be guided by a theory, and scientists try to make it coherent and consistent; this approach works in science because any scientist who dislikes any particular theory can secede and operate with his own. If there is any quality of mind, or settled habit of thinking, that makes it hard for a scientist to become a politician, it is probably this one: he is trained to make the intellectual consistency of various parts of his system a test of its validity.

The politician, on the other hand, is not permitted the luxury of secession at will; he has to learn to work toward common objectives with others whose theoretical principles are quite different from his own. There are obviously, in the political and social sciences, many competing doctrines. If we intended each party to be governed by a doctrine, we would be forced to set up enough parties to go around, or else to decide that only one doctrine can be really true. The former choice leads to the chaos of the multiparty system, the latter to the ideological dictatorship of the single party. In many countries, of course, the multiparty choice has led, after an unhappy experience of political irresponsibility, to the single-party alternative.

The two-party system is based on a quite different idea: it is the most convenient way to organize a periodic contest for power (which is the surest safeguard of responsibility) without letting anyone really expect either party to be much more consistent and principled in its theory than the nation as a whole.

In the context of national politics, a party platform is in some ways like an official statement of military "requirements" in the development of a weapons system. It is a statement of intentions drawn up by people who cannot know what the alternative possibilities are, and cannot foresee the scientific and technological developments (and other changes) that will make it possible to take different roads toward the same general end. The platform is useful and necessary, but it is least useful in dealing with the most basic changes in society. Modern science itself cannot operate on the simple inductive basis that Bacon prescribed for it, but it has forced politics to become an inductive process. The average voter is quite sensible when, refusing to follow the advice of reformers, he votes for the candidate as a man, rather than for his political principles, or supports the party because of what he thinks of its leaders, rather than of its platform.

This is the basis of politics that awards power to the responsible and tolerant center, rather than to the doctrinaire extremes. It is profoundly democratic, since the average man can make a better judgment of the practical effect of choosing John Doe over Richard Roe than he can judge the consequences of scientific hypotheses or economic or social theory. In this respect, the average voter is exactly like any scientist who takes on political or administrative responsibilities: he learns that the most significant judgments are his choices of people, and he is usually shrewd enough not to make those judgments mainly on their professions of principle.

THE MUTUAL DEFENSES OF THE ESTATES

These deep differences between science and politics make possible the system of relative checks and balances in the unwritten constitution. Science can be the basis of an objective criticism of political power because it claims no power itself. Politics can afford to respect the independence of science because science does not attempt to dictate its purposes. Out of their fundamental differences grows the twofold principle discussed in the preceding chapter: (1) the more an institution or function is concerned with truth, the more it deserves freedom from political control; (2) the more an institution or function is concerned with the exercise of power, the more it should be controlled by the processes of responsibility to elected authorities and ultimately to the electorate.

This principle is generally applied by common consent, and in doubtful cases settled on a rather pragmatic and functional basis. It does not depend on the benevolence of political authorities; it is based on the determined self-defense of well-organized interests whose jurisdictional claims the public approves. It is a system of relative, rather than absolutely fixed, checks and balances, but it is nonetheless a system of checks and balances, and not merely of delegation from central authority. The test that is applied, with general public approval, seems to be to ask what kind of discipline, and what controls, are necessary to accomplish a particular purpose, and to protect the general public interest? On the other hand, what kinds of freedom, and how much freedom, are necessary in order to let an institution do its particular kind of work?

At the extremes, these questions are easily answered. An institute for the study of fundamental mathematics, whose members never wished to consult with either government or industry, would obviously do its work best if mathematicians were permitted to run it without outside interference. It would need discipline and controls, but the most effective types would be those that come from the mathematician's publication of his studies followed by criticism from his colleagues. At the other extreme, a member of Congress does not expect that kind of freedom; the purpose of his office is to vote on hard issues that cannot be settled scientifically, and for which he expects to be held accountable to the electorate. But these clear-cut extremes shade off very quickly from one to the other. The typical state university demands academic freedom for its basic research, but it is also engaged in a great deal of applied research designed to serve various economic and social interests, and with respect to that kind of work its claim to independence is less strong. Near the other extreme, even Congress does not operate in all respects on the basis of political conflict; many of its committees deal with policy issues in a nearly nonpartisan way, and some of its committee staffs, along with its Legislative Reference Service, can claim a measure of autonomy because they are engaged in research whose objectivity Congress wishes to safeguard.

Most of the difficulties that are usually attributed to the relation between science and politics are not direct conflicts between the two extremes of truth and power. They arise instead in the middle range between them: in the professional and administrative estates. To consider how such issues arise, and how they are settled, let me emphasize again that the four estates are not corporate entities, or clear-cut classes, but merely four arbitrary groupings along a rather muddled spectrum. If the general public is inclined to speak of "science" in public affairs when what is involved is really technology or engineering or medicine, it is because so many scientists are tempted (or required) to move over into the professional estate in order to help apply their special knowledge to public problems.

The professional estate is like the scientific in basing its work mainly on an accepted body of knowledge, and in organizing itself on the basis of that knowledge to assert a code of internal discipline and responsibility among its members. It is unlike the scientific estate in being directly concerned with the application of knowledge to social purposes. Hence its claim to autonomy is distinctly limited; the doctors are almost (but not quite) independent of control from outside their profession in their relationship with individual patients; they are less so in their administration of a hospital; and very much less so in their views of the enforcement of public health regulations or in the provision of medical care with the aid of public funds. The engineering profession is in a similar status. On aspects of its work that are clearly based on scientific principles, it can demand the right to make the final decision. But most of its work is carried on within the limits and purposes set for it by administrators or politicians.

The administrative estate is like the political in being concerned with the definition of purposes and policies, and with the organization and management of power. It is distinguished from the political estate in not being involved in the electoral campaigns for power and not necessarily affected by the outcome of those campaigns. It should be able to establish a sense of corporate responsibility among its members, and to improve their standards of ethics and efficiency; it often does so by developing standards of performance quite apart from the sanctions of political authority. But its standards can hardly run counter to such authority. It is too close to politics to be granted very much independence from it; a large measure of authority and influence may be given it by delegation, but hardly ever on a basis that it can exercise in its own right. A career ambassador, a general or an admiral, the career staff in the Bureau of the Budget, the administrative assistant secretary or the bureau chiefs of an executive department—these are career officials whose influence is tremendous, but who never (with the occasional exception of the military) demand the right to make decisions against the wishes of their political superiors.

The politician is not willing to give much autonomy to the administrator for two related reasons. He does not concede that administration is based on a set of skills that are fundamentally scientific in nature, especially since they seem so very similar to his own. This reason is debatable, for the body of systematic knowledge involved in modern management has become respectable in volume even though spotty in quality. But the politician's second reason is more easily justified: the administrator, unlike the professional or the scientist, is concerned with the total problems of the organization; to concede that he had the right, on his own authority, to control any general aspect of its affairs would be to open the door to encroachment on the politician's power.

Since the administrator generally exercises his power by delegation from above, and since the professional and the scientist conventionally are depicted on the organization chart as lower still in rank, how can they constitute any effective checks on political power, or defend their own jurisdictions within society? This is the question that would be asked, in a skeptical tone, by anyone who thinks that influence or authority are derived only from formal legal power. But influence and authority come from what men believe, and within their respective fields the scientific and professional estates are likely to command plenty of public faith and confidence to support their position. One might well argue that the politician obeys science in our society more regularly than the scientist obeys the politician; the only reason we do not look at the problem in this way is that nobody notices the compulsion of those forces that are irresistible and are obeyed automatically.

The greatest revolution in American policy in the last two decades, for example, was made promptly as a result of a finding of the scientists which politicians had to take, in a sense, on faith, since it was based on processes and data that laymen could not understand. The scientists devised a secret method of long-range observations, on the basis of which they reported to a skeptical President that the Russians had detonated an atomic (and later a hydrogen) bomb. Their conclusion immediately had a more revolutionary effect on the nature of our foreign and military policies than any amount of purely political debate.

As long as the scientists are united on scientific findings, their findings are taken on faith by politicians, even when profound consequences are involved. This is explained partly by the general moral climate—the element of personal trust within a society. But it is far from the whole explanation, for personal trust exists among politicians and administrators, and they do not take each others' opinions with quite such conclusive faith. The institutions of science and the professions can defend themselves and their opinions and jurisdictions within our system of constitutional checks and balances in several effective ways, even without formal legal safeguards. Here are four of the strongholds in their defenses:

1. The accepted tradition of the self-government of the academic departments within universities gives the politician some assurance that a consensus among scientists is based on the evidence, and not on administrative discipline.

2. The professions recognize the extent to which their effective service, and consequently their influence and independence, depend on the objectivity and reliability of scientific data. Engineers and physicians are trained to respect the methods and the validity of the sciences; all their inner discipline makes them not only take to the defense of science against political interference, but continuously reshape their practice in accord with its new findings. Any challenge to the integrity of science from political authority is taken as an implicit threat to the integrity and autonomy of the related professions.

3. Politicians and administrators, who work in a field of such uncertainty that their decisions are always open to question, are eager to base them on as large an element of certainty as possible. For them, truth must be defined in practice as what the experts agree on. To go against the accepted consensus of either a scientific discipline or a profession—as long as that consensus appears to be based on scientific evidence rather than mere corporate self-interest—is extremely hazardous. Any policy decision, either in the administrative or the political world, has its opponents, and nobody wants to give his opponents a chance to say the decision is unsound from the professional or scientific point of view.

Thus, on the undefinable boundary between a profession and

administration, the professional has a tactical advantage. The administrator has so many problems to deal with at once that he is glad to leave as many of them as he can to be disposed of by settled rules and principles, which will require the minimum of defense against critics. To follow the advice of the doctors or the engineers (or, in other fields, the lawyers) is to play it safe. Far from seeking to attack a scientific consensus, the administrator (or the politician) is often trying to find ways to dodge his hard policy choices by asking the professional expert for some new technological gadget to solve the problem. When we face the social and economic problems of the slum, we try to escape them by prefabricating houses; when we consider the effects of our poor system of regulating transportation, we dream of monorails or helicopters.

4. The influence of the sciences and professions is buttressed by their peculiar right to control the privilege of membership in their respective estates. If a governmental department does not like the general approach of a particular profession to its problem, it cannot organize a new professional association, with new state licensing boards, and write a new code of ethics. The independence of the scientific and professional estates is augmented further by the fact that the movement of individuals from one estate to another, though common enough, is almost always in one direction. A physicist may move from basic research to development engineering quite readily; a chemist or physician may become an administrator in his middle age, and many do. Transfer in this direction along the spectrum from science to politics is relatively easy. But the administrator or politician cannot, in mid-career, become a scientist or engineer or physician, partly because of the procedural restrictions set up by the self-governing professions and disciplines, but mainly because the acquisition of systematic knowledge is too rigorous a process to begin in middle age.

All four of those defenses are strong enough in any modern free society, but they are given special weight in the United States by the nature of the constitutional system. Here is where the formal structure of a written Constitution becomes significant. Its specific procedural restraints on authority may have weakened or become obsolete, but the general division of power between a legislature and an executive, each holding tenure independently of the other, is of more importance than ever.

The President, in the last analysis, is prevented from applying administrative discipline to his subordinate (or insubordinate) scientists and professionals by the fact that he cannot apply political discipline to members of Congress. Unlike the British prime minister, he cannot threaten the tenure of office of legislators, or control their agenda, or limit their ability to take the initiative in matters of legislative or financial policy, or restrict their ability to ask his subordinates at all levels for their opinions on his policies. If a President sought to influence the scientists or engineers or physicians in his administration to suppress data, or to falsify them to further his policy views, or even to refrain from suggesting that they would like to have more money to spend, he would almost certainly invite a rebellion that would be organized around the four defensive points just mentioned. The scientific civil servants, in outrage, would leak information to their professional and academic colleagues; they in turn would involve the influence of their business and civic colleagues and their journalistic supporters to repel this attack on their professional ethics; and the President's normal political opposition in Congress would immediately be increased by the addition of those whose sense of principle and procedure would be offended, and who would be eager to protect their sources of information. This is not to argue that scientists and professionals are absolutely impervious to political influence, but only that the risks of applying such influence go up along with administrative or political rank. Such pressure is least likely to come from the President, who would have much more to lose than to gain by playing that game.

The independent structure of Congress and its committees affects not merely the way in which the President operates, but the way in which the departments under him are organized and staffed. Congress, being independent, wants to get the facts at first hand, and not to hear them interpreted according to the President's policy. Its members tend to share the layman's faith in facts and science: the facts on any given issue can be determined by science, and ought to provide the solution to a problem, if there has been no political hanky-panky to distort them. Scientists are usually terrified by this notion (between the intervals when they are flattered by it) for they realize that facts have meaning only within the framework of some hypothesis or theory, which is a form of policy for science. But a Congressional committee is not willing to concede that it has to handle its specialized subject matter within the framework of any policy assumptions, especially those of the President. It prefers to make up its own, and to deal directly with the experts who can give it the technical information.

This attitude has greatly strengthened the role of the scientists and professionals within the civil service. A Congressional committee will listen with more respect to a man who speaks as an expert, on the basis of evidence certified by some science or some profession, than if he is speaking as a member of a political or administrative team, interested mainly in the coherence and purpose of the government's total program. One reason why it has been easy in practice for professionals and scientists to move into administrative positions in the United States government, is that Congress has not been eager to permit the executive branch to develop a guiding system of policy, a central body of administrative doctrine, within which the several bureaus would be expected to administer their programs. In any bureau that deals with problems with a scientific or professional as well as administrative and political content, it is therefore expected that the scientist or professional can quickly learn the administrative aspects of his job, or get some subordinate to run them for him, whereas no layman could ever learn how to deal with the substance of the professional issues or have the status to command professional support. This is a peculiarly American assumption; the British, as discussed earlier, make the opposite one. Because their top career officials deal only with ministers who are members of a disciplined government, and not with independent members or committees of the parliament, they are expected to be concerned with the general purposes of the government, and to let their subordinates worry about their technical and scientific aspects.

Scientists and professionals in the United States, in their ability to compete for influence and jurisdiction within the constitutional system, are in a far stronger position than one would think by looking at their formal legal power. They have the fundamental advantage of commanding privileged sanctuaries over which they have absolute control, while invading at will the battlefields of administration and politics. In politics, they have the advantage of guerrilla experience in a jungle which the ordinary parade-ground politician has never penetrated: no politics (except perhaps ecclesiastical politics) is as complicated as the politics of academic and professional organizations. The politician, like the conventional political scientist, usually thinks of politics only as contests for power in the public and official campaigns. Professionals, on the other hand, are aware of the potentialities of exerting public influence through private organizations, and of the tactical advantages of possessing special knowledge not subject to public disputation.

The advantages of the scientist and professional are substantial enough so that one might well ask how the administrator and the politician ever manage to protect their side of the constitutional balance. What keeps the President or the Secretary of a department from getting into the position of a sort of constitutional monarch, able to act only on the advice of his professional subordinates?

The first protection of the politician is his ability to define the issues and the assumptions. His legal authority may not make him superior to his scientific and professional subordinates in learning the answers, but it does let him ask the questions. Science cannot claim any special right to determine the purpose toward which a politician is to work, even though it may help him define it by opening up new possibilities and calculating their relative feasibility and cost. When a politician is most successful in changing the policies of an organization which he heads, it is often by discovering that the technical skills of his subordinates have been applied to the wrong problems, and by setting them some new ones. This power, plus control over the allocation of funds, gives politicians the ability to influence the general emphasis of scientific development; they cannot tell scientists precisely what basic problems to work on, but they can provide more money for one field and less for another.

Second, the politician is protected against encroachment by the experts by his ability to detect, and take advantage of, differences of opinion among scientists and professional advisers. The organization of a scientific discipline or of a profession is admirably suited to protect it against interference by the politician; but it is not set up so as to unite its members to impose any particular policy on the politician. He must take a complete consensus among scientists or professionals—within the limits of their proper competence—as the equivalent, for his purposes, of revealed truth. But he finds so many disagreements wherever science touches on policy issues that he is usually left a good deal of room for maneuver.

Third, the politician has (or should have) the authority to sort out the elements of a policy problem, and to decide which ones can be dealt with effectively by various types of professional skills, and which must be determined by his administrative subordinates or by himself. In considering the development of a weapons system, for example, the Secretary of Defense can assert his authority by observing how professional advice from the several services cancels itself out, and how the science of the economist helps to criticize the plans of the engineer. This right to make the jurisdictional decisions among the several estates, so to speak, is the essence of political power, and usually of executive authority.

The politician, as he undertakes to make such jurisdictional decisions, is sometimes tempted to encroach on the normal territory of the scientific estate. Sometimes he interferes directly with the scientist's pursuit of basic science; but he is more likely to interfere when the scientist proposes to publish findings that upset the established political or economic order, or when he joins with the engineering or medical profession in proposing to translate the findings of science into new policies. Who then should decide where the competence of the scientific and professional estates ends? Who, for example, decides whether it is a political or an economic or a scientific issue when a state university in the corn and dairy belt proposes to publish a report that oleomargarine made from cottonseed oil is as nutritious as butter? Or who decides whether the number of inspection stations required as safeguards in a treaty for the control of nuclear testing is to be determined on scientific or strategic or political grounds? Or who decides when the apparent consensus of scientific opinion on the relation of cigarettes to lung cancer is great enough to justify governmental regulatory action, and of what kind? In such issues the problem is less often whether politics will presume to dictate to science than it is how much politics is to be influenced by the new findings of science.

The basis of any system of democratic responsibility is the understanding that issues like these cannot, in any useful sense, be considered merely scientific issues. No science can deal with any such issue in all its major aspects, especially if we wish to keep in mind that the major aspects of a problem are those that relate to the purposes of all types of citizens, not merely of the experts or the rulers. In any given issue, a new scientific development may turn out to be the changing factor in the equation, and thus on balance may determine the political solution of the problem. But it is never possible in advance to define when this will happen, or to determine scientifically how much weight to give to the scientific factor. Accordingly, it is never possible to define a policy question in advance as one that can be left to the scientist or the professional.

Some questions of great public importance, however, are so defined. For example, the law assigns to physicists in the Bureau of Standards the power to determine how long an inch is, and how heavy a pound. So far as I know, no one looks on this as a policy issue, and no politician ever presumes to interfere with it. On the other hand, the politician can never afford to turn over a program to scientific or professional authority to control, unless it is one that includes only those problems that can be solved by processes on which all members of the science or the profession will agree, regardless of their policy views. That is the same as to say that a policy issue is, by definition, one that turns in part on considerations of power and purpose. If the political estate is to be able to deal with those parts of the problem, it has to have the authority, in each particular case, to determine which aspect of the problem it wishes to delegate to other estates, and which it wishes to decide for itself.

The cases in which politicians try to encroach on the proper functions of the scientific or professional estate are relatively rare, and the sciences and professions are well-armed to defend themselves against that kind of attack. They are more vulnerable to a different kind of border incident, in which the politician or administrator, in order to avoid taking responsibility for a hard decision, pretends that it can be made on purely scientific or professional grounds, and pins the responsibility for it on a scientist or engineer or physician. In doing so, he is not intending to encroach on science; he is forcing science to encroach on politics, where it is bound to get involved in political fights.

Consider the case of AD-X2, a battery additive. The Bureau of Standards of the Department of Commerce was asked by the Post Office Department, which is required by law to exclude from the mails advertising that is demonstrably false, whether the manufacturer of AD-X2 was accurate in claiming that his product would increase the power and the durability of automobile batteries. The bureau found that the additive was worthless. The Post Office therefore refused to permit the use of the mails to advertise the additive. But the manufacturer was able to cite enough favorable testimony from users to persuade the new Secretary of Commerce that this action was an unwarranted interference with private enterprise. The Secretary therefore decided to discharge the director of the Bureau of Standards (Dr. Allen V. Astin, a distinguished physicist) on the grounds that on less than certain evidence he had interfered with free private enterprise. The Secretary also persuaded the Post Office to withdraw its ban.

But the case raised so much protest in scientific circles, including institutions like the National Academy of Sciences with great influence among the engineers and businessmen who carried weight with the Secretary of Commerce, that some way had to be found out of the difficulty. The Department of Commerce requested the National Academy of Sciences to make an independent study of both the bureau and its tests of AD-X2. That study was taken as a vindication of the Bureau of Standards, and Dr. Astin was reinstated, a hero in the scientific community.[21]

Cases like these are chronic in American politics. In the typical American city, public health doctors are always having difficulties in enforcing quarantine laws, and municipal engineers in enforcing building codes or safety standards against real estate pressures. These difficulties are ordinarily taken to prove that the scientific or professional estate is weak in trying to defend its own domain against political or administrative encroachment. But the way they occur proves almost the opposite point: that political and administrative authority in American government is so weak that when it deals with an issue in which scientific considerations are mixed with others, it tries to pretend that the others do not exist, so as to require the scientist to bear the public pressure. For the authorities imagine, quite rightly, that the public has more faith in the infallibility of science or the integrity of the medical or engineering profession than in the judgment of an administrator or a political executive.

Thus, in the battery additive case, it was generally assumed by almost everyone concerned that the Postmaster General would not himself decide whether a product was worthless, and that the Secretary of Commerce would not decide personally how conclusive the scientific evidence had to be before the government would interfere with private enterprise. The public and Congress reached past the political and administrative estates and in effect pinned public responsibility for a law-enforcement decision—not a mere scientific opinion—on a scientific agency. And the scientific agency accepted the responsibility for political controversy, as well as for rendering a carefully qualified scientific opinion to its administrative superiors.[22]

This tendency to push decisions that are political and administrative in nature over to the scientific or professional estate for solution is the counterpart to the tendency to encourage scientists and technicians to move up into positions of administrative and political responsibility. Considering these two tendencies together, and the way in which they reinforce each other, one is obliged to conclude that as a nation the United States is less likely to be at fault by encouraging politics to encroach on science, than by forcing scientists and professionals to make policy decisions that go beyond their range of expertise. It does so because it has more respect for specific knowledge than for general responsibility, and is too inclined to think that decisions and policies can be based entirely on knowledge.

THE PLURALIST CONSENSUS

The balance within the constitutional system between the estates that draw their power from scientific knowledge and those that depend on legal authority is necessarily a relative one. No fixed and mechanical system could survive in an era in which science forces such rapid changes in the structure of the economy. But within a tradition that protects the mutual independence of the legislature and the executive, the new strength of the scientific and professional estates can serve to safeguard the pluralism and freedom of the constitutional system. On the one hand, new scientific developments may weaken the autonomy of the older types of institutions (such as local governments and business corporations) that sought to protect themselves against central authority; but on the other hand, the same developments increase the independence and influence of the professions and of scientific institutions. The system gives some promise of being a self-balancing one.

Fundamentally, however, a political system is never automatically self-balancing; how it works depends on what people think and believe. Our twofold principle could easily be turned upside down in a different political tradition. The claim for freedom from political responsibility, on the grounds of a preference for truth, could be asserted by the political as well as the scientific estate: why should not the Congress be as interested in truth as any physicist or mathematician, and why should it not be free enough of the control of ignorant voters so as to apply systematic truth to its policy decisions in the real interests of those voters? On the other hand, if the purpose of truth and knowledge is to serve humanity, why should even an institute of mathematics wish to be free of a political control that is organized by the authority of the people, and in their interests?

These questions seem strange in the light of the English-speaking political tradition; their implications, if we should accept them, would lead us on toward the new totalitarianism, in which science and political power would join to destroy each other's freedom. We are protected by our consensus that science and politics in a free system, while freely interacting through the professions and administration, have to be maintained as mutually independent estates, each able to check and criticize the other. This consensus, for those whose temperaments lead them to insist on an experimental basis for their convictions, is justified by our observations that science works best when it operates in freedom, and that there are practical (if not ultimate theoretical) limits on its ability to comprehend and predict the course of human events.

But the consensus can comfortably include others whose political ideas are shaped more by traditional beliefs or a sense of history: to them, it seems important to remember that free representative institutions and responsible government grew up as a result of the rebellion against the union of the church, which presumed to have a monopoly on revealed truth, and the state, with its monopoly on power. To separate them from each other, it was necessary to permit the creation of many free churches, and to set up effective checks and balances within the state; this was done in the United Kingdom, even though it formally kept an Established Church and a legal unification of powers, as well as in the United States. The work began in England in the seventeenth century. The responsible center of political opinion rejected both the Divine Right of Kings and the Rule of the Saints. And after the Puritan and Whig Revolutions, England laid the foundations of both modern science and of responsible politics. And today free scientific institutions share the political conviction of the free churches: that to use political power to establish any form of truth, whether religious or scientific, does not make politicians into saints or scientists, but only converts men in the churches and laboratories into politicians, and politicians of an especially obnoxious variety.

The series of political revolutions that began in America in the eighteenth century (or perhaps in England in the seventeenth) and ended in Russia in the twentieth has changed the nature of government in the western world. Almost everywhere it has destroyed the actual rule of hereditary monarchs in favor of rule by political parties, and it has destroyed religious authority as the basis of political power while giving more importance to science. In Europe and the Americas, almost all nations seemed to many observers to be driven by the same blind forces in the same direction. And so today most nations like to call themselves democracies; some even like to add emphasis to the term by saying that they are people's democracies, or that they practice economic as well as political democracy.

But the revolutions, in spite of these similarities, were profoundly different in their purposes and effects. To distinguish the constitutional from the Communist system, it does not help to ask whether one is more popular and egalitarian, or more scientific, than the other. These questions were the conventional touchstones of liberalism from the Enlightenment to the twentieth century. Today, however, it is obvious that a system which is both egalitarian and scientific can be just as oppressive as the most superstitious czar.

On the other hand the constitutional systems that have managed to maintain and enlarge our freedoms while strengthening our science have been those with roots that go deeper in history than the Enlightenment, and far deeper than the doctrine of laissez faire. They are rooted in the lesson that freedom depends not merely on the independent exercise of political will, but also on the restraints of truth and law, and on the creation of a broader range of free choices by the discovery of new truth. They are rooted, too, in a disbelief that any abstract form of truth, whether acquired by revelation or research, can solve the muddled and disorderly problems of politics.

These are the systems, therefore, that have begun to work out for the institutions of science a status of independence in relation to politics much like the one long since accorded to the churches and the universities. The checks on centralized power afforded by the separation of the several branches of government are still essential, and those provided by the limited rights of private property are still desirable. But both can be effective only because the new institutions of science, in a world that they are rapidly making over, have allied themselves with the political tradition of the older institutions devoted to humane learning, religious faith, and the common law.

CHAPTER 7

Professionals and Politicians

AMERICANS are notoriously more interested in inventing gadgets than in studying the basic laws of nature. In matters of politics, American scientists run true to national form. They are likely to attack the fundamental problems that exist in the relation of science to politics by proposing new administrative gadgets—such as a Department of Science, or an operations research corporation attached to the presidency, or a staff of science advisers to Congress, or a new system of checks and balances among the scientists within the Executive Office of the President.

All such proposals run into difficulties because they deal with more than the relation between pure science and a disembodied public interest. They also deal with an inevitable conflict between those whose jobs require them to look at the public interest from the point of view of the government as a whole and those who see it from the specialized point of view of particular groups or institutions. And this conflict can never be neatly resolved, because (like subtle types of drama) it is not a conflict between good and evil, but between competing goods. To keep this kind of conflict within limits, it is necessary for the participants either to understand that it cannot be resolved by any scientific method, or else to have a sense of humor. Someone once remarked that the greatest asset in politics is to realize that the present situation, though it may be fatal, is not serious. And the next greatest asset is to understand that the outcome, though it may be fatal, is not fated; science does not require us to give up our political freedom of choice.

Among the difficult free choices that we have to make in politics is the choice of the organization and procedures by which science and the scientific professions are related to the authority of the Congress and the President. I intend to comment on specific proposals that are often discussed, such as the idea of a Department of Science. But first, in order to illustrate what is involved in the problem, I should like to tell the story of a conflict between general political responsibility and one particular scientific and professional interest. This conflict occurred in 1961 and 1962 in a program of science and technology that was one of the oldest in the federal government, and yet the newest.

THE OCEANOGRAPHY PROGRAM

Oceanography was the first large-scale federal scientific program. It began when Thomas Jefferson founded the Coast Survey in 1807 and employed a Swiss scientist, Ferdinand R. Hassler, to bring scientific instruments from Europe and begin the job of charting the seas for the guidance of navigators. Oceanography is a field of basic and applied science in which a great many federal departments and agencies have long been involved. But, for the purposes of my story, the contemporary oceanographic program began in 1956, when a group of government oceanographers decided that their activities needed to be greatly built up. Indeed, the part of the story that I propose to tell begins in March 1961 when President Kennedy included an expanded oceanographic program in his first budget, and it ends twenty months later when he pocket-vetoed the Oceanography Act of 1962.

An idea of the scope of the expanded program is given by the various reports and testimony presented to Congressional committees.[1] At least fourteen operating agencies were concerned, as well as the staff agencies in the Executive Office of the President.

The Navy, which had already revolutionized its strategic doctrine by developing the Polaris submarine and missile system, wanted more knowledge of currents and other ocean phenomena, both to increase its offensive capabilities and to defend against enemy submarines and *their* missiles.

The Geological Survey had its eye on the offshore oil on the continental shelf, and the Bureau of Mines on the promise of vast mineral resources in the ocean depths.

The Bureau of Commercial Fisheries was intrigued by the possibilities of increased protein supplies and even new kinds of food for an overpopulated planet. The Bureau of Sport Fisheries and Wildlife hoped to develop new recreational opportunities.

Medical researchers talked with excitement about the search in the oceans for new biological compounds that might give clues to the biochemistry of sanity and insanity—might even provide a clue for cancer.[2] The Public Health Service, though it soft-pedaled such speculation, was concerned about pollution of our seafoods and our beaches and harbors by sewage and chemical wastes, as was the Atomic Energy Commission about the disposal of nuclear wastes.

Several agencies were interested in oceanographic research because of their roles in aiding navigation. The Coast and Geodetic Survey has the job of mapping the shores and currents; the Weather Bureau makes forecasts; the Corps of Engineers maintains harbors; and the Coast Guard keeps the sea lanes clear of dangers to shipping.

Finally, there were the established research and development programs. The Maritime Administration carries on studies to adjust the design of ships to oceanic conditions; the Smithsonian Institution conducts basic research; the National Science Foundation and other agencies make grants to universities and other institutions for a wide variety of investigations relating to the oceans.

The advocates of a comprehensive federal program knew that they were dealing not merely with a field of science, but a major problem in government organization. As Harrison Brown, chairman of the Committee on Oceanography of the National Academy of Sciences, told a Senate committee in 1960, the decision to be made on the organization of the oceanography program "far transcends oceanography itself." He noted that the undertaking, because of the way in which it cut across the programs of many operating agencies, typified the "problem of decision making, concerning science and technology in Government."[3]

It would be hard to find a better illustration of how the breaking down of the boundaries among the basic sciences is connected with the breaking down of the boundaries among the interests of government agencies, and between the roles of public and private institutions. The testimony of the Academy's Committee on Oceanography emphasized the interrelationships of the several fields of science in studying the oceans; the same data on ocean currents and the same samples from the ocean floor would be useful to biologists, chemists, and geologists, just as they might be of value at the same time to the Navy, the Public Health Service, and the Bureau of Commercial Fisheries. As one Nobel prize winner, Albert Szent-Gyorgi, wrote to the Senate Committee on Commerce, those who seek to solve such practical problems as the cure of cancer by attacking them through the applied sciences are less likely to get results than those who seek to understand fundamental principles; and "the ocean, the cradle of life, offers innumerable possibilities for the approach of its most basic problems." He explained, "For many decades the trend was to subdivide nature and science into new fields. Now we begin to understand the great unity of nature, which is built on a limited number of basic principles."[4]

But it was easier to recognize the unity of nature than to develop unity in the oceanographic program. The difficulty was not that anyone objected in general to an expansion of such research. The problem was rather to devise a system by which its various parts could be related to each other and to the other activities of the government.

The original initiative for the expanded program, of course, had come much earlier than its formal recommendation by President Kennedy, first from scientists in government agencies, and then from the National Academy of Sciences. In 1956 an informal committee of marine scientists within the government, with no secretariat, funds, or staff facilities, worked up the idea. Five federal agencies then engaged the Academy, a private organization, to set up a committee at federal expense to prepare a program for political consideration.[5] The idea was not merely to put together scientific data and scientific ideas, but to muster the kind of support within the scientific and professional communities that can produce political action. Thus was born the Academy's Committee on Oceanography. It included the leading oceanographers of the country, and not only oceanographers; its chairman, Harrison Brown, was a geochemist, and one of its other members, Sumner Pike, was an experienced lawyer and a former member of the Atomic Energy Commission. This committee did its job with such dispatch and energy that by the time President Kennedy had presented the administration's new oceanography program in March 1961, the Academy's program had been under discussion by Congressional committees for almost two years.

Private institutions not only played an important role in bringing the program directly to the attention of Congressional committees but also were built into the program's administrative structure. More than a dozen private institutions, mostly universities, were soon to maintain oceanographic research ships wholly or partly at federal expense, and more than forty colleges and universities undertook to set up some research or teaching in relation to the program. The first emphasis of the expanded program, indeed, was to strengthen the work of the private institutions, which were given well over half the available funds; a special committee of consultants reported later that the 1960–1965 phase of the program had by comparison neglected the government's own laboratories.[6] The role of the private institutions gave them a status of some political as well as administrative influence in the program; within a few years the Navy had approved the request that they had been making repeatedly ever since the Second World War, to declassify and release oceanic soundings for publication. This decision came, no doubt, partly because of a change of heart within the Navy, but it was a change that coincided with organized representations from the Academy's Committee on Oceanography, supported by proddings from the House Committee on Merchant Marine and Fisheries, one of whose part-time staff members was also an adjunct professor teaching oceanography at a private university.[7]

The program found enthusiastic support in the two Congressional committees primarily concerned with oceanography—the Senate Committee on Commerce and the House Committee on Merchant Marine and Fisheries. As translated into financial terms within the Executive Office of the President, the program was to be smaller than such giants as atomic energy and space, for it called for the expenditure of something like two billion dollars in a decade. As Congressman Bob Casey of Texas later remarked a little resentfully, "You do not ask for as much money as we spend on one pad down at Canaveral. I think the benefits we will reap from this are unlimited."[8] Throughout the 87th Congress in 1961 and 1962, the two legislative committees were generally sympathetic with the scientists and professionals who were seeking an increase in the size and scope of the program. The committees were critical of the restraints put on the program by two of the principal groups in the Executive Office of the President, namely the Bureau of the Budget and the office of the President's science adviser. The steps that the two committees took, in disagreement with the Executive Office and its scientific adviser, illustrate some of the key problems of coordinating scientific policies.

THE PROFESSIONAL PEERAGE

Students of government should not take it for granted that the greater the number of political decisions that can be made on scientific grounds, the more effective the policies will be. Similarly, they must not assume that the most effective way to develop a responsible and coordinated program in the United States is to bring more executive actions under the control of the legislature. It is true that in the United Kingdom, the control of a disciplined House of Commons was the means by which a highly centralized administration could be created, and power taken away from the irresponsible Lords. But the American constitutional system does not work like the present parliamentary system. Instead it works more like the older English constitution, in the days when the great barons still maintained a high degree of independent political power in their own domains and conspired in the House of Lords with the bishops against the policies of the King's government.

General Charles G. Dawes, reflecting on the premiership of Ramsay MacDonald and the presidency of Franklin D. Roosevelt, used to wonder why it was that in the United Kingdom politicians were elected on radical platforms and then turned conservative, whereas in the United States they were elected on conservative platforms and turned radical.[9] One important reason for this phenomenon should have already been apparent in General Dawes' time: in the United States, we manage our constitution so as to give a great deal of influence and initiative to the scientific and professional estates. And the influence of the professional estate, which was once predominantly conservative, is now heavily in the direction of political change.

In the early days of the republic, radical democrats were inclined to lump the older learned professions together with the remnants of the historic estates and to distrust them all alike, as vested interests that would always resist progress. The clergy and the lawyers were viewed with some suspicion as natural allies of the established order. Today the scientific wing of the professional estate—which includes the applied scientists, the engineers, the physicians, and others—may be a vested interest, and its members may have conservative ideas, but the influence of their work is usually in the direction of high-velocity change. The common man is far less radical than the professions in what he demands of society; he is likely to prefer to be left alone in his traditional way of life, provided, of course, that technology can supply him with tranquilizers and television, the contemporary version of bread and circuses.

In the early nineteenth century, American radicals were not interested in strong action by the national government, and they accordingly moved toward the decentralization of executive authority and the strengthening of the influence of Congressional committees over executive bureaus. Since this way of thinking weakened the federal government as against the newly developing power of industrial corporations, it became acceptable to twentieth-century economic conservatives. But today, the features of our unwritten constitution that once enabled Congressional committees to team up with lawyers to stop political action are the very ones that enable Congressional committees to team up with engineers and applied scientists to *push* political action.

General Dawes would have had something to think about if he had watched his successor as budget director under President Eisenhower stand by helplessly while the appropriations for research and development continued to multiply in spite of presidential opposition. He would have had even more to think about if he could have heard eminent scientists speculate on the new fields of knowledge that would call for federal support on the scale of the atomic energy or space programs, or that would lead to increased public spending for health and welfare and housing and transportation.[10]

The big question is no longer whether we should give our government control over what private institutions do, but whether we can create a system of responsibility through which it can control what government agencies do. We are not in a dilemma that forces us to choose between freedom and responsibility, and we should be able to distinguish the kind of freedom that protects the integrity of knowledge and the independence of political criticism, from the kind that detaches a piece of government power to run it in irresponsible isolation. It is true that in the dawn of our constitutional history the great barons struck a blow for liberty at Runnymede when they asserted their own privileges against King John. But after that time the extension of popular freedom did not require that the barons be left alone in their feudal privileges; on the contrary, it often required the extension of central authority against their independent power.

If the professional estate in America exercises political influence, it is largely in concert with Congressional committees that share its specialized interests. And if Congressional committees seek such an alliance, it is because the professions have become more powerful as they have become more scientific. With respect to the issue of freedom, the interests of the scientific and the professional estates are very much the same; both demand a measure of institutional autonomy to prevent the objectivity of their work from being corrupted by the purposes of politics. But with respect to public policies which involve the application of scientific knowledge to national purposes, their interests diverge: basic science has no concern with purpose, but the professions (including applied science) are engaged in mixing purposes with their expert knowledge, and hence are more likely to get into the competitive scramble of the administrative and political estates. When they do, they are tempted to claim for themselves something like benefit of clergy—the institutional autonomy that politicians are glad to concede to the basic sciences.

And this claim, of course, suits the taste of committees of Congress, which are much more interested in focusing their attention on particular specialized programs, with the help of expert advisers, than in deliberating on the purposes of those programs and the ways in which they fit into a general policy. Members of Congress used to use their committee positions mainly to protect their local interests, for it was through the committees that they could assert influence over patronage appointments and contracts for public works. But today their functional interests are becoming as important as their geographic interests, and sometimes the two reinforce each other. An active influence in the weapons program, the atomic energy program, or the space program is no handicap to re-election in the eyes of the local constituency.

Thus politicians and professionals work together in natural harmony. The politicians, by bringing the professionals in as their expert advisers, concede to them a status in the legislative process—indeed, almost in the constitutional system—that is something like that of a non-hereditary peerage.

I must resist the temptation to take the constitutional metaphor of the "estates" too seriously, or to make it into a model. Yet it is interesting to recall that the first and the second medieval estates—the clergy and the nobility—did not constitute separate houses of Parliament in England as they did in certain countries on the Continent. Instead the Lords Spiritual and the Lords Temporal sat in the House of Lords together. And there they tried, in their centuries of constitutional struggle against central executive authority, three strategies that in a curious way have their modern counterparts.

First, they tried to keep their rule of their respective domains entirely independent of the authority of the national government; the great barons did not like to have the King's judges come into their territory to enforce the common law against their particular privileges, and the bishops enjoyed their immunities and their independent legal jurisdictions. When they lost that kind of independence, the peers turned to a second strategy: to demand that the King govern in accord with the advice that they would give him in the King's Council. When the King insisted on using different advisers, the peers turned to their third strategy: to demand that the advisers be publicly identified and required to justify their individual policies in Parliament.

Science and technology have accelerated the pace of American politics so greatly that we can see something roughly like these three strategies tried either in succession or all at once within a very few years. As any given field of policy becomes important as a result of technological change, members of Congress and their professional collaborators are tempted first to seek to take the field out of politics and set up machinery to deal with it outside the normal structure of responsibility; second, to insist that political authority act with the help of competent professional advisers; and third, to demand that the professional advisers be publicly identified and held accountable for what they do to further the professional interest, rather than to further the general policy of the government or of the party in power.

These three strategies were exemplified by three legislative proposals that the 87th Congress considered for the organization of the oceanography program. These strategies are followed more often in programs of technology than of basic research, and thus have been more important in the atomic energy and space programs than in oceanography. Nevertheless, in the oceanographic program nearly everyone agreed on its policy objectives, and we can therefore isolate the administrative issues with an unusual degree of clarity. The legislative committees were, as one of them reported, "in full accord as to objectives" with the Executive Office of the President, and they differed with it "solely on the question of whether the coordinating mechanism for a national oceanographic program should operate exclusively under Executive sanction or should have a legislative base with responsibility to Congress, as well as to the President."[11] Throughout this period of disagreement with the Executive Office, the Subcommittee on Oceanography of the House Committee on Merchant Marine and Fisheries reported that Congressmen and their staff members were meeting "on many occasions with the members of the National Academy of Sciences' Committee on Oceanography in a cooperative effort to find the most effective mechanism for fostering and maintaining a well balanced national program."[12] The three strategies that were adopted were not the product of any very systematic advance planning, or of any explicit constitutional theory. In their administrative details, they were the work of Congressional committees and their staffs, and not of scientists and professionals. And yet they represented the characteristic political response of both politicians and professionals to a standard problem in the American constitutional system. And the innocence and good faith that characterized both sides of the dispute illustrate the dilemma of responsible government in an era of scientific progress: to what extent should the constitutional system emphasize central discipline and responsibility, and to what extent should it encourage scientific initiative and technological progress?

INDEPENDENCE FROM POLITICS

The first of the three classic strategies is to try to set up machinery to deal with a field outside the normal structure of political responsibility.

Congressman George P. Miller, chairman of the Subcommittee on Oceanography, introduced H.R. 4276 in February 1961. The bill would have created a National Oceanographic Council, with six operating agency heads as its members. The council members would thus be men whom the President had appointed, but in other ways the council would be taken out of the regular system of presidential supervision over the operating agencies, and would indeed encroach on that system. For the council was to report each year directly to Congress, and to submit in that report a proposed program of appropriations for oceanography for the entire government. It was not only to operate certain research centers directly, but to coordinate the oceanographic activities of the operating agencies, delegate functions to them, and supply them with funds for those purposes.

This bill was opposed by the executive agencies as not in accord with the program of the President, which had assumed that oceanography could be coordinated by the Executive Office without any new statutory machinery. The Bureau of the Budget, which is responsible for making studies of organization and for coordinating the legislative program for the President, went on record against it; and so did the office of the President's science adviser.[13] The spare and polite language used in their reports gives very little clue as to the thinking of the President's staff. It is easy, however, to reconstruct what went on in their staff discussions, if we only recall the background.

Lawyers are usually given the credit for the professional strategy of creating agencies independent of presidential control. This is because the main Constitutional justification for such independence—especially for restraints on the presidential power of removal—is found in their arguments regarding the quasi-legislative and quasi-judicial functions of the independent regulatory commissions, beginning in 1887 with the Interstate Commerce Commission. Yet one of the main reasons for the creation of the regulatory commissions was that they dealt with fields that needed to be governed by experts, rather than by the legislative and judicial processes in which lawyers were skilled. The railroads were to be regulated by what reformers fondly hoped would be the more flexible procedures of the engineers and the economists. And the lawyers who were impressed by this line of argument, and who invented what has later come to be called the "headless fourth branch of government," were a generation or so behind the real innovators. For the first federal agency that was constituted in defiance of the formal Constitutional separation of powers was the first general-purpose scientific agency of the government, the Smithsonian Institution.

The scientists seem to have realized that the power of appointment and removal was not the main issue of constitutional strategy. If the agency could have its purpose defined in scientific or technological terms, and then put formally under the control of a large and clumsy part-time board (or better still, two of them) made up of very eminent and busy men, there was little doubt that the professionals could run it in independence of politics. Thus the Smithsonian's "Establishment" and its Board of Regents are made up of an impressive mixture of members of Congress, the Supreme Court, the President's cabinet, and distinguished private citizens. It is doubtful that these two boards have ever interfered to any troublesome extent in the actual conduct of the Institution's professional activities.

The essential point in the strategy of independence turns on the definition of purpose. If an agency can be set up with its mission defined not in terms of general political purpose, which would require it to be properly subordinate to presidential direction, but in terms of a professional or technological interest, then it may have a plausible claim on a status of independence.

This was the rationale behind the creation in 1915 of the National Advisory Committee for Aeronautics. That agency was not advisory at all, though it was headed by a committee of eminent part-time members. It conducted a program of applied research and development that was intended to serve the purposes of both military and civilian agencies of the government, and of private business as well. At the end of the Second World War, the atomic energy program was visualized in much the same terms by men who had taken part in the NACA; it was an important field of technology that deserved to be set aside in an independent agency, whose technological program would be related to the political purposes of several operating agencies. The leaders of the Office of Scientific Research and Development recommended that atomic energy be put under a commission made up of eminent private citizens, serving the government only part time under tenure arrangements that would minimize their accountability to the President, and make them as independent of politics as possible. The Congress finally decided, on the President's recommendation, to have the commission members serve full time; this would make clear their legal responsibility to the President. But the professionals had won their essential point: the Atomic Energy Commission had become the most important federal agency organized on the basis not of a political purpose but of a field of science and technology.[14]

The proposal for a National Oceanographic Council mustered comparatively little political support. One reason was that oceanography was not a field in which the average citizen had been impressed by any spectacular technology; his imagination had not been fired by anything like the mushroom cloud of the nuclear bomb, or the drama of plans for a landing on the moon.

Another reason was that the field called not for an entirely new program, but for the strengthening of activities that were firmly embedded in the programs of the regular operating agencies. But there was yet another reason for political coolness: the strategy of taking a field out of politics had come to seem less attractive. The strategy did not seem to suit the needs of an age of positive government action in which the scientific professions had become less worried about political interference and far more interested in mustering the political support that was necessary for large-scale financing.

The independent regulatory commissions, set up in order to apply technology to major fields of policy, had done less to further technological progress than the ordinary departments and agencies. Nobody could imagine a first-rate scientist working for the Interstate Commerce Commission. And though the fields of aviation and telecommunications had escaped the technological stagnation of the railroads, this was not because of the Civil Aeronautics Board or the Federal Communications Commission, but only because those fields were rescued by the research programs of the military and space and aviation agencies, none of which had been set up under an independent board.

The independence of the regulatory commissions had been great enough to keep the government from developing any coherent policy in their respective fields, but not enough to let them resist meddling by politicians who were interested in favors for their friends.[15] Political interference had not been much of a problem in those scientific programs that were not regulatory in nature. The Smithsonian Institution was pretty well insulated from partisan politics. So were the Coast and Geodetic Survey, the Geological Survey, and the Office of Naval Research, all of which were in regular executive departments. And no scientist who compared the Smithsonian and the Office of Naval Research with respect to recent influence in the scientific community would be attracted to the formula of independence.

Although complete independence was no longer the ideal, it

was still tempting to try to convert a professional field—a branch of technology that would normally be considered a means to a political purpose—into an end in itself. Thus the space program was a transformation of the National Advisory Committee for Aeronautics, which had been a service agency for the operating agencies. In the transformation, NACA's unwieldy governing board was abolished so as to make the administrator of the National Aeronautics and Space Administration (NASA) directly responsible to the President. Moreover the agency got a definition of purpose in terms of policy objectives, not merely in terms of technology or science. What brought the big appropriations was not the advancement of science; it was the purpose of beating the Russians to the moon, which enlisted the passions of the cold war, and at the same time the purpose of reserving the exploration of outer space to peaceful civilian means, which reassured those who feared a hot war.

The Air Force and most of the members of the President's Science Advisory Committee were unhappy about the amounts of the space program's appropriations, for quite different reasons. The Air Force was unhappy because it would have preferred that rocket development be kept a means toward Air Force ends. The basic scientists were unhappy because so large a proportion of the nation's scientific talent was being devoted not to the basic-science aspects of space exploration but to its spectacular political purpose. But the combination of purposes pleased the alliance of the applied space scientists and the Congressional committees that assumed the function of overseeing NASA and took political credit for it. And the combination had its effects on the organization of the executive branch, for the Congressional committees that watched over NASA undertook to protect its jurisdiction as their own. For example, the House Committee on Science and Astronautics intervened to make sure that NASA, rather than the Weather Bureau, would put a weather satellite into orbit,[16] and vigilantly protected NASA against the jealousy of the Air Force.

223

The atomic energy program, however, was an even better illustration of the way in which a field of technology was transformed into a political purpose or an end in itself, so as to be deeply enough in politics to get money, but not enough to be subordinated to the policy judgments of the traditional operating agencies. Like NASA it illustrates the alliance between specialized professional interests and a Congressional committee preoccupied with a field of technology, against the basic scientists and the general administrators.

The atomic energy program was set up under two supervisors: the Joint Committee on Atomic Energy in the Congress, and the Atomic Energy Commission in the executive branch. Of the two, the joint committee was inevitably the more powerful, for the simple reason that it had the legal responsibility to oversee the commission and the practical ability to take all sorts of disciplinary action against its program. Of course the Atomic Energy Commission had no corresponding influence over the joint committee. The result was an illustration of how best to violate the eighteenth-century constitutional maxim of James Wilson: "The legislature, in order to be restrained, must be *divided*. The executive power, in order to be restrained, should be *one*."[17] Not that the joint committee and the commission did a poor job within the field of nuclear science and technology; as far as any layman could tell in that field, their joint performance was superb. Rather the way in which they were organized made it far more difficult to ask the important questions of purpose and priority that are at the heart of political responsibility.

In Congress, the joint committee became the advocate of the use of atomic energy over and above the levels which departments of the government, trying to make decisions as to the best and cheapest way to accomplish their purposes, would have chosen. The nuclear-powered submarine, airplane, and aircraft carrier were all pushed by the joint committee more enthusiastically than the Department of Defense would have chosen, or the President's Science Advisory Committee would have recommended.[18] The development of civilian power reactors was surely pushed past the point that would have seemed economical to a department interested in the general purpose of providing power instead of in a particular technology. Similarly, if the "atoms for peace" program had been left entirely to the State Department or the foreign aid agency, there would be many fewer reactors in the underdeveloped countries today.

The case for a special agency to push the development of any new field of technology is a defensible one, especially since any new field is always neglected by established organizations and often actually resisted by them. James T. Ramey, formerly staff director of the Joint Committee on Atomic Energy and now a member of the Atomic Energy Commission, argues that technological progress would be greatly impeded if the government always counted the cost in advance by undertaking only those developments for which some department foresaw a requirement and an economical use.[19]

This is an argument which the joint committee and the commission together are obliged, by the nature of their assignment, to maintain against other parts of the Congress and executive branch. The joint committee, to maintain its positive influence, has insisted on reviewing each year, and specifically authorizing, the entire budget of the Atomic Energy Commission, a move which transfers to it, and from the Appropriations Committee, a large measure of the actual control over atomic energy expenditures. Similarly, the commission is obliged to support not merely basic research, but also engineering development, without regard to the "requirements" of other agencies. Thus the special arrangements for the control of atomic energy which a frightened Congress enacted in 1946 have turned into a system not for its restraint, but for its promotion.

In no field, ironically enough, has this been more true than in military affairs. The great purpose of the Atomic Energy Act was to take the atom away from the soldiers and devote it to peaceful purposes. But the result of detaching the program from the departments concerned with general purposes, and putting it in an agency concerned only with one type of technology, has been just the opposite. For more than a decade every military staff planner, as he computed the alternative advantages and costs of using different types of weapons to accomplish any particular objective, was given a powerful incentive to choose nuclear weapons because they were free. That is to say, the warheads were provided not out of the budget of the military service, as were conventional weapons, but by the Atomic Energy Commission.[20]

It was no wonder that in 1962 the five members of the commission concluded that things would be run better if the commission as such were abolished and the program organized under a single administrator, apparently believing that it would thus be less subject to the control of the joint committee and more responsive to the direction of the President. And it was no wonder that the man who had been the first chairman of the commission, David E. Lilienthal, concluded in 1963 that the time had come to convert the program from its unique status and bring it back into the main stream of government affairs, so that the government would treat all aspects of science equally.[21] Many scientists and administrators alike began to ask whether it would not be desirable for the field of atomic energy to be organized on a different basis, so that it would be easier for decisions in this field of technology, as well as in others, to be made not according to the judgments of the enthusiastic specialists, but according to the advice of scientists with more general interests and the priorities of those administrators and politicians who calculate how much a particular technological development will contribute to the ends of public policy.

Some considerations such as these must have been in the minds of the scientists and administrators in the Executive Office of the President when they recommended against the original version of H.R. 4276, the oceanography bill of Representative Miller. After hearing their objections, the Committee on

Merchant Marine and Fisheries proved, by the revisions that it then made in its bill, that it knew exactly what it intended to accomplish, and that it was not persuaded by the Executive Office arguments. It chose to accept, instead of the Executive Office proposals, proposals for revision that it attributed to the Committee on Oceanography of the National Academy of Sciences. These would have strengthened the proposed National Oceanographic Council as a separate entity, to make it more clear that oceanography was an end in itself and not to be judged merely in the light of departmental priorities. Thus the revised draft would have (1) reinforced the powers of the council to make decisions; (2) given it a staff of its own and an "executive director to whom the Congress could look for regular periodic reports"; and (3) provided more clearly for the appropiation to the council of funds that could be used to support work in any of the operating agencies.[22] Incidentally, it would have given the House committee a jurisdictional claim over all the pieces of the oceanography program, which would otherwise remain subject to the "oversight" of various committees.

But the House Subcommittee on Oceanography had to give up its preference for the strategy of independence. It was not possible to take the pieces of the program away from the operating agencies so as to make oceanography truly an independent program. The Executive Office continued to oppose the House subcommittee's proposal, and the Senate did not agree to it.

PROFESSIONAL ADVICE

The Senate had committed itself much earlier to the second type of strategy, which is to see that a specialized field be organized so that the political executive will be more or less obliged to act according to expert advice.

As the House committee saw it, the essence of the Senate strategy was that it "would have assigned the coordination function to the National Science Foundation."[23] This statement sums up the intention, but fails to do justice to the subtlety of the strategy. The proposal, as stated in S. 901, the bill submitted in 1961 by the Senate Committee on Commerce, would indeed have put the central responsibility for the program in the National Science Foundation, but on an advisory basis. In accord with the recommendations of the National Academy of Sciences and the budget message of the President, most of the program—that is, the operations—would be left in the regular executive departments. But the National Science Foundation would be directed by law to develop a national policy and program for oceanographic research; to encourage the cooperation of federal agencies in dealing with problems relating to the seas and the Great Lakes; and to evaluate the scientific aspects of the oceanographic work of the entire government and of private institutions receiving government funds.

The Foundation would do all this through a new Division of Marine Sciences to be created by S. 901. That division was to be headed not simply by an officer of the Foundation, but by a committee, to be made up partly of representatives of federal agencies, partly of scientists from nonfederal institutions. In an earlier draft of the bill the federal agencies were to be represented by anyone they might wish to designate, and the outside scientists were to be chosen by the Foundation "from the universities and institutions receiving assistance" from the same federal agencies. But, by the summer of 1961, the bill clearly wanted to make the Division of Marine Sciences more independent: it required that the federal representatives had to be scientists, and that the members from outside the government were, in unspecified number, to be "designated by the National Academy of Sciences and National Research Council to serve on this committee."[24]

The Senate committee reported that the changes from the earlier to the later version of its bill included "supplementary provisions recommended by the Committee on Oceanography" of the Academy, and the Academy's committee later formally recommended the bill, pronouncing it an improvement over the earlier version. Yet with respect to the proposal to put the co-ordination function in a partially independent division of the National Science Foundation, the position of the Academy was less clear. Roger Revelle, testifying for the Academy's committee, had identified the problem of coordination as a most difficult one, and had opposed the specific proposal to make the Foundation responsible for coordination, but he had not come up with a specific alternative. And he and other witnesses had put great stress on the need to give representatives of oceanography within the government "a way of bypassing the Bureau of the Budget, at least in part," and reporting to Congress as well as to the executive branch.[25]

It may be too much to call the Senate bill subtle, but it was subtle at least to the extent that it is less crude to bring a king under the control of advisers than it is to depose him. The House bill would have crudely given an independent agency, reporting directly to Congressional committees, authority to issue coordinating instructions to the operating agencies and to prepare a budget in the field of oceanography without respect to the President's instructions and the President's budget. The Senate bill would have only given the National Science Foundation more money and the authority to advise, and would have specified how the advisers were to be chosen.

American politicians are just beginning to appreciate the potential uses of "advice" in constitutional maneuvering, and political scientists are generally unaware of its significance. But to the staff of the Executive Office, even to the comparatively new scientific staff, this strategy had already become a well-recognized ploy against which they put up their guard automatically.

The strategy of advice was first used, in a rather unimaginative way, in the direct relationship of the Senate and the President, as prescribed by the Constitution. The "advise and consent" provisions of course let individual Senators initiate as well as control most presidential appointments in their respective states. But now this strategy is employed in a much more complex way:

it depends on a combination of (1) the influence Congressional committees acquire by prescribing in statutes the sources from which executive agencies must receive advice, (2) the influence Congressional committees acquire by the advice they give operating agencies, and (3) the influence they acquire by advising other Congressional committees and the Congress as a whole. All of this was involved, as we shall see, in S. 901 of 1961.

"Advice," in the world of politics, can mean anything from literal advice to complete control. If a legislator or executive gets advice privately from a consultant of his own choosing, and if he also has available competing advice from others of equal competence, the advice is indeed merely advisory, and his responsibility for action is unimpaired. But that kind of advice is never what Congressmen argue about. Step by step, that kind of advice can be converted into something like the advice to a constitutional monarch from his prime minister, which means full control.

The successive steps by which advice to an executive becomes power over him run something like these: (1) the adviser is given formal legal status as an adviser; (2) his advice is given publicly and formally, so that if the executive turns it down he is likely to lose some political or legislative support; (3) the adviser is also in charge of administering the function on which he advises; (4) the advice is in the form of an operational plan or general program that the executive needs, and cannot get anyone else to prepare for him; (5) the executive does not have a free choice in naming his adviser, or dismissing him, but is more or less obliged to take the recommendations of someone whose influence may rest either on political or professional authority; of the two, professional authority may be harder for a political executive to challenge.

The best example in American government is the status of the Joint Chiefs of Staff. Their function may be mainly political and administrative in nature (in terms of my metaphor of the four estates) but they base their prestige on the expertise of the military profession. And they base their power on their statutory right to give advice collectively to the Congress and the President as well as the Secretary of Defense, and individually to the Secretaries of their respective military departments. They have acquired the influence that comes with the first four steps noted above, although their monopoly has recently been diluted by the Defense Secretary's use of civilian staff as well. And even the fifth step (namely, the executive does not have a free choice in hiring and firing his adviser) is not completely beyond the Chiefs; no one would doubt that the President must sometimes consider the opinion of Congressional committees as he chooses (or thinks of dismissing) a Chief of Staff.

As the example of the Joint Chiefs suggests, the strategy of transforming advice into power is used in the United States not to extend the control of a disciplined political party over the government as a whole, but to extend the combined influence of a Congressional committee and a professional group over a particular aspect of policy.

The Congress as a whole does not use its power to usurp the power of the President, as it legally could, and as Woodrow Wilson, for example, imagined in the late nineteenth century that it might do. If only the legal barriers of the Constitution stood in the way, Congress could have used its authority to appropriate funds and to enact laws in any desired degree of detail, controlling organization and procedure as well as the substance of policy, and could have made the President into a mere figurehead. But it does not do so because it does not believe it should, and that belief is not merely a matter of the personal consciences of Congressmen, but of the sense of legitimacy that they share with the American people. The House of Commons was obliged to usurp the constitutional power of the King and the House of Lords because people quit believing in hereditary authority and began to believe that political power should be responsible directly to the people. The American House was unable to make its Speaker (as Wilson predicted) into a prime minister, because the President and the Senate had, contrary to the original intention of the Constitution, come to be chosen by the electorate, so that their claim to anointment by election was just as legitimate as that of the House. Far from setting up its own disciplined leadership to take executive authority away from the President, Congress chooses to lean on him as its principal leader of legislative policy. It is only the rather scholarly legislators like Senator J. William Fulbright and the late Senator Estes Kefauver who can imagine that the election of a Congress that is out of sympathy with the President destroys his mandate for leadership, or that Congress wishes to find ways to hold the administration as a whole accountable to it.[26] The hard-bitten pros in the pure American tradition know better; President Truman took the opposition of a "do-nothing" Congress as his great political opportunity, and Senate Majority Leader Lyndon B. Johnson proclaimed that during the administration of President Eisenhower it was not the duty of the Opposition to oppose.

But although the Congress does not wish to run the government as a whole, individual Congressional committees are less inhibited about their particular fields of interest. Members of Congress are able and ambitious men, with not only a liking for power, but a desire to do things for their country. They have no taste for the role of being only one cog in a voting machine by which general policy is enacted on the recommendation of their party leader. They want to have a hand individually in making policy. And the discovery of the glamorous new potential policies that science had made possible opened up all sorts of new fields to them.

The more conscientious Congressmen did their chores for constituents, and took care of the home states' interests, but they smarted under the knowledge that these errands were beneath their dignity and intellectual capacity, and brought politicians generally into disrepute. It would be a relief to a Fogarty or a Lister Hill to find that he could do more than any Secretary of Health, Education, and Welfare to advance medical research, or to a Hickenlooper or Pastore to find that he had more influence over atomic energy than the Atomic Energy Commission, or to a Mahon or Symington to be more expert than the military secretaries with respect to the weapons program, or to a Lennon or a Magnuson to think that in oceanography his committee had found a new road to technological glory.

Constitutionally, Congressional committees have no power. Congress can neither delegate its legislative power nor grant executive authority to its members or committees. But the potentialities of advice are considerable. And in the last few years, while talking a great deal about the ways in which the complications of technology have helped the Executive encroach on the Congress, Congressional committees have been finding ways to collaborate with the professionals to acquire a measure of actual control over pieces of the executive branch. The strategy of advice comprises three tactics.

Undisciplined advice

The first is hardly ever thought of as a deliberate tactic, but follows from a sense of the general fitness of things. Looking at a particular field of policy, a Congressional committee sees the scientific professionals within the executive branch as right-thinking men, dedicated to high technical standards and the accomplishment of their particular mission. It sees their political and administrative superiors, who try to subordinate the professional specialty to considerations of general national policy, as political meddlers. Most Congressional committees are surprisingly nonpartisan in their operations, and those members who by the seniority rule come to dominate them find it comfortable to work, year after year, with the professionals in the operating agencies who continue to dominate substantive programs no matter which party is in power. Accordingly, they think of the professional and technological aspects of policy as the real policy; what a budget officer does, or the Secretary of a department, is not the responsible policy, but political meddling with it.

So a Congressional committee, in looking for advice on a program, thinks in terms of a caste system. The highest caste consists of professionals (and scientists) in private institutions; they can give advice without being influenced by politics. Next come the professionals in the operating agencies; they may be subordinate to political superiors, but there are various ways of protecting them against those superiors and getting their real (as contrasted with their disciplined) opinions. Lower still come the general administrators, whose efforts at coordination are seen as something of a handicap on any particular program. This caste system then becomes the basis for the curious scale of compensation by which people are paid out of government funds. The highest salaries go to the managers and the professionals of the corporations that take part in the government programs under contract (the very highest, of course, to those in the profit-making corporations, and the next highest to the nonprofits). Within the operating agencies, under the top political officers, come the professionals; and somewhat lower come the administrators.[27]

All this seems so natural in the United States (no matter how odd it might seem to various other countries) that ordinarily very little formal action is needed to make effective the tactic of direct access to professional advice. The main thing is to make sure that the Congressional committees have full and free access to the policy views, as well as the technical views, of the professionals, and that they are not constrained by administrative or political discipline. In departments where the power stakes are very high, as in the Department of Defense, such access is guaranteed by specific legislation and reaffirmed regularly in committee hearings; the Joint Chiefs are authorized by statute to give their independent views on military policy to the appropriate Congressional committees, regardless of the opinions of the Secretary of Defense and the President. In most departments, the line of communication between the professionals and the Congressional committees is so well recognized that it is never challenged, and does not need to be defended. Congressional committees also find it useful to require the operating agencies to consult with professional advisers from private institutions; these arrangements counterbalance the political supervision of the department heads, and give the Congressional committees a further guarantee of full access to professional advice.

Leverage against operating agencies

The second tactic within the strategy of advice is to make sure that the operating agencies accept the instructions of the Congressional committee. Executive agencies are not expected merely to comply with the law, but with the will of Congress, which is interpreted not by the courts but by the Congressional committees. In the annual process of asking for money and legislation, each bureau or agency is asked in detail how it proposes to use them; if it wishes the power and the funds to do its job, it has to satisfy its committees, and then (unless it has a very good excuse) it has to stand by its bargain as recorded in the legislative history. This process used to be only periodic and general, but now techniques have been invented to bring operating agencies back for the committee's approval of particular actions. At first laws were enacted that required operating agencies to "come into agreement" with Congressional committees before taking specific actions; this was given up as unconstitutional. It was found less offensive and just as effective to require that certain executive actions be taken only subject to subsequent veto by the Congress as a whole, or by certain committees of Congress; or to require that specific actions be reported to Congressional committees a certain period ahead of their effective dates.[28]

An even more ingenious variation, and one that illustrates the way in which the old geographic patronage of the committees is being converted into the new patronage of research and development, is one that gives to a legislative committee complete control over particular projects of the executive agencies. The historic ties of the Army engineers to the legislative subcommittees on Rivers and Harbors, and to the appropriations sub-committees on Public Works, have been so intimate that no Secretary of War or Defense, and no President, has been able to interfere; when President Roosevelt tried to have his National Resources Planning Board take a hand in that area, he only got the board abolished for its pains. The legislative committees dealing with the Bureau of Reclamation in the Interior Department have had a similar relationship for half a century, but in addition they have recently found a way to assert specific control over local projects in a quite Constitutional way: the Small Reclamation Project Act of 1956 (as amended in 1957) provided that Congress would appropriate no money for any particular project until sixty days after Interior had submitted the project to Congress, and then only if neither of the two Interior and Insular Affairs Committees (House and Senate) had disapproved the project. Thus the Congress, under the guise of an internal pro-cedural rule, actually delegates control of an executive action to particular legislative committees. And now the technique, having been tried out on the traditional pork barrel, is being applied to research grants: the Water Resources Research Act of 1964 enacted this same procedure with respect to Interior's research grants to universities.

Leverage against appropriations committees

That technique, of course, gives the legislative committee extra leverage not only against the executive agencies, but against the Congressional appropriations committees, and accordingly it is also a part of the third tactic, which has to do with the influ-ence of advisory procedures within the Congress. In order to give an executive agency money, Congress has to take two quite different actions. It must pass legislation authorizing the appro-priation of funds, and then by a separate act it must appropriate the funds. Each House does the first on recommendation of one of its specialized legislative committees; the second, on recom-mendation of the appropriations committee. Until after the

Second World War, most authorization acts were on a continuing basis, and generally in indefinite amounts, as they still are for many agencies. The Department of Agriculture, for example, has permanent authority to conduct research in a wide variety of fields; its statutory authorization is good until repealed, and the amount to be spent each year is controlled by the appropriations committees.

But in recent years it has come to be the practice in certain fields for a legislative committee to authorize appropriations for a particular program for a fixed period of time, such as one year, and in a specific amount. It had long been the tradition for the civil works of the Army Engineers to be handled in that manner, but that was considered an embarrassing exception, and not the rule. Now the newer technical and scientific programs are following suit, namely the military procurement of aircraft, missiles, and ships, and research related thereto; the atomic energy program; the space program; and the program of Arms Control and Disarmament. With the possible exception of the last of these, the motive is not to insist on economy (any more than it is in the case of the civil works program of the Army Engineers), but to give the legislative committee greater leverage against the appropriations committee in expanding the program. The legislative committee, of course, cannot require higher appropriations; its influence is only advisory. But if the legislative committee, which includes those members with the greatest depth of special knowledge of a particular program, can persuade the Congress to pass a law authorizing expenditures at a higher level, it is much harder for the appropriations committee to hold them down.

These three tactics are usually thought of as part of a strategy by which a legislative committee may increase its control over the executive. But the issue is not really one between the Congress and the executive branch. In the first place, these extensions of committee control are, more often than not, initially suggested by executive agencies, which think that they can get more protection and support by acknowledging their fealty to Congress. Second, the legislative committee is engaged in strengthening its power of initiative, and its independence, against the appropriations committee and the Congress as a whole even more than it is against the Executive. The only important machinery by which Congress tries to discipline its own specialized interests is that of the appropriations committees, which were set up by the great financial reform of 1921, the Budget and Accounting Act, which also created the Bureau of the Budget as the President's agency. If Congress had really wished to do so, it could have used the unified appropriations power (in collaboration with the Budget Bureau) to get the same kind of disciplined control over expenditures that is exerted by the British Treasury. But the specialized legislative committees, in collaboration with the independent professionals in the executive branch, have had an effective alliance that has made that kind of discipline impossible.

When a legislative committee is concerned not merely with the program of a particular operating agency that is organized on the basis of purpose, but with some field of applied science or technology that is a means toward the purposes of several agencies, the problem takes on a new dimension, or a new degree of complexity. In that case, the legislative committee comes into jurisdictional conflict not only with the appropriations committee, but with the other legislative committees whose operating agencies are affected by the field. At this point, the committee has to find some point in the executive branch to build up as a basis for its own influence.

That is what the Senate Committee on Commerce was doing when it proposed to build up a part of the National Science Foundation as the center of coordination for the oceanography program. S. 901 would have given to a committee with a strongly specialized interest the duty of recommending a government-wide program. The preparation of that program would probably be dominated by specialists designated by the National Academy, and by their scientific colleagues who would not be particularly sensitive to administrative discipline; and that program would give the interested legislative committees of the Congress a foundation on which to put forward their recommendations for Congressional action.

This strategy of advice neatly combined all three component tactics. To understand why it failed to work, one has to recall the history of the National Science Foundation. When Congress was considering its creation at the end of the Second World War, it was assumed (in both of the alternative versions of the bill) that the Foundation was to have responsibilities not only for basic research but for certain applied research programs as well, and that it was, moreover, to coordinate the basic research programs of the operating agencies. In the bill favored by the leadership of the Office of Scientific Research and Development, the Foundation was to be headed by a board of eminent private citizens, serving on a part-time basis, and with authority to appoint their own executive director. When President Truman objected to this formula, and the bill was held up, the War and Navy Departments sought to continue their wartime collaboration with scientists and engineers from private institutions by setting up in the National Academy of Sciences a Research Board for National Security, which would have been in effect a continuation of the OSRD program. That proposal was rejected; the weapons research programs were picked up enthusiastically by the military services themselves; and when the Foundation was finally established its proposed function in applied research and development had been forgotten, but it was still assigned by law the responsibility to coordinate the basic research programs of the entire government.

In this role, the Foundation was a failure—or perhaps it would be fairer to say that it was too realistic ever to try to play the part. Its disappointed supporters were inclined to attribute this failure to political prudence, maybe even cowardice; this was unfair because, in crude terms, a new agency with a budget of a few million dollars does not realistically undertake to give orders to the great departments with budgets of billions, no matter what the law may say. Managerial theorists were inclined to say that the Foundation failed because it was not located in the Executive Office of the President; operating departments will accept directions from the President's staff agencies, but not from other agencies in the regular line of operations. This explanation is hardly adequate, since both the Department of State and the Department of Justice serve as staff agents of the President in giving instructions to other departments. Two other explanations seem more cogent.

First, although the director of the Foundation was appointed by the President, the highest formal authority in the Foundation was still the National Science Board, made up of men on part-time duty, nominated to the President by a variety of scientific associations and institutions. The success of the director turned on a delicate balance between his loyalties to this board, representing the scientific community, and to the President. In such a relationship, neither he nor the chairman of the board was in a position to be an effective full-time staff agent of the President, or to work out the relationship of continual compromise with other staff agencies, representing other types of interests and concerns, in the President's Executive Office.

Second, the Foundation had been organized not on the basis of purpose, like the operating agencies, and not even on the basis of the applied fields of science or development engineering, but on the basis of the scientific disciplines, in order to be prepared to deal with its clientele, the universities, and to handle its main type of business, applications for the support of basic research projects. This did not give the director of the Foundation the kind of staff (in terms of either organization or personnel) that would enable him to consider effectively the relation between an operating agency's basic research program and the applied research and development program that provides the payoff in terms of its end purposes.

It is this background that explains the fate of S. 901, the 1961 bill to coordinate the oceanographic program through the

National Science Foundation. For when the Foundation itself gave the Senate Commerce Committee its advice on the bill, it made a statement of firm opposition, and in terms that seemed to go beyond the call of duty as that duty may have been defined by the Bureau of the Budget. For the director of the Foundation reaffirmed its commitment to a form of organization founded on the basic scientific disciplines. He noted that oceanography was not a basic discipline, but a field of research to which all the disciplines contributed. And he argued that to set up a division based on this field would inevitably lead to a demand for other divisions for similar fields, which would overlap intolerably with each other and with the basic disciplines. Most important, perhaps, the resulting confusion would have made much more difficult the Foundation's channels of communications, and its organized advisory relations, with the university world.[29] Most of the universities cooperating in the oceanographic program did not have teaching departments or degrees in oceanography at all, but divided their oceanographic research and teaching among such disciplines as geology, biology, and chemistry.[30]

So now two strategies for the federal oceanography program had been tried. One of them would have turned a field of applied science into an operating program with a separate budget of its own, and therefore would have treated a part of the professional estate as if it were in the political estate. This strategy failed because it came into conflict with a principle of organization that was prevalent in the Congressional committees as well as the operating agencies—the principle of organization by purpose. The second strategy sought to have the professional field governed by the advice of the scientific estate; that proposal failed because it came into conflict with the scientific estate's preference for organization by discipline. Oceanography, as a field that included both basic and applied science, could not be governed either as a political purpose in its own right or as a field of pure knowledge.

The two Congressional committees accordingly got together on the third strategy.

PUBLIC ACCOUNTABILITY OF
PRESIDENTIAL ADVISERS

They were able to unite on the third strategy because a new possibility was opened up to them in the spring of 1962: the President made the office of his scientific adviser accessible to Congress. In Reorganization Plan No. 2 of that year he created the Office of Science and Technology (OST) as a part of the Executive Office of the President, with the purpose of enabling it to give advice to Congress as well as the President.

If oceanography had become too firmly embedded in the structure of politics either to be detached and given a status of independence, or governed by advice from the professional and scientific estates, perhaps it was necessary to admit that it could be directed only from the center of political power, the presidency itself. In that case, the obvious strategy to be tried, on the reasonable assumption that the President would not personally be either expert or deeply concerned with this field, was to see whether his advisers in this particular field might not be formally designated so as to be held accountable, to some degree, by the Congressional committees and the parts of the scientific and professional community concerned.

Accordingly, the House and Senate committees abandoned their two earlier strategies and agreed in 1962 on a new version of S. 901.[31] This bill provided that the Office of Science and Technology should "establish, advance, and develop a national program of oceanography. In order to insure that the greatest possible progress shall be made in carrying out this national program, the Office shall issue a statement of national goals with respect to oceanography, which shall set forth methods for achieving those goals and the responsibility of the departments, agencies, and instrumentalities of the United States to carry out the national program on an integrated, coordinated basis." To translate that program into operations, the OST was to be required to make an annual report to Congress as well as the President, not only giving a general account of the state of the program, but also presenting a "detailed analysis of the amounts proposed for appropriation by Congress for the ensuing fiscal year for each of the departments, agencies, and instrumentalities of the Government to carry out the purposes of this Act."

The bill authorized the appointment, within the OST, of an Assistant Director for Oceanography, to be appointed by the President with the advice and consent of the Senate. It also required the establishment of an Advisory Committee for Oceanography, which would consist of "scientists selected on the basis of competence from universities and other non-Federal institutions and agencies, and from industry."

President Kennedy had set up the OST by transferring out of the White House Office (which is the inner and most intimate circle of Presidential advisers in the Executive Office) the staff organization that served the President's Special Assistant for Science and Technology. So the Special Assistant, in his new additional capacity as director of the OST, was no longer bound by the tradition that prevented members of the White House Office from testifying before Congressional committees; his new status was analogous to that of other members of the broader Executive Office, like the director of the Budget Bureau and the chairman of the Council of Economic Advisers. He was still to serve, in addition, as chairman of the President's Science Advisory Committee, made up of eminent scientists from outside the government, which remained in the White House Office, and also as chairman of the Federal Council of Science and Technology, with a membership comprising a high scientific or professional officer of each of the major operating agencies.

The strategic significance of the new S. 901 was that it would attempt to control the organization of the Executive Office of the President, and its inner procedures, to an unprecedented degree. Previously, the inner organization of the President's staff agencies had been left substantially to his discretion. The assumption that they were responsible primarily to him, and took no important policy action on their own authority, had distinguished them from the operating agencies. The assumption had been established when the Budget and Accounting Act of 1921 had let the President appoint the director of the Bureau of the Budget without Senate confirmation, to emphasize the unique line of responsibility of that official. But now, just as the legislative committees had been looking for ways to break down the exclusive influence of the appropriations committees over the government's financial program in the Congress, they were beginning to look for ways to do the same thing within the Executive Office. The proposed "detailed analysis" of expenditures for oceanography would in effect be a special budget, which the Congress would be free to adopt even if it were higher than the President's regular budget for that field. And if, as might be expected, the President were to use his political authority to require the Office of Science and Technology to set a limitation on the amount of money asked for in its "detailed analysis," the members of the OST's Advisory Committee for Oceanography from private life would be likely to communicate that fact to the Congressional committees. And Congress is free to exercise its Constitutional privilege to increase, as well as to decrease, the budget recommended by the President.

This procedural point, of course, is the heart of the contrast that General Dawes drew between the inherent conservatism of the British constitution and the inherent radicalism of the American. If American conservatives ever seriously meant to stop what they call irresponsible federal spending, they might well organize a movement to require that the Congress, like the Parliament, should not appropriate funds except on the request of the executive, or at least to give the President the authority enjoyed by the governors of many states to exercise an item veto over enacted appropriations.

The function which S. 901 prescribed was no less than the direction and coordination of the executive departments, and the organization of the President's staff for that purpose. A conference committee of the House and Senate, after putting the bill into its final form, reported that it "gave serious and extended consideration" to one question of special significance.[32] This question was whether the direction-and-coordination function should be assigned by law to the Office of Science and Technology or to the President himself. The decision was unanimous: legal responsibility should be placed in the OST. The medieval barons had considered the person of the king inviolate but had had no scruples about impaling his advisers. The committees of Congress had been finding more effective ways to maintain "oversight" over the operating agencies; it seemed only right and proper to extend this principle to the staff agencies in the Executive Office. Both houses of Congress accepted the conference report and approved S. 901.

This put before President Kennedy the issue whether the coordinating mechanism for the oceanographic program should remain a part of the President's staff, completely subject to his discretionary control, or should be defined by law and responsible to Congress as well as to the President.

Jurisdictional questions arise, of course, whenever programs cut across the jurisdictions of operating agencies; but they are especially difficult in fields of rapidly developing technology, because executive agencies and Congressional committees alike see in them the key to future policies and programs. Each specialized interest is alert to this possibility. Industries seek research and development contracts as the best way to make sure to get future production contracts in any given field. Military services build up their research and development programs on particular weapons systems in order to expand their potential claims on strategic roles and missions. Executive departments and agencies know that by starting in on programs of applied science and technology they may in effect stake out claims on future operating programs, and commit the government to new lines of policy that as a practical matter the President and Congress will be obliged to support.

In a classic (and perhaps apocryphal) case in the nineteenth century, Congress gave a federal agency only half as much money as it requested, and it proceeded to build a bridge halfway across a river. Congress still had the legal power to refuse to appropriate any more money for the purpose, but its political choice was gone. Since then, it has learned that, in order to have any actual control, whether in the direction of stimulating or constraining an agency, it must apply the control at the early planning stage, rather than after projects are under way. And now, with so many important programs depending on the application of science and technology, and so many fields of technology being of interest to several departments at once, it is becoming clear that the problem cannot be dealt with by individual operating agencies, or by the individual legislative committees of the Congress that review their particular programs. Some central authority has to guide the planning of interagency programs. The more complex and basic and unpredictable the nature of the science or technology, the more it calls for a system of coordination that can let decisions be made from a broader point of view than any single agency.

Oceanography, for example, was to each of more than a dozen agencies an important means toward its particular purpose. But each agency, if left to itself, would have planned its research and development work in the way that would contribute to its own purposes, regardless of the interests of others. To make the program into an effective whole, the Office of Science and Technology had to work with the agencies concerned. If possible it had to persuade each of them to include the appropriate share of the total program in its budget, even though this meant that each had to undertake some work not directly relevant to its own purposes as it saw them, and consequently that, in order to stay within its budget, it would have to cut out something that it would prefer to do.

This was hard enough within the executive branch, but even harder when the program reached Congress. For it got there as a part of a dozen or more separate agency budgets, and they were promptly distributed in each house among seven appropriations subcommittees which looked at them from points of view that were just as parochial as those of the executive agencies. In many cases, the several parts of the program required legislative authorization before coming up for appropriations, and the program as a whole was under the jurisdiction of six legislative committees (and nine of their subcommittees) in the Senate, and eight legislative committees (and thirteen of their subcommittees) in the House, and the Joint Committee on Atomic Energy to boot.[33]

The result, of course, as Dr. Jerome B. Wiesner, director of the Office of Science and Technology, told Congress in 1963, was that "we are not completely successful in holding interagency programs together through the realignment common to the budget process." He said that "several committees in the Congress review pieces of a coordinated program, without the over-all perspective developed at such effort in the original planning; and legislative authorizations therefore often diverge sharply from Executive proposals."[34] The chairman of the House Subcommittee on Oceanography later acknowledged that this was indeed a problem, but reminded the executive witnesses rather acidly that for fiscal year 1965 the Congress had cut the oceanography program budget only from $138 to $124 million, whereas the Budget Bureau had already made an even deeper cut, from $175 to $138 million.[35] But there is no point in trying to apportion blame in such a matter between the executive and legislative branches: the Congressional committee acts largely on the recommendations of the operating agency and the agency acts largely in anticipation of (and in response to) Congressional committee pressures. About all that one can say in general terms about such decisions is that the specialized interests of particular Congressional committees, and particular executive agencies, work together to frustrate the general program of the Congress and the President and whatever special interagency programs they may try to devise.

If an interagency program could be directed by Congress by either of the first two strategies—independence or advice—the problem would be simple. But the essence of the difficulty is that each of the actions and decisions that must go together to make up an interagency program is also an action or decision that one of the operating agencies must take to further its particular purpose. The agency cannot ignore its own purpose—it is legally responsible to its executive superiors and accountable to the specialized Congressional committees with which it regularly deals. The actions and decisions cannot be pulled out and put in an independent agency, set apart from the political pressures that determine the operating agency's policy. Nor can any independent adviser or coordinator be given legal authority to direct them, for that authority would be directly in conflict with the primary authority of the head of the operating agency itself, and it would be impossible to define in advance the respective limits of the two authorities.

Even aside from political considerations, the problem is inherent in large-scale organization. No administrative department likes to do things in the interest of another department's purpose, even if a superior authority tells it that it should. No department likes to rely on another department to supply it with services that it considers essential to its purpose, even if a superior authority thinks that this will save money for the organization as a whole. The political system does make the problem more difficult in the United States government, if you wish to consider it as one big organization to be appraised in administrative terms, because each department is given legal authority directly by the Congress, and held accountable for its exercise directly by specialized Congressional committees. But the problem would be difficult enough (although less obvious to the public) even if the Congress, like the House of Commons, had no committees with the power to make policy decisions.

Moreover, though the essence of the difficulty lies in the overlap between an interagency program and the programs of the several operating agencies concerned, the difficulty is compounded by another overlap. Each interagency program overlaps also with other interagency programs. It is not the whole story to say that oceanography overlapped with the operating programs of the Navy, the Coast and Geodetic Survey, the Weather Bureau, and so on—leading the Federal Council for Science and Technology to create an Interagency Committee on Oceanography. Also, the council had a similar committee on atmospheric sciences.[36] Since in fact the atmosphere and the oceans interact with each other all over the world, the concerns of these two committees and their interagency programs intersected with each other. So, to a lesser extent, did both of them with the programs of other interagency committees in such fields as natural resources, water resources research, and laboratory astrophysics.[37]

None of these interagency programs was organized as a separate administrative entity. Each was only a phase of the programs of a number of operating agencies, which took the primary responsibility for getting the funds from Congress and doing the work. The question was not whether Congress was to pass on the interagency programs; it had to authorize them all, and appropriate money for them all, but it normally saw them in fragmented form, as phases of the programs of operating agencies that came before many committees and subcommittees. How should Congress deal with this problem if it wished to have a hand in some of the more novel and important aspects of government policy?

One way, of course, would have been to reorganize the committee structure of Congress itself, in order to be able to develop the interagency programs and policies directly within Congress. It must have been assumed that this was not a practicable course. Students of government would do well to speculate why.

Congress undertakes to deal with more details than it can consider by deliberation in its houses as a whole, just as the President must deal with more than he can consider personally. Both have to delegate, but the ways in which they delegate are fundamentally different. The President delegates to subordinates in a hierarchy. Congress delegates (in practice, though not in legal theory) to its committees, and in its delegation there is no hierarchical rank; some members acquire more influence by seniority or leadership than others, but each has an equal vote, equal status, and equal responsibility. Each member properly considers himself responsible only to his constituents; his independence is buttressed against party (or any other) discipline by the seniority system and by his personal connections in his state or district. Difference of opinion among members can be settled only by the processes of deliberation, debate, and voting, mostly under the scrutiny of the public. And when committees are set up with overlapping jurisdictions, issues between them have to be settled by those processes within the House or Senate as a whole. Though deliberation and debate in a large assembly can do many things, it cannot itself draft a complex program; such a task has to be referred to some committee, or delegated to the Executive.

Quite aside from the difficulties of dealing with technical and abstruse subjects, Congress, as a deliberative body of equals, is limited by the very nature of its processes. The number and variety of interagency programs is almost limitless, for they are simply all of the special phases common to the programs of the operating agencies that seem worth singling out for special attention. To the OST, a single type of observation at sea by the Weather Bureau, for example, may be a part of the interagency program on oceanography, and also of the one on atmospheric sciences, and perhaps others. From the point of view of the Budget Bureau, the same act of making that observation requires the provision of staff and money, so that it has to be thought of also as personnel policy and budgetary policy—quite aside from the question whether the Weather Bureau or someone else should do the job, which is organization policy.

It is one thing to permit one particular specialized committee to decide that one particular interagency program is of special urgency and importance, and to press for its expansion. It is quite another thing to make sure that all the relevant aspects of policy have been considered and kept in balance. To do that requires a continuous study of the relationships among the operating agencies, between them and the interagency programs, and among the interagency programs. An elementary calculation of the permutations and combinations in all these relationships will suggest that they will not be reconciled by the processes of deliberation and voting among committees of equal status. They can be blended together only by a system in which some discretionary authority can make decisions and assign priorities.

Within the Congress, the only possibility is the appropriations committee. But even though it is given a great deal of delegated authority from Congress, and in turn gives it to its subcommittees, it too has to operate within a system in which voting by equals is the ultimate sanction. The chairman of an appropriations committee can have it handle a very large quantity of decisions by dividing its work among subcommittees. But the jurisdiction of the subcommittees has to be determined in advance, and each has to work either by agreement among its members or by voting. For that reason, the chairman of the committee is not able to make subcommittees work together on a problem that cuts across their jurisdictional boundaries, or to change their assignments from week to week or to transfer members at will from one subcommittee to another, or to disregard their advice when it seems motivated by too specialized an interest. Nor can he systematically have every major aspect of policy considered simultaneously and in teamwork by subcommittees whose responsibilities are deliberately intended to overlap, so that he can have the benefit of seeing how the same actions look to men with different specialized points of view.

All these things have to be done, and can be done only in a disciplined organization. Congress understands that responsible legislative action can be taken only on the basis of a program that has been proposed by disciplined and responsible leadership, and it would rather look to the President for such leadership than to subject most of its membership to the party discipline of a few of its own leaders. Its members and committees can retain more freedom of action if they act on a recommendation from the President, whose status will not be affected if they disagree with him, than if they submit to a leader or leaders chosen from within Congress, who would then have the right to insist that they demonstrate their confidence in him by supporting his policies.

A political program cannot be created either by debates among equals, or by the processes of research. It can be created only by a leader who can first select his goals (which means to reject an infinite number of others) and then guide his staff and his operating agency heads in building up a program to attain those goals. If the President undertakes to prepare such a program (which the Congress can then consider, and may either revise or reject) he needs to be able to subject the staff units of his Executive Office to the kind of discretionary control which the chairman of an appropriations committee cannot exercise over his subcommittees. He needs to decide the assignments that each staff unit will have; he needs to make sure that it is not committed so strongly to a specialized point of view that it cannot subordinate its expertise to his policies; and he needs to protect against the possibility that it will get to be tied so closely to an outside clientele, or to a particular Congressional committee, that it cannot serve his purposes. He needs, in short, to keep it from getting past the stage where the adviser is given formal legal status—the first of the five successive stages by which (as noted above) advice can be converted into political control.

In this effort, Presidents have so far been reasonably successful. Staff members have indeed been formally denominated as economic advisers, or science advisers, or budget advisers, and assigned to help the President on particular aspects of substance or procedure. But their power stops there: they are not permitted to reveal publicly their advice to the President, or to administer the operations on which they advise him, or to prepare an operational plan which in practice it would be awkward or embarrassing for him to amend or reject. And above all they are not selected for Executive Office positions by any procedure which seems to leave their loyalties or responsibilities running to any authority other than the President.

Only one conspicuous exception had ever been made, and it turned out to be only an apparent one. Against the wishes of President Eisenhower, the National Aeronautics and Space Council was set up by statute in the Executive Office, as a result of the keen interest of Senator Lyndon B. Johnson, then chairman of the Senate special committee considering the creation of the new space program. President Eisenhower exercised his discretion, in a negative way, by refusing to appoint an executive secretary for the council (though the statute had provided for such an appointment) and by keeping the council from meeting very often to transact business. When President Kennedy and Vice President Johnson agreed that the space program was one in which the Vice President should take the lead, the National Aeronautics and Space Council was activated. When the President appointed as its executive secretary Edward C. Welsh, who had been serving as legislative assistant to Senator Stuart Symington, a member of the Senate Committee on Space, it began to seem possible that this committee had intended, and had managed, to gain control of a part of the Executive Office of the President. During the first hearing at which Dr. Welsh appeared in his new capacity, several Senators reminded him rather pointedly that he was expected to continue to report to them as well as to the President on the affairs of the council, and that he could count on them for support.[38]

Nothing came of this possibility, and this was perhaps in part because Dr. Welsh had the good judgment to accept the normal obligations of membership in the Executive Office, but also because the chief poacher had turned gamekeeper. As chairman of the Space Council, Vice President Johnson considered himself a part of the executive branch. And the council was evidently given no monopoly on the space program within the

Executive Office: the Office of Science and Technology and the Bureau of the Budget continued their roles of influence over it.

Nevertheless, it must have been disturbing to the President's advisers that certain members of Congress were using the space program as the precedent for their thinking about the oceanography program. In the space field a technological program that was maintained largely in support of the purposes of operating departments had been converted into a major operational program in its own right. And it was clear that the pattern might become fashionable. Oceanography as an interagency committee was one subcommittee of the Federal Council on Science and Technology. If it were converted into a major post, occupied by a man who was confirmed by the Senate, who was allied with a specialized committee of independent advisers, and who reported directly to Congress, there would be not only potential conflicts with operating agencies but even worse potential conflicts among committees that had been set up to resolve conflicts. Truly terrifying were the complications that could be imagined if the Interagency Committee on Oceanography were made a statutory power and if similar status were given to the committees on atmospheric sciences, natural resources, water resources research, and others with equally plausible claims.

It was of course conceivable that Congress would decide that the case of oceanography was really of unique importance, and that it should absorb some of its counterparts, such as atmospheric sciences. This was indeed suggested later in one committee hearing.[39] To have the interagency program on oceanography swallow up the one on atmospheric sciences might please the Navy and the Coast and Geodetic Survey, but it would surely upset the Weather Bureau and the Federal Aviation Agency and especially the Air Force, which would see this as another move by which the Navy was seeking to aggrandize its missions. The possibility of letting this kind of jurisdictional rivalry among the operating agencies move into the Executive Office, and make it a political battleground, was an alarming one. There were danger signals all around that this process might begin. Some of those who wished to build up the importance of education as a federal responsibility, but had given up on their hopes to make the Office of Education into an executive department, had begun to advocate a statutory council on education in the Executive Office. Other suggestions of the same kind were arising in various fields.

In the minds of the President's advisers, the possibility that Congress might begin to specify the assignments within the Executive Office, and to prescribe the nature of their authority and their order of importance, was a major threat to the system of political responsibility. For that system depends on the ability of Congress to hold the operating agencies accountable for accomplishing the major purposes of national policy. If the heads of the executive departments and agencies were to be made legally subject to orders from staff units in the Executive Office, responsibility would have to be focused on the professional specialties by which the Executive Office staff is organized, rather than the general political purposes of the operating agencies.

As long as the subdivisions of the Excutive Office have no legal power in their own right, and no assignments except those that the President wishes to give them, this danger that professional experts will exceed their staff roles, and take over decisions that ought to be judged in the light of more general political considerations, is minimized. For if a staff unit in the Executive Office gives instructions that a department head thinks go beyond the President's real wishes, the department head is free to appeal, and unless his case is poor he is likely to be sustained by the President. No chief executive wishes to break down the prestige and responsibility of his major political subordinates. And staff advisers, as long as they have no public political responsibility and report to no outside constituency, can always be reversed with little embarrassment.

If Congress wishes the President to present it with a program for which it can hold him and his department heads politically responsible, it will do well not to make the staff members in the Executive Office independent political operators in their own right, and not to bring them under the control of legislative committees. To make technology a political end in itself is not the best way to keep it under responsible political control.

Considerations of this kind had been developing as a part of the doctrine of presidential staff work, under presidents of both parties, ever since General Dawes set the imprint of his ideas on the Bureau of the Budget. As presidential advisers considered the nature of the oceanography program, and the extent to which S. 901 would give a measure of independent political power within the Executive Office to a professional pressure group, it must have seemed obvious to them that the President had no alternative, no matter how much they sympathized with the scientific and technological purposes of the bill. They recommended against its approval, and the President gave it a "pocket veto" as the Congressional session of 1962 came to an end.

I might well drop the oceanography story at this point, since it was meant only to illustrate the procedural ways in which professional purposes come into conflict with general political responsibility. (The substantive issue had long since been won by the oceanographers; the National Academy's Committee on Oceanography was entitled to take great pride in the extent to which it had increased the recognition of, and support for, an important field of science.)[40] It may be useful, however, to take note of the fact that stories like this have no end. In 1963, the House Subcommittee on Oceanography negotiated with staff members of the Executive Office to find out what kind of bill could be passed that would not be vetoed by the President; as a result of that negotiation, the earlier measure was revised to eliminate the ways in which it had sought to make it possible for a part of the Executive Office to be held accountable by an outside professional constituency.

The new bill (1) declared that oceanography was important, and that the United States should have a program to further it;

(2) required the President to submit annually to the Congress recommendations to carry it out, including budgetary and legislative recommendations; and (3) authorized the President to use for these purposes such advisory arrangements as he might find appropriate, including an advisory committee to meet on his call. This bill met the President's objections, since in the main it authorized and directed him to do what he was already doing. The House passed it. But the Senate ignored it, and its Committee on Commerce began again to think of alternatives.

THE MAJOR PROPOSALS

But even if this story has no end, it has a moral. What can it teach us about the major proposals that have been recently made to relate science and the scientific professions to the political authority of the Congress and the President?

A Department of Science?

The central issue in the oceanography program turned on the fact that applied research is, and must be, intimately related to the programs of the operating agencies. Research is indeed the pioneer on the frontier of policy, and the nation gains if each agency, and the Congressional committees that are interested in it, look on research as a principal means for accomplishing their purposes and opening up new opportunities.

Since the late nineteenth century many have believed that scientific activities should not be scattered among various departments but centralized in a Department of Science,[41] partly to get additional status for science, and partly to keep it from being subordinated to departmental purposes. In the mid-twentieth century, however, the idea that it would really be possible to separate the big research programs from their parent departments has come to seem highly unrealistic, and undesirable even in theory. Leading scientists, with few exceptions, have come to rely instead on more effective and flexible coordinating arrange-

257 |

ments, including both interagency collaboration and guidance from the President's Executive Office.

There is a more limited, and more attractive, version of the Department of Science proposal: to bring together in a new department those agencies of applied research that, by the very nature of their programs, are not tied mainly to the purposes of a single operating agency. If, so the proposal runs, the Bureau of Standards, the Weather Bureau, the Geological Survey, the Naval Observatory, and several others were brought together, the total collection would get more support and attract better scientists. It could also prepare a more balanced program for each of its constituent units—more balanced in terms of its contribution to the national policy as a whole and to the programs of the government's operating agencies.[42]

There is a great deal of merit in this argument. In a government of completely centralized legislative responsibility, it should be feasible to set up such a Department of Science, and to decide on purely pragmatic grounds whether or not a particular applied research bureau should be included in it. Would the Geological Survey, for example, benefit more from a closer association with other research bureaus, and a better balanced relationship with various operating agencies, than from its present connection with the Department of the Interior? But under the Congressional system, which is far from centralized, that cannot be the only criterion. Programs of applied research get their legislative support, and their funds, because of their apparent connection with the programs of operating agencies, and the political support of those agencies and of their constituencies. It is highly doubtful that a group of research bureaus, if taken out of the operating agencies and put in a Department of Science, would continue to get as much support from the operating agencies and as much money from the Congress as they do under the present system.

Basic research, of course, is a different matter. It commands a certain amount of political support in its own right, quite apart from the fact that the universities of the country provide it with a constituency of considerable influence. Should it be made into an executive department? Would the status of a Secretaryship and a post in the cabinet help basic science either to get more funds, or to be administered on a more rational basis with less obligation to the operating agencies? In the past, a few half-hearted efforts have been made to take responsibility for the support of basic research away from the operating agencies and give it to the National Science Foundation. The results have been generally disappointing; the appropriations system does not yet operate in quite so rationalized a manner. It seems clear, on the basis of experience, that more money will be provided for basic research if each operating agency will, in effect, tax itself to contribute to the basic science that is linked to its applied sciences, than if the total basic research program were handled in a single budget and defended before a single appropriations subcommittee. If practical politicians ever agree to centralize all support for basic research in a single department, it will probably be from the same motive that leads business corporations in many cities to support the creation of a united Community Chest: it would lead to a more rigorous centralized review of applications, tighter controls, and a smaller total budget. It is partly for this reason, but even more because the plurality of sources of support keeps any one agency from dominating them, that the universities and research laboratories do not generally advocate the creation of a centralized federal department for basic research.

But if the idea of centralization were to be forgotten, the case for strengthening the present arrangements for the support of basic research would be a strong one. A more important agency than the National Science Foundation might well be created. The support of basic research, as the National Science Foundation demonstrated in the oceanography story, carries few implications for particular policies or programs. The National Science Foundation and the National Institutes of Health would obviously provide the nucleus of such an agency. But to propose to raise it to departmental status would bring up two questions that should be faced: how is federal support for scientific research to be related to support for research on other subjects, and how are all kinds of research to be related to general educational policy? There is no question that present federal activities tend to distort the programs of the universities, which are able to keep a proper balance between the sciences and the humanities, and between research and teaching, only by great ingenuity in finding and juggling funds from other than federal sources. A department of basic research and education could help to bring about a better balance. It would need to build into its grant-making procedures enough scholarly advisory committees to satisfy even the academic world without doing any damage to Congressional or Presidential responsibility. If this could be managed, such a department might be an appropriate instrumentality for dealing with the new importance of the scholarly estate in our constitutional system.

An operations research corporation for the President?

The privately incorporated agencies for operations research have been extraordinarily useful to the military services. Hence it was inevitable that from time to time scientists in Washington would suggest that what is good for the Army or Navy or Air Force ought to be even better for the President. Why should not the Executive Office have a private subsidiary corporation to study issues involving the application of science to policy?

There are three main reasons for the success of the operations research corporations. The first and least important is money; they can pay their professional staff members higher salaries than would be possible in the civil service, though much less than comparable persons are paid by industrial corporations. The second is that they can offer an environment that is attractive to the scientist or professional, who tends to be repelled by either the routines of the civil service or the constraints of working in an atmosphere dominated by military rank, tradition, and conformity. Third and most significant for our question, they provide a basis of independence from which scientists and professionals can criticize, on a confidential basis, the technological and operational doctrines of the moment and make alternative suggestions to military leaders. This is not a matter of applying pure science to military problems, but of seeking to find better ways to blend scientific and professional and economic and psychological thinking in accomplishing the mission of a service.

This all works well at the level of a particular military service, where an operations research corporation can take the service's mission for granted. As you go up in the hierarchy, however, the problems get further away from those in which the scientific and professional issues are crucial, and take you into more conflicts of departmental purpose. It has been much harder to make a success of the Institute for Defense Analyses (IDA), set up to serve the Secretary of Defense and the Joint Chiefs, than of the operations research corporations attached to the several services. For the IDA's recommendations are not presented to a unified and strongly disciplined system of authority which can take them or leave them but which finds them useful as stimuli to thought even when it rejects them. They go instead to an arena of competing purposes, in which there is considerable danger that the professional recommendations will be misinterpreted by higher political authority. Hence, the Joint Chiefs must give the IDA far less leeway in setting the assumptions on which it bases its studies, and in choosing the subjects on which to report, than a military service may permit its particular private subsidiary.

As the oceanography story illustrates, the President needs little help from his Executive Office in thinking of new scientific programs that may be needed; he can get that from the operating agencies, from the National Academy of Sciences, or from a multitude of willing volunteers. He needs scientific advisers who can help him evaluate proposals from operating agencies, identifying proposals that are based on scientific and professional certainty and those for which equally attractive alternatives are available. These advisers must be able to work with others in the

Executive Office to blend scientific advice with advice on the financial, diplomatic, legal, and many other aspects of policy. Above all they must protect him from being presented with advice, ostensibly based on scientific considerations, that will really represent an invasion of his general policy by a special interest. The purpose of his scientific and professional advisers should not be merely to enable him to rely on science in making his policy decisions, but, even more, to protect him from having to adopt special-interest programs that pretend to be based on scientific necessity.

The President does not need a single operations research corporation, though he might usefully employ the services of several. He should not entrust his staff work to the control of any single private agency, and he can use a variety of private agencies only if he has the protection of adequate technical advice that is fully responsible to him.

A science advisory staff for Congress?

Bills were introduced in both houses of Congress in 1963 to establish a Congressional Science Advisory Staff, or a Congressional Office of Science and Technology (H.R. 6866, H.R. 8066, and S. 2038).

To the question whether Congress should have at its disposal any scientific advice that it needs, there can be only one answer: it should. But there remain questions as to whether Congress really wants a central office for this purpose, and how it would use such an office.

The need of Congress for scientific advice is roughly the same as that of the President. On public policy it wishes not only to consider the ends but to understand the proposed means, and it wishes to understand not only the current programs of operating agencies, but the ways in which current research may offer promise of future developments. Unlike the President, however, the Congress, being made up of two equal houses, each of which includes many equal members, has to subdivide itself in order to get its work done, and this process of subdivision into committees creates problems quite different from those of organizing the staff divisions within the Executive Office.

The President can keep the lines of responsibility within the executive branch at least tolerably clear by distinguishing sharply between his operating agencies, which he holds responsible for running their programs, and his staff agencies, which he holds responsible for advising him on national policy as a whole and helping him to control the means used by the operating agencies. Political responsibility can be enforced only in a single line of operations. And the staff agencies are subject to two types of discipline, both of which serve to prevent scientists from exaggerating their competence to help determine policy: first, the staff agency has less status in executive councils, and less political claim on the President, than the responsible heads of the operating agencies; second, the science advisers' opinions are checked by others within the Executive Office. Their opinions are checked by criticism and competing opinions, not only of others within the same field of science but by experts in other fields, and also by the various types of administrative staff work by which the President makes sure that all aspects of any particular policy are considered. Moreover, the discipline of the Executive Office prevents a scientific adviser from making a public issue of one of his dissenting opinions.

The main potential danger in the creation of a single Congressional office or advisory staff for science and technology is that it would be subject to none of these restraints. If a particular committee should choose to rely on the advice of that office, and to publicize it in committee hearings without reconciling it with the opinions of other committees and the judgments of other types of experts, the Congress and the public would be presented with an issue which laymen are not competent to judge, and ought not to be asked to judge. It is all too likely that the creation of such an office in the Congress might have the opposite effect from the one intended; it might give a few scientists who have no responsibility for the conduct of government business, and are under no disciplined compulsion to submit their opinions to the criticism of other experts (and especially of experts from other fields) an opportunity to push their personal views on policy beyond the extent which their scientific knowledge would justify.

There are three alternative ways by which Congress has obtained independent scientific advice in the past. One is to employ scientific members of committee staffs; this has the advantage of relating the professional staff member closely to the policies and programs on which he is advising, and giving the members of Congress a chance to understand his limitations as well as his competence. The second, which was adopted late in 1964, is to employ scientific staff members in the Legislative Reference Service; this has the advantage of putting them in a staff together with experts of other types of background, and within some framework of general responsibility. The third is the original plan of a century ago, which may yet prove the best of all: to make use of the advisory services of the National Academy of Sciences. This enables Congress to get, at any time and on any problem, advice from scientists of the highest order of competence in the particular field in question, and the very fact that they are chosen for particular assignments, rather than kept on retainer, is a guarantee of their objectivity and freshness of point of view.

Some combination of all three of these methods would seem preferable to the creation of an institution that would put scientists in the position of commenting with authority on political issues without subjecting their science to expert appraisal of its limitations. And all three methods put together are much less important to Congress than the way in which its senior members understand that the most important issues are not determined by scientific considerations at all, and that they can get at them more effectively by close questioning of responsible administrators and professionals than by any amount of expert staff work.

If, as politicians, they have an eye first on who is to have authority and how much are we to trust him, and second on what are
the main purposes he proposes to pursue, they can safely leave
most of the technical issues to be determined by the consensus of
the scientific and professional estates.[43]

Divide the roles of the President's science adviser

Scientists greeted President Eisenhower's appointment of a
Special Assistant for Science and Technology, and a Science Advisory Committee of scientists from private institutions, with a
chorus of enthusiasm. But the unanimity of that enthusiasm was
no more enduring than the unanimity of any other political opinion among scientists. Among the Science Advisory Committee's
panel members themselves there was occasional grumbling that
their scientific advice did not get to the President undiluted, and
that the committee's chairman was too responsive to nonscientific
considerations in dealing with major issues. And when some scientists on the outside naturally became dissatisfied with various
aspects of science policy—for example, with the extent to which
research grants were concentrated in a comparatively few universities—they reacted in the best Jeffersonian tradition and proposed to break up what seemed to them too great a concentration
of power at the center. They did not like a single individual to be
presidential adviser, chairman of the Science Advisory Committee, and chairman of the Federal Council on Science and Technology. And when Dr. Jerome B. Wiesner resigned from those
jobs in 1963 the editor of *Science,* Dr. Philip H. Abelson,
charged that the combination of functions had led to an undesirable concentration of power that was exercised arrogantly and
in secret, and proposed that the several positions be separated.[44]

The critics are concerned, of course, not merely with the actions taken in person by the science adviser, but with what his
subordinate staff members do in his name and the President's. It
is inevitable that scientists and engineers in operating agencies
will not like to have their plans interfered with by professional

265 |

staff members in the Executive Office, especially by men who are junior to them in rank and professional eminence. It is even likely that some of the actions of staff members are the result of the itch of any aggressive staff member to interfere more than he should with the operating agency's plans. But the remedy for this type of meddling (which is very hard for anyone to distinguish from the desirable type of staff work) is not to break up the staff, but rather for the head of the operating agency either to refuse to accept the views of the President's staff man, or appeal to the President against him.

For example, *Science* has cited an illustration of the type of problem on which it is right for Executive Office staff to raise issues, and on which it may be equally right for the operating agency to refuse the recommendations and be sustained by the President. The Office of Science and Technology considered the plans of the National Aeronautics and Space Administration for landing on the moon. Those plans called for sending a space vehicle directly into an orbit around the moon. The OST instead thought it would be better to have an intermediate stage in the operation—to put into orbit around the earth a vehicle from which a smaller moon vehicle could be launched. The OST "contended that, since the military potential for space appears to be in the near-earth regions, an earth orbit in the lunar program would help develop techniques that could be adapted for military purposes." NASA argued instead that it was cheaper and faster to employ a lunar orbit, and NASA won.[45]

Whether or not this is an accurate summary of the technical considerations involved in the OST argument, the story illustrates the key administrative issue. An operating agency may properly propose to do a major job in a way that best suits its own particular purpose. If a staff agency can then discover a way in which the operating agency can do the same job in a way that will also contribute to the purposes of other parts of the government, it should speak up. If it can get the agency's voluntary agreement to such a course of action, all the better; if not, it may recommend it to the President. And the President may take the advice, or he may prefer to support the judgment of his operating agency. It is by deciding which to support—his staff agency or an operating agency—that he makes some of his most crucial decisions.

What is essential is that the staff advice on which the President acts must not be partial and fragmentary. On any major problem, the staff advice which comes to him may need to be a blend of technology, economics, diplomacy, and domestic politics; it must be put together by collaboration among specialists of various types in the Executive Office, all of whom must do their best to become generalists. Personally, the President could never deal with the myriad of problems on his desk by trying to puzzle out for himself how, with respect to each one, a great many competing types of expert knowledge fit together.

A single principal science adviser may bring together advice from outside experts and from scientific administrators inside the government, and help blend that advice with the views of the Bureau of the Budget and other staff in the Executive Office. He can do so most effectively if, as director of the Office of Science and Technology, he also remains the chairman of both the Science Advisory Committee and the Federal Council on Science and Technology. If he were replaced in these jobs by three scientists, equal in status, the odds are heavy that none of them would ever get the ear of the President, because to the rest of the Executive Office it would simply become too complicated to deal with all three of them on any difficult issue.

To consider the members of the Executive Office staff publicly accountable for their advice seems, at first glance, a democratic idea. But it ignores the fact that the electorate and the Congress, even more than an executive, have to focus and concentrate responsibility in order to enforce it. It ignores the further fact that political responsibility is most efficiently enforced with respect to operating responsibility for major purposes, not with respect to the technological means to accomplish those purposes.

And it ignores, even more, the need that any responsible executive has for staff advisers who will be motivated to operate as members of a team, adjusting their several specialized interests to his common policy objectives, and who cannot be called to account by anyone for their failure to defend a special professional point of view within the executive's confidential councils.

Congress must not give up its right to review the scientific and technological aspects of policy from time to time, just as the President must not give up his right to intervene in details of departmental administration. These are the ways by which democratic political authority may purge the government of the ills of bureaucracy, and of the pretensions of professional subordinates to extend their authority beyond its proper limits into policy decisions. But a purgative is not to be confused with a healthy diet; no one should think that the quality of democratic responsibility is measured by the extent to which professionals take part in political controversy, or politicians preoccupy themselves with technology, even though a little of both may be a good thing.

In our system of constitutional relativity, it is impossible to prescribe precisely the proper balance between special professional interests and the public interest as defined by responsible political authority. The balance must be maintained in the actual conduct of public business. But it cannot be maintained unless the Congress permits the President to use scientific advisers, and other staff advisers, who are not forced to acquire political influence in their own right to maintain their positions, or obliged to represent any special professional interest within the Executive Office. The President ought not to be given the authority to make the final decisions on the big policy issues; that can be done only by the processes of legislation. But he ought to be given a chance to formulate the questions, and to propose answers for consideration by the Congress.

The technical ideas of scientists and professional men can be judged most effectively in the councils of their peers. On the other hand voters can best judge those types of general issues on which they are as wise, or at least as entitled to a preference, as any expert. The reconciliation of these two types of judgment is the most difficult responsibility of political leadership and administrative staff work.

CHAPTER 8

Science and Freedom

SCIENTISTS, EVEN THOSE WHO have no other political interest, are interested in freedom. They are manifestly concerned for the freedom of their own research, cherishing the privilege of unhampered investigation and teaching in academic institutions. They also like to think of science as the intellectual force that challenged the authority of the church and the old forms of learning. They like to believe that the inner spirit of science is one of freedom, that the processes of scientific research require freedom, and that therefore the political influence of science must be in the direction of freedom—not merely for scientists but for mankind.

And so, in an ideal sense, it should. But that is like saying that, since the spirit of religion is one of love, the political influence of religion must always be in the direction of charity and peace. History suggests that there is a political fallacy in both statements. Just as churches, once they are organized in association with worldly power, do not always conform to their ideals, so scientists seem to be able to accommodate themselves to political systems that destroy freedom, or even able to support the basic theory of such systems. It is obvious on the record that scientists who are highly sophisticated in their own disciplines are quite capable of supporting authoritarian political theories on either the right or the left, or at least passively accepting them —and this seems to be as true in the social as in the physical and biological sciences.

Scientists in the free nations have been clearly committed to the cause of freedom, and have done much to increase the spirit of independence and open criticism within their free institutions.

But this does not mean that science as such, in a different setting, would necessarily have the same result. For wherever science tries to become a unified and authoritative system of thought that pretends to explain all types of knowledge and to guide all types of actions, it becomes more a rationalization of a will to power than a valid intellectual discipline. And there is little reason to think that science, in countries that are now under dictatorial rule, will by educating the masses necessarily give them a greater spirit of political freedom.

The countries that have been the most successful in establishing free governments are those in which the essentials of freedom were established before science became a powerful force in society. In Great Britain, the skepticism of the classical scholar and the passionate independence of the dissenting clergy did more than science to break up the unity of ecclesiastical thought on which the traditional authority of the sovereign depended. Indeed, science had a chance to flourish, and develop its own independent institutions, only after this revolution in both intellectual and political affairs that had been led by the theologians.[1]

Bacon was of course correct in thinking that science was in conflict with Platonic theology in that science opposed teleology —the way of thinking that explained events in terms of their purposes. But by his day theology had, over the millennia, taken broad steps in his direction. After all, the idea of monotheism was a major step away from the belief that specific human purposes were promoted by particular gods, and toward the idea that there was a coherent system of order in the universe. Another step was embodied in the myth of the expulsion from the Garden of Eden, which suggested that man was not a god, and not to share in the knowledge of ultimate purpose—a myth much more congenial to the mood of modern science than that of Prometheus, whose ambition was merely technological, to break up, so to speak, the Olympian patent monopoly. And then in later centuries had come the two most pertinent changes in theological ideas: first, the doctrine that Divine purpose had not been

271 |

summed up by a revelation of specific commandments or rules of conduct, but depended instead on an indefinable personal relationship; and second, the belief that no human organization could be trusted with authority to define the nature of truth or of Divine purpose.

It was this last step, culminating in the Puritan rebellion, that left England in the seventeenth century a freer place for the development of science than anywhere else in Europe. For though the Puritans themselves had no intention of being tolerant, their doctrines undermined the kind of hierarchical organization that was needed to enforce intolerance, and to maintain traditional sovereignty on a national scale. As James I so grimly summed up the issue, "No Bishop, no King." And neither the Puritans nor the skeptical trimmers who succeeded them in political power expected that man could discover a doctrine or a theory by which he could be made perfect on earth. That expectation, which tempts men to entrust their rulers with unlimited authority in order to gain unlimited ends, reappeared during Robespierre's worship of Reason, and then again in the utopian vision of Karl Marx. It is not based on science as scientists now understand science, though it may well be based on a popular faith in science as an approach to a new Utopia.

Indeed it is clear that science alone, without the intellectual checks and balances provided by other intellectual disciplines, will not fortify a political system against this temptation to use power to force men to be free. And it is equally clear that science and theology alike are unable to define with authority the ends of public policy. Though science has given mankind greater certainty of knowledge, it has gained that certainty by renouncing the concern for purpose that must remain at the heart of politics and administration—in both their practice and their theory.

Any constitutional system that undertakes to protect freedom by dividing power has to be based first of all on a separation between the institutions that exercise political power and those that are engaged in the search for truth. And this separation seems to be based in turn on a way of thinking that accepts and defends the mutual independence of various disciplines, and of various forms of knowledge. The maintenance of the privileges of private property, or the defense of the prerogatives of the several branches of government, is important but secondary. The most fundamental threat to freedom would be an effort of a science faculty in a university, with the help of political authority, to suppress a faculty of law or theology, or vice versa.

The case for the mutual independence of the several disciplines does not depend mainly on the objective validity of the ways by which they acquire and verify knowledge. It depends even more on the political value of maintaining free competition and free mutual criticism in the search for truth. And this is a value on which men in every university tacitly agree—men who believe in the infallibility of Divine Revelation along with men who believe that the only way in which anyone can know anything is by the rigorous method of science. And along with men who say they believe hardly anything.

It would be ridiculous today to think that the natural sciences are trying to extend their dominion over other forms of learning, even though in Communist countries Marxist theory undertakes to base its notions of justice and of the purpose of politics on the principles of a materialist science. For the natural sciences in the Western world, even while they are rapidly developing the concepts and principles that they have in common, are not moving toward an authoritarian unity in the government of their several disciplines, or of their own scientific societies. However scientists might conceive of the ideal unity of the sciences, they are not inclined to make it the basis of a unified organization that could control their scholarly interests, much less the basis of a political theory to control public affairs.

So far I have been talking about freedom from politics, a freedom which scientists enjoy in countries that follow the Western tradition, though they have probably done less to achieve it than they have taken credit for. But scientists are beginning to develop also an increased interest in a more positive freedom—freedom *in* politics. And they have probably done more to extend this kind of freedom for themselves—freedom to participate in government and engage in policy innovation—than they have been willing to admit. Their freedom *from* politics depends on the assumption that science cannot authoritatively define our ends. But that is not to say that it does not influence them, or that it can deal only with means. The scientists' freedom in politics, and the politicians' ability to control technology in a responsible manner, depend on the assumption that science can influence our political ends as well as our technical means.

Politically, science has a profound influence on the way we all think about ends and values, and the political system has to accommodate itself to that fact. This has nothing to do with the abstract question whether science can provide any knowledge of ultimate purpose or of ideal values. Some would say that only theology and philosophy and the arts afford such knowledge, and that science never can. Others would say that ultimate purpose and ideal values are concepts without real (that is, scientific) meaning, being at worst mere rationalizations of irrational preferences, and at best mere verbal statements of propositions which for the time being science has not yet reduced to systematic knowledge. But this dispute can be ignored in dealing with the political problem; in politics, ends and values are those purposes and policy judgments on the basis of which politicians in a free system have to be responsible to the electorate. And obviously science has a profound effect on the ways in which a political system makes its most important choices.

Science supplies much of the great body of factual knowledge that men must agree on (at least they must agree on most of it) if their arguments about the choices that are open to them are to be conducted on some rational and orderly basis. It sweeps away superstitions that paralyze political responsibility. It opens up new opportunities and new possibilities for cooperation, and thus makes the concept of a public interest more meaningful, though at the same time more complicated and difficult to define. Accordingly, it is impossible to expect either science or scientists not to be deeply involved in the major issues that confront a modern government.

So science cannot either solve our policy problems for us or stand aside from them. And that is why the scientific community and the politicians need to develop the clearest possible idea of the working rules that govern their relationship. But it is not easy to define the ways in which scientists should be given support by government and permitted to exercise their initiative or influence in policy issues of interest to government.

Disestablishment is obviously no longer an acceptable formula. In other times the government of the United States left the support of education and research, except in fields related directly to governmental programs, to state and local governments and private philanthropy. But it now considers the direct support of fundamental science a primary national purpose. And the change is a profound one in ways that are more important than the appropriation of funds; politicians now recognize that their decisions depend on scientific considerations, and that their established policies may be upset by new scientific discoveries. They stand in some awe of the scientists. It seems we have come a long way from the Jacksonian belief that the duties of government are so simple that they can be discharged by any ordinary citizen.

Yet in a way we remain as overconfident as ever of the competence of our fellow citizens. If science is involved in policy, then we expect science to solve our problems for us. And so we look to elected politicians to base their decisions directly on the advice of pure scientists, or even less plausibly we think that scientists as such should be given positions of political authority.

It is very hard for Americans to admit that practically all policies are based on a mixture of ideas that only scientists can understand with other ideas that most of them do not bother to— such as considerations of cost, administrative effectiveness, polit-

275 |

ical feasibility, and competition with other policies. As a result, policy questions cannot either be solved like an equation or disposed of by a statute. On the contrary, political authorities can deal with them only within the context of a politically responsible organization. They do so partly by coming to understand the facts themselves, but mainly by granting their support and confidence to an appropriate balance of scientific, professional, and administrative talents within the public service. The United States finds it hard to adjust itself to the idea that it must now seek to maintain effective control over the experts not by the tactics of pure individualism, and not by breaking up the power of established institutions and professional corps within the government, but by maintaining a proper balance among competing estates.

It should be possible for political leaders to encourage the initiative of scientists in matters of policy, and at the same time to distinguish between their precise scientific knowledge and their political prejudices. (And if the politicians cannot tell the difference themselves, the scientists' colleagues and rivals will help them do so.) Nevertheless, politicians are obliged to be on their guard in such matters. For whether or not most scientists wish it, laymen are likely to push scientists into the position of prophets. A sophisticated generation that has given up much of its faith in traditional religion may be beginning to worship science mainly for the magical benefits that it can provide through technology. As a result, the established institutions of science are now under as much temptation to resort to casuistry as any ecclesiastic: to what extent are they to advocate the appropriation of billions to support particular programs of technological magic in order to dazzle the vulgar voter into letting them have millions for the advancement of scientific truth?

As a practical matter of institutional politics, science is no longer seriously threatened by the rivalry of the magic of religion; its own technological magic is what it has to worry about. The advancement of basic science will doubtless get still larger appropriations as a result of the emphasis on the purposes of military or nuclear or space technology or the demand for new wonder drugs. But it may also suffer considerable distortions in the directions of its development and in the distribution of its best talents, and its leaders are fearful of threats to the autonomy of its institutions. For this reason, the selection of men concerned with basic research as advisers to the President is an appropriate one. It is not at the level of the Presidency that a combination of secret bureaucracy and technology is likely to dominate the policies of the United States in irresponsible and inhumane directions. The Presidency is too open to public scrutiny, and too effectively checked by a variety of bureaucratic interests and Congressional committees, and too sensitive to its quadrennial accountability to the nation as a whole, to become committed to highly specialized technical purposes. The threat of technocracy is more likely to come through an alliance between particular Congressional committees and the professional interests within a particular agency or department. For though the committees of Congress have been multiplying the procedures by which they can hold the executive branch accountable, no one has yet found ways by which the committees themselves can be regularly called to account by the Congress.

Five successive Presidents, from Roosevelt to Johnson, brought to their Executive Office science advisers drawn mainly from basic research and academic institutions. The main reason why the President has turned to the scientific rather than the professional estate for his advisers is probably that the basic scientists, on issues that do not affect their own types of establishment, are relatively able to give objective advice. On the issues of political action, entailing the largest expenditures, they tend to be somewhat less committed to particular ways of thinking, and particular projects and policies, than are the industrial engineers and the physicians in private practice—less committed, and less subject to charges of conflict of interest. With their help, and with an understanding of the limitations on the contribution that they can make to issues of policy, a political leader has a better chance to

277 |

maintain responsible control over the technological programs of government and to prevent his subordinates from presenting him with recommendations to which he can find no practicable alternative.

The establishment of science (and other forms of learning) in free universities and professional societies, governed on principles quite different from those of politics, has provided an essential counterbalance in the American constitutional system to the democratic competition for political power. It has provided the answer to those who feared, after the abolition of aristocracy and an established church, that democracy could never foster the arts or the theoretical sciences, and would steadily decline in intellectual energy and in the freedom and initiative of its independent institutions. At the same time, science has turned loose technological forces in society which we have not yet learned to control in a responsible manner, and it shows little promise of discovering a new system of absolute values by which to judge them.

In view of the way in which science seems to condemn us to live in a world of rapid social change, we may have to get used to a constitutional system that does not operate according to absolute rules or fixed procedures, but one that adjusts itself to meet new conditions in a world that we do not expect to become perfect in the predictable future. Perhaps indeed a nation can be free only if it is not in too great a hurry to become perfect. It can then defend its freedom by keeping the institutions established for the discovery of truth and those for the exercise of political power independent of each other. But independence should not mean isolation. Only if a nation can induce scientists to play an active role in government, and politicians to take a sympathetic interest in science (or at least in scientific institutions) can it enlarge its range of positive freedom, and renew its confidence that science can contribute progressively to the welfare of mankind.

Notes

Chapter 1: Escape to the Endless Frontier

1. Vannevar Bush, *Science the Endless Frontier: A Report to the President* (Washington: U.S. Government Printing Office, July 1945), pp. 6, 14.

2. Tolstoi's *Aelita*, published in 1923, is discussed in Peter Yershov, *Science Fiction and Utopian Fantasy in Soviet Literature* (New York: Research Program on the U.S.S.R., 1954), pp. 19–22.

3. Ivan Yefremov, "The Heart of the Serpent," in *More Soviet Science Fiction*, ed. Isaac Asimov (New York: Collier Books, 1962), pp. 50, 57.

4. Asimov in the introduction to the book just cited, p. 11.

5. E.g., W. M. Miller, Jr., *A Canticle for Leibowitz* (Philadelphia: Lippincott, 1959); C. S. Lewis, *That Hideous Strength* (London: John Lane the Bodley Head Ltd., 1945); A. E. Van Vogt, *Slan* (New York: Dell, 1961); or Frederik Pohl and Cyril M. Kornbluth, *The Space Merchants* (New York: Ballantine Books, 1953).

6. J. D. Bernal, *The Social Function of Science* (London: George Routledge & Sons, 1939), p. 381.

7. For example, Loren Eiseley's "Man: the Lethal Factor," the Phi Beta Kappa–Sigma Xi Lecture to the American Association for the Advancement of Science, December 29, 1962, published in *American Scientist*, March 1, 1963, pp. 71–83.

8. S. I. Vavilov, *Lenin and Philosophical Problems of Modern Physics* (Moscow: Foreign Languages Publishing House, 1953), pp. 12, 32.

9. Michael Polanyi, *Personal Knowledge* (Chicago: University of Chicago Press, 1958), p. 239.

10. For a brief summary of the comparative degree of success of physicists in the Soviet Union to escape from the control of the "diamat," but the greater difficulty in other scientific fields, see the annotations by Herbert Ritvo in *The New Soviet Society: Final Text of the Program of*

the Communist Party of the Soviet Union (New York: New Leader, 1962), pp. 221–222.

11. Fred Hoyle, *The Black Cloud* (New York: New American Library, 1959), p. 87.

12. Leo Szilard, *The Voice of the Dolphins* (New York: Simon & Schuster, 1961), pp. 25–26.

13. For example, George C. Sponsler (of the Bureau of Ships, Navy Department), "Needed: Scientists on Top," *Bulletin of the Atomic Scientists,* June 1962, pp. 17–20.

14. Max Born, *Physics and Politics* (New York: Basic Books, 1962), pp. 83, 66.

15. Eugene Rabinowitch, "The Scientific Revolution," *Bulletin of the Atomic Scientists,* October–December 1963.

16. C. P. Snow, *Science and Government* (Cambridge, Mass.: Harvard University Press, 1961).

17. Text in *New York Times,* Jan. 22, 1961, p. 4E.

18. Adams predicted that "the future of Thought, and therefore of History, lies in the hands of physicists," and went on to speculate that a rapid acceleration of thought in the direction of the abstract sciences might "reduce the forces of the molecule, the atom, and the electron to that costless servitude to which it has reduced the old elements of earth and air, fire and water." His prediction was uncanny, except for the term "costless." *The Degradation of the Democratic Dogma* (New York: G. P. Putnam, 1958), pp. 277, 303 (first published in 1919). For a critique of Adams' loose use of scientific metaphors in dealing with history and politics, see Joseph Mindel, "The Uses of Metaphor: Henry Adams and the Symbols of Science," *Journal of the History of Ideas,* January–March 1965, pp. 89–102.

19. See the authorized interpretation by the President's Special Assistant for Science and Technology, George B. Kistiakowsky, in *Science,* Feb. 10, 1961, p. 355.

20. See for example the editorial in *Science,* June 28, 1963, p. 1365; also the study of government-university relationships conducted by the Carnegie Foundation for the Advancement of Teaching, "Twenty-six Campuses and the Federal Government," *Educational Record,* April 1963; and Committee on Science and Public Policy, *Federal Support of Basic Research in Institutions of Higher Learning* (National Academy of Sciences, 1964).

21. Gibbon was ostensibly speaking of ancient Rome. *The Decline and Fall of the Roman Empire,* vol. I, chap. ii.

22. Jacques Maritain, Miguel de Unamuno, and Jose Ortega y Gasset represent the conservative critics of the Enlightenment; J. D. Bernal may

be taken as a sample on the socialist side. Judith N. Shklar, whose *After Utopia: The Decline of Political Faith* (Princeton, N.J.: Princeton University Press, 1957) begins with the observation that "nothing is quite so dead today as the spirit of optimism that the very word Enlightenment evokes," goes on (p. 3) to admit that "the less reflective public, certainly until 1914, remained cheerfully indifferent to the intellectual currents of despair." In this optimistic category I would include many American scientists, and bring the date up to the present.

23. Paul M. Gross notes that the "estate" metaphor is by no means new; it was used by Arthur D. Little forty years ago. See Gross' "The Fifth Estate in the Seventh Decade," *Science,* Jan. 3, 1964, p. 13. Alvin M. Weinberg made a similar use of the metaphor in a commencement address at the University of Chattanooga, later reprinted in the October 1963 *Yale Scientific Magazine.*

Chapter 2: The Fusion of Economic and Political Power

1. *Boston Globe,* Jan. 24, 1963, p. 1.

2. For example, see J. W. Kendrick, *Productivity Trends in the United States,* National Bureau of Economic Research, 1961, esp. p. 110; R. Solow, "Technical Change and the Aggregate Production Function," *Review of Economics and Statistics,* vol. 39 (1957), p. 312; and E. Denison, *The Sources of Economic Growth in the United States and the Alternatives before Us* (New York: Committee for Economic Development, 1962).

3. Address by Secretary of Commerce Luther H. Hodges to Chamber of Commerce of the United States, Jan. 23, 1963 (Department of Commerce press release, same date).

4. Message to Congress, Jan. 29, 1963.

5. Wilfrid C. Rodgers, "Politicians See Gold in Space," *Boston Sunday Globe,* Feb. 3, 1963.

6. *Science,* March 15, 1963, p. 1036.

7. Address by Governor James A. Rhodes of Ohio at the Governors' Conference, Miami Beach, July 21–24, 1963 (official press release). See also *Business Week,* Jan. 26, 1963, p. 32.

8. Committee for Economic Development, *A Confidential Analysis of Economic Developments,* December 1962. Quoted by permission.

9. James Wilson, for example, based his "general principle of law and obligation" on a thoroughly Newtonian view of the cosmos, and looked for a set of principles by which law and politics could be made as reliable as mathematics and physics. He made an effort not only to think in terms of analogies between scientific and political systems, but

to base "the science of politics" not on Platonic argument but on the same principles of "induction from experiment" that "My Lord Bacon first delineated" and Newton perfected. *The Works of James Wilson,* ed. James DeWitt Andrews (Chicago: Callaghan & Co., 1896), I, 49, 130–131, 369, 508–511. Americans, however, did not originate this comparison, or the mood of complacency about their Constitution that seemed to go with it. J. T. Desaguliers, Fellow of the Royal Society and Chaplain to the Duke of Chandos, published in 1728 *The Newtonian System of the World the Best Model of Government, An Allegorical Poem.* In it, he remarked, "among my Philosophical Enquiries, [for "Philosophical" a modern would read "scientific"] I have consider'd *Government* as a *Phaenomenon,* and look'd upon that Form of it to be most perfect, which did most nearly resemble the Natural Government of our *System,* according to the Laws settled by the *All-Wise* and *Almighty Architect* of the Universe." For the Rev. Mr. Desaguliers, the Newtonian system was the basis of the *"limited Monarchy,* whereby our Liberties, Rights, and Privileges are so well secured to us, as to make us happier than all the Nations round about us."

10. Samuel P. Huntington, "The Founding Fathers and the Division of Powers," in *Area and Power,* ed. Arthur Maass (Glencoe, Ill.: Free Press, 1959).

11. Carl L. Becker, in his *The Heavenly City of the Eighteenth-Century Philosophers* (Yale University Press paperbound edn., 1959, pp. 49 ff.), discusses the connections between the scientific and political thought of the period. As Becker notes (p. 60), these connections did not depend on any critical understanding. He quotes Voltaire: "Very few people read Newton because it is necessary to be learned to understand him. But *everybody talks about him."*

12. As Philipp Frank noted, "Recent advances in science have increasingly revealed unifying traits connecting the different fields . . . A century ago it was believed that chemistry was essentially different from physics . . . Today we can scarcely distinguish between the two fields . . . We notice equally the increasing intrusion of physics and chemistry into some fields of biology." *Relativity—A Richer Truth* (Boston: Beacon Press, 1950), p. 58. Much the same point was made, in more detail, by Frank L. Horsfall, Jr., "On the Unity of the Sciences," *Science,* April 7, 1961, p. 1059.

13. *Report of the Committee for the Study of Engineering Education at Yale University,* submitted Oct. 23, 1961.

14. Quotations in this and the next paragraph from *Report of the Dean,* School of Engineering, Massachusetts Institute of Technology, 1959, pp. 8–12.

15. A. N. Whitehead, *Science and the Modern World* (New York: Macmillan, 1946), p. 141.

16. Alvin H. Hansen, "Federal Tax Policy for Economic Growth and Stability," paper submitted to the Subcommittee on Tax Policy, Joint Committee on the Economic Report, Nov. 9, 1955, pp. 15–16.

17. Sumner H. Slichter, "Technological Research as Related to the Growth and Stability of the Economy," in *Proceedings of a Conference on Research and Development and Its Impact on the Economy,* National Science Foundation, Washington, 1958, pp. 107–117.

18. Dexter M. Keezer in same *Proceedings,* p. 145.

19. "Government Contracting for Research and Development," a report to the President by the director, Bureau of the Budget, April 30, 1962, Annex 4 (mimeo.), reprinted in *Systems Development and Management,* Hearings before a Subcommittee of the Committee on Government Operations, House of Representatives, 87th Cong., 2d Sess., 1962, Part 1, Appendix I. See also National Science Foundation, *Reviews of Data on Science Resources,* December 1964, p. 5.

20. Charles J. Hitch in *Systems Development and Management,* just cited, Part 2, pp. 539–540. These were "items, in some phase of development" which might involve "development and investment costs in excess of $1 billion."

21. A. W. Marshall and W. H. Meckling, *Predictability of the Costs, Time and Success of Development,* RAND Corporation, Santa Monica, Calif., 1959.

22. Hitch, p. 543.

23. Committee on Appropriations, U.S. House of Representatives, Department of Defense Appropriations Bill, 1962, Report No. 574, 87th Cong., 1st Sess., pp. 40–41.

24. "The field of atomic energy is made an island of socialism in the midst of a free enterprise economy." James R. Newman and Byron S. Miller, *The Control of Atomic Energy* (New York: Whittlesey House, 1948), p. 4. Mr. Newman, writing a preface to this book a year after the text was completed, noted that "only one major policy formulation, the decision by the Atomic Energy Commission not to conduct research in its own laboratories, departs sharply from the interpretations of the Act set forth in these pages" (p. xi).

25. The comparison is made on the basis of financial reports for the 1960–61 academic year.

26. By tax dollars, this statement refers to the so-called "administrative budget funds," which do not include trust funds and certain revolving funds. For a general discussion of this problem from the legal point of view, see Arthur S. Miller, "Administration by Contract: A New Concern

for the Administrative Lawyer," *New York University Law Review,* vol. 36 (1961), pp. 957–990. The economic aspects are discussed in a study by Carl Kaysen, "Improving the Efficiency of Military Research and Development," *Public Policy XII,* the 1963 yearbook of the Graduate School of Public Administration, Harvard University. The general problems of weapons development and procurement programs are discussed in a study published by the Harvard Business School: Merton J. Peck and Frederic M. Scherer, *The Weapons Acquisition Process: An Economic Analysis,* 1962.

27. "Government Contracting for Research and Development" (note 19, above). In *Systems Development and Management,* see Appendix I, pp. 204–209.

28. U.S. House of Representatives, Third Report by the Committee on Government Operations, "Air Force Ballistic Missile Management," House Report No. 324, 87th Cong., 1st Sess., May 1, 1961, p. 50.

29. Operations Research Office, Johns Hopkins University, *Defense Spending and the U.S. Economy,* vols. I and II, 1958. See also National Science Foundation, *Research and Development in Industry 1960,* Washington, 1963, p. 11.

30. Robert A. Solo, "Gearing Military R & D to Economic Growth," *Harvard Business Review,* November–December 1962, pp. 49–60.

31. Address by Luther H. Hodges to Chamber of Commerce of the United States, Jan. 23, 1963 (Department of Commerce press release, same date).

32. Jacob Perlman, "Introduction," *Proceedings of a Conference on Research and Development and its Impact on the Economy,* National Science Foundation, Washington, 1958, p. 9.

33. *Science* (June 28, 1963, pp. 1380–1382) discusses the reasons for Congressional disapproval of this proposal.

34. National Science Foundation, *Federal Funds for Research, Development, and Other Scientific Activities,* vol. XII (1964), table XVII.

35. Local pride has not been destroyed by science: a friend from the Los Angeles area objects indignantly to my failing to mention the superior contribution of that vicinity to the development of long-range missiles.

36. Major John Wesley Powell, who did more than anyone else to build up the earth sciences in the federal government in the late nineteenth century, made a similar point in testifying before a Joint Commission of Congress in 1886: "Possession of property is exclusive; possession of knowledge is not exclusive; for the knowledge which one man has may also be the possession of another." A. Hunter Dupree, *Science in the Federal Government* (Cambridge, Mass.: Harvard University Press, 1957), p. 227.

37. Milovan Djilas, in his *The New Class* (New York: Praeger, 1957), notes the effect on a Marxist theorist of this not very surprising discovery.

38. "And the flaw that we saw in the STL [Space Technology Laboratory], of course, was the commercial aspect which was developing within it, and which, in its way, would in our opinion adulterate the objectivity, even as I think the dedication and loyalty to a specific service . . . does to some extent destroy complete objectivity in the eyes of the military." Chet Holifield in *Systems Development and Management* (hearings cited in note 19, above), Part 3, August 1962, p. 975.

39. For the best summary of this point of view, see Charles J. Hitch and Roland N. McKean, *The Economics of Defense in the Nuclear Age* (Cambridge, Mass.: Harvard University Press, 1960).

40. Richard E. Neustadt, in his *Presidential Power* (New York: John Wiley, 1960), outlines a theory of political management that is analogous to Mr. Hitch's theory of the management of research and development programs. For a similar approach see the economist Charles E. Lindblom, *Bargaining: The Hidden Hand in Government,* RM–1434–RC, RAND Corporation, Santa Monica, Calif., 1955.

41. James R. Killian, Jr., "Research and Development in a Dynamic Economy," in *Proceedings of a Conference on Research and Development and Its Impact on the Economy,* National Science Foundation, Washington, 1958, p. 164.

42. Both are published in *Preventing Conflicts of Interest on the Part of Special Government Employees,* President's memorandum of May 2, 1963 (U.S. Government Printing Office).

43. Thus the Holifield (Military Operations) Subcommittee of the House Committee on Government Operations played a leading role in influencing the Air Force to change the corporate nature and functions of the private corporation through which its most important systems engineering was being handled. The Executive followed by sorting out more completely and systematically the appropriate roles of various types of institutions in its 1962 report on "Government Contracting for Research and Development" (note 19, above).

44. Helge Holst and others to David E. Bell, director, Bureau of the Budget, April 17, 1962. Reprinted in *Systems Development and Management* (hearings cited in note 19, above), Part 1, p. 339.

45. For example, see Michael Polanyi, *The Logic of Liberty* (London: Routledge & Kegan Paul, 1951). Or see Congress for Cultural Freedom, *Science and Freedom* (London: Martin Secker & Warburg, 1955).

46. These developments are of course not peculiar to the United States; they are illustrated by the ways in which the Socialist parties of

285 |

Western Europe have become less doctrinaire Marxists in recent years, while conservative governments have undertaken to support scientific programs. Minister of Science Hans Lenz, in a recent speech in the German Bundestag, remarked that "the German people must take account of the fact that education and research assume for our generation the same priority as social questions assumed in the nineteenth century." Kenneth Lindsay, *Introductory Report to Second Parliamentary and Scientific Conference,* Council of Europe and Organisation for Economic Cooperation and Development, Vienna, May 1964, p. 23.

Chapter 3: The Diffusion of Sovereignty

1. *Establishment of a Congressional Science Advisory Staff,* Hearing before the Subcommittee on Accounts of the Committee on House Administration, House of Representatives, 88th Cong., 1st Sess., Dec. 4, 1963, p. 11.

2. Edward McCrensky, in his *Scientific Manpower in Europe* (New York: Pergamon Press, 1958), pp. 27–29, gives the general picture with respect to salaries and personnel policy. As for the classic attitude of the Administrative Class regarding its relation to the scientific civil service, see the testimony of Sir Warren Fisher, Permanent Secretary of the Treasury, before the Royal Commission on the Civil Service, 1929–1931, *Minutes of Evidence,* pp. 1276, 1282. For its contemporary attitude, see C. H. Sisson, *The Spirit of British Administration* (London: Faber & Faber Ltd., 1959). Sisson discusses the substantial differences between the British and Continental administrative traditions; the Continental administrator may be more likely than the British to have had some scientific or technical education, but he operates within a bureaucracy that relies equally on a closed career system.

3. As A. Lawrence Lowell put it, "The great professions, which have secured general recognition in the community, have been strong enough to insist that strictly professional work must not be intrusted to men who have had no professional training or experience." *Public Opinion and Popular Government* (New York: Longmans, Green, 1926), p. 274. Detailed illustrations for specifically scientific fields may be found in the series of "Service Monographs of the United States Government" published by the Institute for Government Research, notably those on the Steamboat Inspection Service, the Office of Experiment Stations, the General Land Office, and the Public Health Service. See also Lewis Mayers, *The Federal Service: A Study of the System of Personnel Administration of the United States Government* (New York, London: D. Apple-

ton, 1922), p. 21; and Lewis Meriam, *Public Personnel Problems from the Standpoint of the Operating Officer* (Washington: Brookings Institution, 1938), p. 317.

4. Data supplied by the Rockefeller Public Service Awards office, Princeton University.

5. These figures included civil servants of GS–14 class and above; they excluded the military and public health services, the Foreign Service, and political appointees. W. Lloyd Warner, Paul P. Van Riper, Norman H. Martin, and Orvis F. Collins, "A New Look at the Career Civil Service Executive," *Public Administration Review,* December 1962, pp. 188–194.

6. Michael E. Smith, "Bureau Chiefs in the Federal Government, 1958," in *Public Policy X,* the 1960 yearbook of the Graduate School of Public Administration, Harvard University, p. 62. This study brings up to date some of the data first developed by Arthur W. Macmahon and John D. Millett in their classic study, *Federal Administrators* (New York: Columbia University Press, 1939).

7. U.S. Civil Service Commission, *The Federal Top Salary Network,* Washington, 1960.

8. "From 1951 to 1961 the number of scientists and engineers at grades GS–13 and up in federal service more than tripled." Committee for Economic Development, *Improving Executive Management in the Federal Government,* New York, 1964, p. 28.

9. Macaulay put it more pointedly in 1833: "If astrology were taught at our universities, the young man who cast nativities best would generally turn out a superior man." Quoted in Royal Commission on The Civil Service, *Fourth Report,* Cd. 7338, 1914.

10. "From the beginning the membership of the Academy included many officers of the Government . . . On one occasion at least this led to some embarrassment, for the reason that through this double relationship it was thought that the view of subordinate officers might control the action of those higher in authority." Frederick W. True, *A History of the First Half-Century of the National Academy of Sciences* (Washington, 1913), p. 202. The same fear, or hope, exists in the present relationship between the Academy and the Federal Council for Science and Technology. This history of the Academy, and A. C. True's *History of Agricultural Experimentation and Research in the United States* (Misc. Pub. No. 251, U.S. Department of Agriculture, Washington, 1937), tell a great deal about the role of scientific societies in the development of new federal programs.

11. For example, the story of the origins of food and drug legislation in the work of Harvey Wiley, chief chemist of the Department of Agriculture and leader in various private scientific societies, is told in Oscar

E. Anderson, *The Health of a Nation* (Chicago: University of Chicago Press, 1958).

12. J. Walter Jones, *Historical Introduction to the Theory of the Law* (London: Oxford University Press, 1940), p. 53.

13. The National Research Council, created by President Wilson to do in the First World War (in a rudimentary way) what the Office of Scientific Research and Development did in the Second, was supported not by appropriations but by the Rockefeller and Carnegie Foundations. Richard G. Axt, *The Federal Government and Financing Higher Education* (New York: Columbia University Press, 1952), p. 78. For an account of a number of cases in which private philanthropy was used at governmental request (for example, to pay for the study that led to the devaluation of the dollar and the abandonment of the gold standard) see Louis Brownlow, *A Passion for Anonymity* (Chicago: University of Chicago Press, 1958), esp. pp. 280–281.

14. *Report of the Science Advisory Board,* Washington, Sept. 20, 1934, p. 15.

15. *Ibid.;* also *Second Report of the Science Advisory Board,* Sept. 1, 1935, esp. p. 75; and Lewis E. Auerbach, "Scientists in Government during the New Deal: A History of the Science Advisory Board" (unpublished paper for the Science and Public Policy Seminar, Harvard University, 1964).

16. See the first volume of the official history of the Atomic Energy Commission: Richard G. Hewlett and Oscar E. Anderson, Jr., *The New World* (University Park: Pennsylvania State University Press, 1962).

17. Julian Huxley, *Man in the Modern World* (New York: New American Library, 1952), pp. 120–121. See also his *Religion without Revelation* (New York: Harper, 1957).

18. The record of the Oppenheimer security hearing gives the best single story on the policy initiative of scientists in such fields. U.S. Atomic Energy Commission, *In the Matter of J. Robert Oppenheimer: Transcript of Hearing before Personnel Security Board,* 1954. But almost any number of *Aviation Week and Space Technology,* or of *The Bulletin of the Atomic Scientists,* would provide additional illustrations.

19. For an account of the way in which the leaders of the American Revolution came to refuse "to believe that the transfer of sovereignty from the crown to Parliament provided a perfect guarantee that the individual would be protected from the power of the state," and a discussion of the way in which the leaders of the Revolution finally denied that there was any sovereignty except in the people, see *Pamphlets of the American Revolution 1750–1776,* ed. Bernard Bailyn, vol. I, (Cambridge, Mass.: Harvard University Press, 1965), pp. 35, 115–139. As for

the early nineteenth century, it would be hard to find any theory further from John Austin's doctrine of sovereignty than the roughly contemporary views of John C. Calhoun, e.g., his *Disquisition on Government*. For the effect of such views on the conduct of the Civil War, see Frank L. Owsley, *State Rights in the Confederacy* (Chicago: University of Chicago Press, 1925).

20. Among the beneficial results which Jefferson expected from "immense advances in science" was that of "clearing the mind of Platonic mysticism." His correspondence, for example, shows repeated references to the role of science and rationalism in freeing mankind from oppression, and to the "Platonic Christianity of the Priests," or the "Platonizing successors" of the primitive Christians, as the corruptors of morals and the instruments of tyranny. E.g., see *The Life and Selected Writings of Thomas Jefferson* (New York: Modern Library, 1944), pp. 687, 632, 637.

21. Walter Bagehot, *The English Constitution* (London: Oxford University Press, 1928), and Thomas Woodrow Wilson, "Cabinet Government in the United States," *The International Review,* August 1879 (reprinted 1947 by the Overbrook Press, Stamford, Conn.). By the turn of the twentieth century, Wilson had apparently changed his mind, in view of the new role of the presidency, especially in international affairs; see his *Congressional Government,* preface to 15th edition.

Chapter 4: The Established Dissenters

1. Jerome B. Wiesner, "Science in the Affluent Society," address at centennial celebration of the National Academy of Sciences, Oct. 23, 1963 (mimeo.).

2. Simon Ramo, address at the University of California at Los Angeles, May 1, 1961 (mimeo.). The idea was subsequently noted in the *Report of the American Assembly: 1962–63* (New York: Columbia University Press).

3. Jacob Boehme, *The Signature of all Things* (New York: E. P. Dutton, Everyman's Library, 1934), p. 3.

4. This passage appears, with only slight variations, in *The Proficience and Advancement of Learning, Divine and Human,* Book II, and in *De Dignitate et Augmentis Scientiarum,* Book V, chap. iv. I am indebted to Dr. Marjorie Hope Nicolson for calling it to my attention (see her *The Breaking of the Circle*), and I have used her translation, except for the substitution of the word "science" where she read "philosophy." In this context, Bacon's "philosophy" clearly meant what we mean by science; it was translated as "Natural Philosophy," for example, in *The*

Philosophical Works of Francis Bacon, ed. John M. Robertson (London, 1905), pp. 119, 517.

5. Jefferson, in a letter to John Adams, April 8, 1816, affirmed his confidence in human goodness and social progress, and based that confidence on a refutation of the determinism of Diderot, D'Alembert, and D'Holbach and on a belief in both a theistic "first cause" and the effective workings of "final causes." Jefferson was strongly anticlerical, and opposed all forms of ecclesiastical establishment, but was a little contemptuous of the tendency of scientific radicals in the Catholic countries to turn atheist; he noted that the Protestants, when they defected from Platonic Christianity, turned Deist. See also his Letter to Thomas Law, June 13, 1814, *The Life and Selected Writings of Thomas Jefferson* (New York: Modern Library, 1944), pp. 667–668, 636–640.

6. Jefferson to David Williams, Nov. 14, 1803, *The Writings of Thomas Jefferson,* ed. Albert E. Bergh, 1903, X, 429.

7. A facsimile of Franklin's "Proposal" is given in each of the recent Year Books of the American Philosophical Society, Independence Square, Philadelphia. The Robert Hooke quotation is from C. R. Weld, *A History of the Royal Society with Memoirs of the Presidents* (London: John W. Parker, 1848), I, 146–147.

8. Weld, I, 146–147.

9. Thomas Sprat, *History of the Royal Society,* 1667, reprinted in Washington University Studies (St. Louis, 1958), p. 152. Edwin G. Conklin, "A Brief History of the American Philosophical Society," *Year Book* of the Society (Philadelphia, 1962), pp. 39–40.

10. Jefferson to Roger C. Weightman, June 24, 1826, *Life and Selected Writings,* Modern Library, p. 729.

11. Lewis Feuer argues to the contrary: that science is held back by religion, and fostered by a kind of Epicurean materialism. See his *The Scientific Intellectual* (New York: Basic Books, 1963).

12. Everett Mendelsohn, "The Emergence of Science as a Profession," in *The Management of Scientists,* ed. Karl Hill (Boston: Beacon Press, 1964). See also Sir Eric Ashby, *Technology and the Academics* (London: Macmillan, 1959). For a delightful account of the persistence into the twentieth century of the unreformed establishment at Oxford, see E. L. Woodward, *Short Journey* (New York: Oxford University Press, 1946).

13. I. Bernard Cohen, *Science and American Society in the First Century of the Republic* (Columbus: Ohio State University, 1961).

14. Brooks Adams in his introduction to Henry Adams, *The Degradation of the Democratic Dogma* (New York: Macmillan, 1920), p. 58.

15. Niels H. Sonne, *Liberal Kentucky 1780–1828* (New York: Columbia University Press, 1939).

16. Cohen, p. 6.

17. Jefferson to David Williams, cited above, pp. 429–430.

18. For a summary of Jefferson's views on the expectation that a natural aristocracy would be produced by the progressive forces of science, see his letter to John Adams, Oct. 28, 1813, *Life and Selected Writings*, Modern Library, pp. 632–634. For a very suggestive discussion of the political consequences of the lack of philosophic depth in the thinking of Jefferson and his associates, see Daniel J. Boorstin, *The Lost World of Thomas Jefferson* (Boston: Beacon Press, 1960).

19. For the legal ancestry of the private foundation and its roots in the status of the medieval church—but also in the political radicalism of the fourteenth century—see Henry Allen Moe, " 'The Vision of Piers the Plowman' and the Law of Foundations," American Philosophical Society, *Proceedings,* 102 (1958), 371–375. For the subsequent story of the development of foundations in England, see W. K. Jordan, *Philanthropy in England, 1480–1660* (London: Allen & Unwin, 1959), and David Owen, *English Philanthropy 1660–1960* (Cambridge, Mass.: Harvard University Press, 1964). Owen (p. 326) quotes Thomas Hare, who is better known for his advocacy of proportional representation than as a leader in the Social Science Association and in the organization of philanthropy, as remarking in 1869, "I regard endowments as an important element in the experimental branches of political and social science."

20. Memorandum of 1923 by Wickliffe Rose, General Education Board, quoted in Raymond B. Fosdick, *The Story of the Rockefeller Foundation* (New York: Harper, 1952), p. 141.

21. *Political Science Quarterly,* June 1887, reprinted in *Political Science Quarterly,* December 1941, p. 481. Wilson's essay actually recognized and gave priority to the role of administration in policy: "It is the object of administrative study to discover, first, what government can properly and successfully do, and, secondly, how it can do these proper things with the utmost possible efficiency." But he put such strong emphasis on the second point that the influence of his essay was heavily in the direction of making administration a value-free science.

22. Clark Kerr, *The Uses of the University* (Cambridge, Mass.: Harvard University Press, 1963).

23. *Tax-Exempt Foundations,* Report of the Special Committee to Investigate Tax-Exempt Foundations and Comparable Organizations, House of Representatives, 83rd Cong., 2d Sess., House Report No. 2681 (1954), pp. 17–19, 56, 60, 67, 73, 200.

24. Among the scholars who propounded systematic conservative theories was Richard M. Weaver, of the University of Chicago, who

argued in his *Ideas Have Consequences* (Chicago: University of Chicago Press, 1948) that the defeat of logical realism by nominalism in the theological debates of the Middle Ages was the great turning point in Western history, from which resulted our modern liberal and scientific decadence. William of Occam, he argued, led a philosophic attack that, with later support from Bacon and Hobbes, is responsible for the current onslaught on our "last metaphysical right" of private property.

25. *Tax-Exempt Foundations,* p. 422.

26. *Ibid.,* p. 425.

27. The lack of a genuinely conservative political tradition in the United States is discussed by Louis Hartz, *The Liberal Tradition in America* (New York: Harcourt, Brace, 1955).

28. Ernest Nagel remarks, for example, on the decline in the early belief in mechanics as the perfect and potentially comprehensive science, and the growing belief that the reduction of one science to another that is more abstract and simple—for example, biology to physics—does not necessarily produce a more useful method. See his *The Structure of Science* (New York: Harcourt, Brace & World, 1961), pp. 154, 363. For a classic example of the reductionist and deterministic type of biology, see Jacques Loeb, *The Mechanistic Conception of Life,* ed. Donald Fleming (Cambridge, Mass.: Harvard University Press, 1964); the first edition was published in 1912.

29. Einstein noted that James Clerk Maxwell's equations, which could not be interpreted mechanically, made it necessary to give up mechanics as the foundation of all physics. See his "Autobiographical Notes" in Paul A. Schilpp, *Albert Einstein: Philosopher-Scientist* (Evanston: Library of Living Philosophers, 1949), p. 25. As for Kelvin's view, see Nagel, p. 114.

30. Albert Einstein and Leopold Infeld, *The Evolution of Physics* (New York: Simon & Schuster, 1938), p. 33.

31. P. W. Bridgman, in *The Way Things Are* (Cambridge, Mass.: Harvard University Press, 1959), pp. 170–172, makes this point, even while citing the effect on human conduct of belief in determinism, with the history of Calvinism as an example. "A deterministic universe was demanded by the religious and philosophic notion of an omnipotent and all-knowing God."

32. James B. Conant, *Modern Science and Modern Man* (New York: Columbia University Press, 1952), p. 54.

33. Gerald Holton, "Über die Hypothesen, welche der Naturwissenschaft zugrunde liegen," in *Eranos-Jahrbuch* XXXI (Zurich: Rhein-Verlag, 1963), p. 408.

34. René Dubos, "Logic and Choices in Science," American Philosophical Society, *Proceedings,* 107 (1963), 370. See also Theodosius

Dobzhansky, "Evolutionary and Population Genetics," *Science*, Nov. 29, 1963, p. 1131.

35. See, for example, the various quotations from Teilhard de Chardin's writings available in Nicolas Corte, *Pierre Teilhard de Chardin: His Life and Spirit* (New York: Macmillan, 1960). Edmund W. Sinnott, in *The Biology of the Spirit* (New York: Viking Press, 1953), argued for a new and biologically respectable concept of purpose. George Gaylord Simpson criticized their positions in his *This View of Life* (New York: Harcourt, Brace & World, 1964). At the same time he took an antireductionist position and dealt at length with the special problem of considering purpose in biological science.

36. Ernst Mayr, "Cause and Effect in Biology," *Science*, Nov. 10, 1961, pp. 1501–1506.

37. Bernard Berelson and Gary A. Steiner give a summary of the current accomplishments of the behavioral sciences in their *Human Behavior: An Inventory of Scientific Findings* (New York: Harcourt, Brace & World, 1964).

38. "Science and the Race Problem," *Science*, Nov. 1, 1963. See also letter of rebuttal in *Science*, Feb. 28, 1964, pp. 913–915.

39. National Academy of Sciences–National Research Council, *Scientific and Technical Societies of the United States and Canada, 1960–61*, ed. John H. Gribbin (Washington, 1961).

40. "The Contribution of Science to Christianity," in *Henry Drummond, an Anthology*, ed. J. W. Kennedy (New York: Harper, 1953), p. 75.

41. British Association for the Advancement of Science, *Report of the Annual Meeting* (1934), p. 13.

42. Jacques Maritain, *The Range of Reason* (New York: Scribner, no date), pp. 406, 87, 210.

43. John Dillenberger, in *Protestant Thought and Natural Science* (New York: Doubleday, 1960), gives an excellent summary of these developments. "There is a great danger of filling the gaps in science with theological answers, or of seeing too readily the footprints of God in the world, or of assuming that one is thinking God's thoughts after Him. Few indeed are those who see an argument for free will in the concept of indeterminacy or who follow du Nouy in finding a theistic frame of reference in biology . . . The respect for mystery which has emerged in contemporary science does not necessarily imply a spiritual or religious interpretation of the world" (pp. 283–284).

44. Paul Tillich, *Dynamics of Faith* (New York: Harper, 1958), p. 33.

45. Karl Barth, in his major theological work, looked on politics and

political questions as "fundamentally uninteresting." *Community, State and Church* (New York: Doubleday Anchor Books, 1960), p. 23. Dillenberger's comments are pertinent: "While theologians and scientists previously crossed into each other's territory, Barth and Tillich have so separated these spheres that they have disregarded the knowledge of the world contributed by natural sciences . . . To be sure, the thrust of existentialism was not merely against science: it protested wherever men became an object . . . The emergence of existentialism in the theological renaissance of the twentieth century stands for a recovery of man more congenial to classical theology, than the notion of man as the embodiment of value or as moral personality." Dillenberger, pp. 262–264.

46. Reinhold Niebuhr, *The Nature and Destiny of Man* (New York: Charles Scribner's Sons, 1947), Part I, pp. 198–203, 298–299.

47. Not only does the Inter-Varsity Christian Fellowship attract student support from among those concentrating in the sciences, but the faculty advisers at two thirds of the colleges reporting came from the natural sciences, and the academic members of the National Board are predominantly from the sciences. Lawrence Neale Jones, "The Inter-Varsity Christian Fellowship in the United States," unpub. Ph.D. dissertation, Yale University, 1961.

48. *The Leviathan,* Part I, chap. i.

49. Hermann Weyl, "Wissenschaft als Symbolische Konstruktion des Menschen," in *Eranos-Jahrbuch* XVI (Zurich: Rhein-Verlag, 1948), pp. 427–428. I am indebted to Gerald Holton for calling this article to my attention, and for the translation of this passage.

50. Bridgman, pp. 43–44, 259.

Chapter 5: The Spectrum from Truth to Power

1. Robert Dorfman, in his survey of "Operations Research" for the *American Economic Review* in September 1960, noted types of problems that were not susceptible to solution by operations research, and went on to say, "Fortunately, this galaxy of unsolvable problems is less obtrusive in narrow operational contexts than in broad strategic ones. It is easier to ascertain the objectives of a department than of a firm, of a section than of a department, of a particular phase of the work than of a section" (p. 611). Much the same distinction is apparent in Herbert A. Simon's discussion of programmed and nonprogrammed decisions, and their relation to hierarchical organization, in his *The New Science of Management Decision* (New York: Harper, 1960), pp. 5–7, 49–50.

2. Albert Wohlstetter, "Defense Decisions: Design vs. Analysis,"

abstract of paper presented at Second International Conference on Operational Research, Aix-en-Provence, September 1960.

3. The story of the fire ant is only one of many interesting cases that led to the concern exemplified in Rachel Carson's *The Silent Spring* (Boston: Houghton Mifflin, 1962), and in the subsequent report of the President's Science Advisory Committee on the use of pesticides. For the fire ant story, see W. L. Brown, Jr., "Mass Insect Control Programs: Four Case Histories," *Psyche: a Journal of Entomology*, June–September 1961, p. 75, and Edward O. Wilson, "The Fire Ant," *Scientific American*, March 1958, p. 36. Brown said in his 1961 article that some of the insect control programs amounted to "scalping in order to cure dandruff." The articles by Wilson and Brown show how the scientific journals may be ahead of the popular authors, and even further ahead of political action.

4. There is an interesting analogy here between the politician's use of science and the scientist's use of the discoveries of other scientists, for example by using mechanical or electronic aids in searching for citations. H. Burr Steinbach observes that "the importance, to a scientist, of *knowing the literature* is (i) inversely proportional to the size of the idea (many people think of many small things) but (ii) directly proportional to the proximity to technology (finding out someone else did something saves time—sometimes)." "The Quest for Certainty: Science Citation Index," *Science*, July 10, 1964, p. 142.

5. P. M. S. Blackett, "Operational Research," *The Advancement of Science*, April 1948. This paper had been written and circulated privately during the war.

6. Similar testimony as to the extent to which operations research is progressively less able to deal precisely and completely with problems that have to be faced by higher levels of authority may be found in Bernard Brodie, *Strategy in the Missile Age* (Princeton, N.J.: Princeton University Press, 1959), p. 388, and Charles J. Hitch and Roland N. McKean, *The Economics of Defense in the Nuclear Age* (Cambridge, Mass.: Harvard University Press, 1960), pp. 125–128.

7. Unpublished lecture by Dr. Panofsky at Tufts University, March 7, 1964.

8. See for example Senator Henry M. Jackson's comment in *Arms Control and Disarmament*, Hearings before Senate Committee on Armed Services, Preparedness Investigating Subcommittee, 87th Cong., 2d Sess., 1962, p. 26. Also Senator J. W. Fulbright's comment in *Nuclear Test Ban Treaty: Hearings*, Senate Committee on Foreign Relations, 88th Cong., 1st Sess., 1963, pp. 639, 642. Also Representative Jack Westland's comment in *Technical Aspects of Detection and Inspection Controls of a Nuclear Weapons Test Ban*, Hearings before the Special Subcommittee on

Radiation and the Subcommittee on Research and Development of the Joint Committee on Atomic Energy, Part 1, 86th Cong., 2d Sess., 1960, p. 75.

9. Richard Bellman, for example, warns the mathematician of the difficulties of determining which problems will or will not be "susceptible to the collection of devices, tricks, and legerdemain called mathematics." He goes on to note that the "classical techniques are ineffectual as far as decision making in the face of complexity and uncertainty is concerned," and emphasized the value of the "engineering attitude," which is "partial control with partial understanding." *Challenges of Modern Control Theory*, RAND Corporation, Santa Monica, Calif., RM 3956–PR, January 1964.

10. John C. Whitehorn, M.D., Professor Emeritus of Psychiatry, Johns Hopkins, "Education for Uncertainty," a lecture at the Massachusetts General Hospital, 1961, printed by the University of Rochester School of Medicine and Dentistry.

11. Col. Francis X. Kane, USAF, "Security Is Too Important to Be Left to Computers," *Fortune*, April 1964, p. 146.

12. U.S. Atomic Energy Commission, *In the Matter of J. Robert Oppenheimer*, transcript of hearing before Personnel Security Board, 1954. See esp. pp. 384–394, 709–727, 742–770. See also Robert Gilpin, *American Scientists and Nuclear Weapons Policy* (Princeton, N.J.: Princeton University Press, 1962).

13. "Raffiniert ist der Herr Gott, aber boshaft ist er nicht." The remark, taken from a conversation, adorns the professors' lounge in the Princeton University mathematics department. *Albert Einstein: Philosopher-Scientist*, ed. Paul A. Schilpp (Evanston, Ill.: Library of Living Philosophers, 1949), p. 691.

14. If the reader's taste runs to science more than theology, he may compare the following by Bernard Berelson and Gary A. Steiner, in their *Human Behavior* (New York: Harcourt, Brace & World, 1964): "But there is another way in which man comes to terms with reality when it is inconsistent with his needs and preferences; and it is here that the behavioral-science model departs most noticeably from the others. In his quest for satisfaction, man is not just a seeker of truth, but of deceptions, of himself as well as others" (pp. 663–664).

15. Nigel Calder, "Parliament and Science," *The New Scientist*, May 28, 1964, p. 534.

16. Thornton Read, in his *Command and Control* (Center of International Studies, Princeton University, 1961) gives a very lucid summary of the problem. The difficulties that result from too much reliance on the computer are summed up in Anthony G. Oettinger, "A Bull's Eye View of Management and Engineering Information Systems," *Proceedings of*

the 19th ACM National Conference, Association for Computing Machinery, New York, 1964, pp. B.1–1 to B.1–14.

17. Roberta Wohlstetter, in her *Pearl Harbor: Warning and Decision* (Stanford, Calif.: Stanford University Press, 1962), points out that the blunder at Pearl Harbor was not the result of lack of warning, but of poor strategic analysis, and that this in turn came less because we did not understand the Japanese than because we did not understand the deficiencies in our own system of responsibility.

18. Sidney Hook criticizes the political and fictional critics of the command and control system in *The Fail-Safe Fallacy* (New York: Stein & Day, 1963).

19. For an impression of the significance of the distinction, see the way in which the Army Chief of Staff system was contrasted with the Navy's Commander in Chief of the Fleet system by Henry L. Stimson and McGeorge Bundy, *On Active Service in Peace and War* (New York: Harper, 1948), pp. 32–33, 450–451, 506.

20. Brockway McMillan, address before the First Congress on the Information System Sciences, Nov. 19, 1962.

21. Sir Robert Watson-Watt, *The Pulse of Radar* (New York: Dial Press, 1959), pp. 277–278.

22. "In this setting there exists a considerable danger that complex decision systems involving human parameters will be broken down into routine segments which are more or less independent of human reaction, and that the combination will then be called a credible simulation of the total system . . . Also, there is an attractive but dangerous precedent for restricting value parameters in the interest of simplicity and neatness; the result . . . may be satisfactory in a 'game' situation but is disastrous in application." David L. Johnson and Arthur L. Kobler, "The Man-Computer Relationship," *Science,* Nov. 23, 1962, p. 876.

23. Read, p. 21; Johnson and Kobler, p. 877.

24. Read, p. 15.

25. Calder, p. 534.

26. Zbigniew Brzezinski and Samuel P. Huntington vigorously disagree with the theory that the systems of the U.S.A. and U.S.S.R. are converging; one of their reasons is that in the U.S.A., unlike the U.S.S.R., the policy-making process is dispersed among groups whose power depends not on legal power or on property but on special knowledge. See their *Political Power: USA/USSR* (New York: Viking Press, 1964), p. 413. See also Sheldon S. Wolin, *Politics and Vision* (Boston: Little, Brown, 1960). In his last chapter Wolin discusses the ways in which modern business has believed that it could assume essentially political functions.

27. "Khrushchev's Report to the Party Plenary Session," Nov. 19,

1962, in *The Current Digest of the Soviet Press,* vol. XIV, no. 47, p. 5.

28. *Ibid.,* pp. 5, 13.

29. S. Kheinman, "Sozdanie material'no-tekhnicheskoi bazy kommunizma i nauchno-tekhnicheskaya revolyutsiya," *Kommunist,* no. 12, August 1962, pp. 47–48. The title in English: "The Establishment of the Material-Technical Basis of Communism and the Scientific-Technological Revolution."

30. Boris N. Ponomaryev, "Leninism Is Our Banner and All-Conquering Weapon," *Current Soviet Documents,* vol. I, no. 8, May 13, 1963 (Crosscurrents Press, New York). The italics in the quotation were in the original.

31. L. Ilichev, "Nauchnaya osnova rukovodstva razvitiem obshchestva; nekotorye problemy razvitiya obshchestvennykh nauk," *Kommunist,* no. 16, November 1962, p. 34. The title in English: "The Scientific Basis of the Management of the Development of Society; Certain Problems of the Development of the Social Sciences."

32. The theoretical problems of the relation of science to materialist dialectic, which denies positivism and reductionism almost as vigorously as idealism, are summarized by Maxim W. Mikulak, in "Philosophy and Science," *Survey: a Journal of East European Studies,* July 1964, pp. 147–156. See also Richard Pipes, "Foreword to the Issue 'The Russian Intelligentsia,'" *Daedalus,* Summer 1960, and other essays in that number, especially those by David Joravsky and Gustav Wetter.

33. To illustrate the difference between Orthodox and Roman Catholic theology with respect to perfectibility, as seen from the Roman point of view: Gerhart B. Ladner argues that the idea of reform (as distinct from revolution or renaissance) was inhibited by the Eastern Orthodox belief, as typified by St. Gregory of Nyssa, who held that "the reform of man had been purification of the soul which would thus mirror God more and more clearly; a resulting vision of God is not excluded even on earth." By contrast, "Augustine did not think that the terrestrial condition of even the holiest man warrants the expectation of a vision of the fullness of God this side of heaven." See Ladner's *The Idea of Reform* (Cambridge, Mass.: Harvard University Press, 1959), pp. 190–191. On the issue of perfectibility and its relation to ecclesiastical government, see also Reinhold Niebuhr, *The Nature and Destiny of Man* (New York: Charles Scribner's Sons, 1947), Part II, p. 133.

Chapter 6: Constitutional Relativity

1. Burke argued that civil freedom was not "a thing that lies hid in the depth of abstruse science," or having "any resemblance to . . . propo-

sitions in geometry or metaphysics." He blamed the academic and professional world—"too much confined to professional and faculty habits" and thus made unfit for a comprehensive view of public affairs—for the intellectual leadership of the French Revolution. "We have seen all the academicians at Paris, with Condorcet, the friend and correspondent of Priestley, at their head, the most furious of the extravagant republicans." This would lead France, he predicted, to a predicament in which "some popular general . . . who possesses the true spirit of command, shall draw the eyes of all men upon himself." *Burke's Speeches and Letters on American Affairs,* Everyman's Library (London: J. M. Dent & Sons, 1931), p. 221; *The Works of the Right Honourable Edmund Burke* (London: Oxford University Press, 1934), IV, 48, 358, 243.

2. For a concise statement of this position by an English politician of Burke's persuasion, see L. S. Amery, *Thoughts on the Constitution* (London: Oxford University Press, 1947).

3. "On Conciliation with the Colonies," *Burke's Speeches and Letters on American Affairs,* p. 95.

4. This required a reversal of the original revolutionary tendency; under the influence of thought like Paine's, unicameral legislatures were established in Pennsylvania, Georgia, New Hampshire, and Vermont; the governor was elected by the legislature (usually for a one-year term) in ten of the original thirteen states; and executive power was divided between the governor and a council elected by the people or the legislature in nine states. Jean H. Wheeler, *The Meaning of the Constitution* (to be published).

5. For a general account of their views and influence, see Daniel J. Boorstin, *The Lost World of Thomas Jefferson* (Boston: Beacon Press, 1960).

6. Senator Barry Goldwater, speech accepting nomination as candidate for the presidency, Republican National Convention, 1964.

7. Thomas S. Kuhn, *The Structure of Scientific Revolutions* (Chicago: University of Chicago Press, 1962).

8. The Soviet Union, by generally separating advanced research from the universities, and supporting it in institutes that do not have the educational function, may diminish the independent self-government of science and bring it more under potential political or administrative control.

9. C. P. Swanson, "Photobiology: A Splinter Discipline That Crosses Departmental Lines," *Science,* June 26, 1964, pp. 1561–1562.

10. For an impression of the way in which the Continental European system is now loosening up as the result of new research funds from U.S. Government grants, and of the research experience of influential European

scientists in the United States, see Victor K. McElheny, "Research in Biology: New Pattern of Support Is Developing," *Science,* Aug. 28, 1964, pp. 908–912.

11. Martin Kilson, "Authoritarian and Single-Party Tendencies in African Politics," *World Politics,* January 1963, pp. 262–293.

12. At this point I am challenged to define "discipline." For the purpose of this discussion, a discipline is what its professors say it is. The fact that they, and not lay authority, can alone define the discipline is the operationally significant point, rather than the fact that a discipline is a blend of objects of study and a peculiar methodology, both of which are always changing.

13. Michael Polanyi, "The Republic of Science: Its Political and Economic Theory," *Minerva,* Autumn 1962, p. 54.

14. Kuhn, p. 37.

15. National Science Foundation, *Reviews of Data on Research and Development,* September 1963, p. 3.

16. Allan Nevins, in *The State Universities and Democracy* (Urbana: University of Illinois Press, 1962), and Clark Kerr, in *The Uses of the University* (Cambridge, Mass.: Harvard University Press, 1963), give illuminating interpretations of this process.

17. These figures, unlike those cited in note 15, include special contract research centers. National Science Foundation, *Federal Funds for Research Development, and Other Scientific Activities,* vol. XII (Washington: Government Printing Office, 1964), table xvii.

18. For a description of the grant system, see *Administration of Research and Development Grants,* Report of the Select Committee on Government Research of the House of Representatives, 88th Cong., 2d Sess., July 31, 1964. The study noted that "the two agencies which awarded the greatest number of grants, with the highest aggregate dollar value, reported using the services of advisory panels," and that "almost all agencies which do not maintain advisory panels for specific projects, do employ panels of experts to provide counsel on the general areas of research to be supported by grants" (pp. 11, 16).

19. The report of the Science and Public Policy Committee of the National Academy of Sciences, *Federal Support of Basic Research in Institutions of Higher Learning,* 1964, is impressively restrained on this topic. See pp. 95–98.

20. The style of thought of a politician may be more like the tacit than the explicit part of a scientist's knowledge, if we may borrow Michael Polanyi's distinction. See his *Personal Knowledge* (Chicago: University of Chicago Press, 1958).

21. Samuel A. Lawrence, "The Battery Additive Controversy," in

Case Studies in American Government, ed. Edwin A. Bock and Alan K. Campbell (Englewood Cliffs, N.J.: Prentice-Hall, 1962), pp. 325–368.

22. One of the recommendations of the National Academy of Sciences was that similar difficulties could be avoided if the Bureau of Standards would thereafter confine its responsibility to the technical side of product testing, and the Secretary of Commerce bear responsibility for the policy and the nontechnical procedures. *Ibid.,* p. 359.

Chapter 7: Professionals and Politicians

1. See especially National Academy of Sciences–National Research Council, *Oceanography 1960 to 1970, Vol. I—Introduction and Summary of Recommendations* (Washington, 1959); also Interagency Committee on Oceanography of the Federal Council for Science and Technology, *Oceanography—The Ten Years Ahead* (Washington, 1963).

2. *Advancement of Marine Sciences—Marine Sciences and Research Act of 1961,* U.S. Senate, 87th Cong., 1st Sess., Calendar No. 399, Report No. 426, June 20, 1961, p. 13. This will be cited hereafter simply as *Advancement of Marine Sciences.*

3. *Marine Sciences and Research Act,* report to accompany S. 2692, 86th Cong., 2d Sess., Senate Report No. 1525, June 7, 1960, p. 17.

4. Dr. Albert Szent-Gyorgi, Director of the Laboratory of the Institute for Muscle Research, in *Advancement of Marine Sciences,* p. 67.

5. *Advancement of Marine Sciences,* pp. 39–43.

6. *National Oceanographic Program—1965,* Hearings before the Subcommittee on Oceanography of the Committee on Merchant Marine and Fisheries, House of Representatives, 88th Cong., 2d Sess., Serial No. 88–23, 1964, lists the research ships (p. 42) and the cooperating universities (Appendix 3), and summarizes the report of the committee of consultants (p. 54). Hereafter cited simply as *National Oceanographic Program—1965.*

7. *National Oceanographic Program—1965,* pp. 53, 224.

8. *National Oceanographic Program—1965,* p. 11. This document contains in its appendices the official reports from the Executive Office summarizing the program. For the two billion estimate, see p. 433.

9. Charles G. Dawes recorded this question in his *Journal as Ambassador to Great Britain* (New York: Macmillan, 1939), p. 66. He used to recall it and apply it to subsequent experience in personal conversations.

10. The Republican Platform Committee, for example, on July 9, 1964, heard Alan T. Waterman, former director of the National Science Foundation, testify that "science will continue to bring to light research

or development programs of greater and greater import for mankind. These will be impressive but some will also be very expensive." Later, he alluded to the possibilities of doubling the life span, predetermining the sex or other characteristics of children, or altering the earth's environment in ways that would require government action to ensure human survival. Mimeographed statement.

11. *Providing for a Comprehensive, Long-range, and Coordinated National Program in Oceanography,* Committee on Merchant Marine and Fisheries, House of Representatives, 87th Cong., 2d Sess., Report No. 2221, Aug. 14, 1962, p. 8.

12. *Ibid.,* p. 6.

13. Letter of May 9, 1961, from Philip S. Hughes, Assistant Director for Legislative Reference, Bureau of the Budget, to Chairman, Committee on Merchant Marine and Fisheries.

14. The issue between the May-Johnson bill, as endorsed by the OSRD leaders, and the McMahon bill, which the President and the more vocal young nuclear physicists supported, turned primarily on the issue of degree of independence of the proposed commission. Contrary to the charges in the great debate among the scientists of the period, the two bills did not differ with respect to their potentialities for military domination of the program. Ironically enough, by the time of the security hearings in the case of J. Robert Oppenheimer, who had been for the May-Johnson bill, the chairman of the commission created by the McMahon bill was Admiral Lewis L. Strauss, and its general manager was General Kenneth D. Nichols.

15. See, for example, the 1959 hearings on the "administrative procedure" legislation, especially the delicious passage in which Senator Everett Dirksen made it clear to the unhappy representatives of the American Bar Association that none of their proposals for a code of procedure would keep him from getting in touch with staff members of the independent commissions on behalf of his constituents. *Administrative Procedure Legislation,* Hearings, Subcommittee on Administrative Practice and Procedure, Senate Judiciary Committee, 86th Cong., 1st Sess., Senate Resolution 61, July 1959, pp. 91–92.

16. *The National Meteorological Program,* Preliminary Staff Report of the Committee on Science and Astronautics, House of Representatives, 87th Cong., 1st Sess., July 13, 1961. This report states the case for centralizing in NASA of space activities for all civilian purposes, against the plan of the executive branch to let the Weather Bureau fund the meteorological satellite.

17. *The Works of James Wilson,* ed. James DeWitt Andrews (Chicago: Callaghan & Co., 1896), I, 353–359.

18. See the claims of the Joint Committee on Atomic Energy to this effect in, for example, its release no. 436, Jan. 10, 1964.

19. James T. Ramey, address to Ninth Institute on Research Administration, American University, Washington, D.C., April 1964. He quoted Edward Welsh as saying that "if we had required a clear-cut prior mission, we would probably have developed no airplanes, no spacecraft, or, in fact, no wheel."

20. Elinor Langer, "Nuclear Stockpile," *Science,* May 8, 1964, pp. 660–662.

21. See David E. Lilienthal, *Change, Hope, and the Bomb* (Princeton, N.J.: Princeton University Press, 1963), p. 118; also John W. Finney, "Is the AEC Obsolete?" *The Reporter,* Nov. 19, 1964, pp. 44–46.

22. Letter from Committee on Oceanography of National Academy of Sciences dated July 27, 1961, published in *Providing for a Comprehensive . . . Program* (note 11, above), pp. 24–25. See also pp. 7–8 of that report. It must be noted that the interests of the scientists and the Congressional committee were not identical; the Academy's committee recommended that the National Oceanographic Council should be in the Executive Office of the President and report to Congress only through the President. But the two groups were alike enough in their interests to form an alliance against the Executive Office.

23. *Providing for a Comprehensive . . . Program,* p. 7.

24. The two stages noted were represented by S. 2692, reported by the Senate Committee on Commerce in Senate Report No. 1525, June 7, 1960, and S. 901 (a revised version of the same bill), reported in 1961 in the Senate report, *Advancement of Marine Sciences.* A summary and analysis of the bill begins on p. 44 of that report. Thus the Senate strategy was, in one sense, the first rather than the second to be considered by Congress; the Senate had indeed passed S. 2692 in 1960. But the full elaboration of the advisory strategy did not appear until S. 901, and for this reason, and because S. 901 became the basis of conference-committee action in the later compromise between the two houses, it seems proper to consider it second.

25. *Advancement of Marine Sciences* (1961), p. 43; *Providing for a Comprehensive . . . Program* (1962), p. 32; *Marine Science,* Hearings before the Committee on Interstate and Foreign Commerce, U.S. Senate, 87th Cong., 1st Sess., on S. 901 and S. 1189, March–May 1961, pp. 85–87, 35–36.

26. As, for example, when Fulbright suggested, after the Democrats lost the Congressional elections of 1946, that President Truman should resign, or when Kefauver brought up from time to time variations on the old proposal that cabinet members should have seats in Congress. Senator

Fulbright's suggestion is summarized in *Newsweek,* Nov. 18, 1946, p. 36, and Senator Kefauver's in chap. vi of his *A Twentieth-Century Congress* (New York: Duell, Sloan & Pearce, 1947), pp. 65–79.

27. Alvin M. Weinberg, director of the Oak Ridge National Laboratory (a nonprofit contractor), was concerned enough about the effects of this salary arrangement in putting "the most mature, experienced people . . . in the contractor establishments, not in the Government," that he proposed that Congress make it possible for the contractors to lend staff to the agencies which supplied their funds. Testimony before Select Committee on Government Research, House of Representatives, Nov. 20, 1963.

28. William E. Rhode, *Committee Clearance of Administrative Decisions* (East Lansing: Michigan State University Bureau of Social and Political Research, 1959).

29. *Advancement of Marine Sciences,* pp. 93–94.

30. See the nationwide listing of university curricula in this field in Interagency Committee on Oceanography of the Federal Council for Science and Technology, *University Curricula in Oceanography,* 1963.

31. The new bill carried the same number as the earlier Senate bill, S. 901, although it took only the enacting clause from that bill and substituted a new House bill for the rest. *Oceanographic Act of 1962,* Conference Report to accompany S. 901, 87th Cong., 2d Sess., House of Representatives, Report No. 2493.

32. *Ibid.*

33. *National Oceanographic Program—1965,* p. 32.

34. Jerome B. Wiesner, statement before Subcommittee on Science, Research and Development, House Committee on Science and Astronautics, Oct. 16, 1963, mimeo.

35. Chairman Alton Lennon, *National Oceanographic Program—1965,* p. 50.

36. The budget for research and development in meteorology, under the coordination of this committee, and under the administration of a dozen bureaus and agencies, was $108 million for Fiscal Year 1965. This was nearly as large as the entire oceanographic program ($138 million), and much larger than its research and development aspects exclusive of ship construction, instrumentation, and facilities. *The Budget of the United States Government, 1965,* pp. 418–423.

37. *Providing for a Comprehensive . . . Program,* p. 9.

38. *Amending the National Aeronautics and Space Act of 1958,* Hearing before the Committee on Aeronautical and Space Sciences, U.S. Senate, 87th Cong., 1st Sess., April 19, 1961.

39. *National Oceanographic Program—1965,* p. 19.

40. The extent of support for the oceanographic program, and the conviction of its potential economic benefits, were illustrated by two reports published in Washington in 1964. One was Committee on Oceanography, National Academy of Sciences–National Research Council, *Economic Benefits from Oceanographic Research,* Publication 1228. The other was National Security Industrial Association Ad Hoc Committee on Ocean Science and Technology, *A National Ocean Program.*

41. A. Hunter Dupree, *Science in the Federal Government* (Cambridge, Mass.: Harvard University Press, 1957). See chap. xi, "The Allison Commission and the Department of Science, 1884–1886."

42. This and other proposals are analyzed in Dael Wolfle, "Government Organization of Science," *Science,* May 13, 1960, pp. 1407–1417.

43. Argument in favor of a special staff of science advisers for Congress may be found in *Establishment of a Congressional Science Advisory Staff,* Hearing before the Subcommittee on Accounts of the Committee on House Administration, House of Representatives, 88th Cong., 1st Sess., Dec. 4, 1963. The negative point of view may be found in Senator Clinton Anderson, "Scientific Advice for Congress—Need Is Clear But Solution Isn't," *Science,* April 3, 1964. The opposition of the House Appropriations Committee is reported in *Chemical and Engineering News,* Dec. 30, 1963, pp. 24–26. An excellent summary of the problem appears in *Government and Science No. 3, Scientific-Technical Advice for Congress—Needs and Sources,* Staff Study for the Subcommittee on Science, Research and Development of the Committee on Science and Astronautics, House of Representatives, 88th Cong., 2nd Sess., 1964.

44. Editorial, *Science,* Nov. 22, 1963.

45. Daniel S. Greenberg, "Science and Government: A Survey of Some of the Major Elements in Growing, Troubled Relationship," *Science,* July 26, 1963, p. 340.

Chapter 8: Science and Freedom

1. The connection between the rapid development of science in England in the late seventeenth century and the doctrines and institutions of Puritanism and the dissenting churches is traced by Robert K. Merton in the chapter called "Puritanism, Pietism, and Science," in his *Social Theory and Social Structure,* rev. edn. (Glencoe, Ill.: Free Press, 1957), pp. 574–606.

Index

Abelson, Philip H., 265
Abstract theory: trend toward, 28, 30–32; application to reality, 120–122, 127. *See also* Basic sciences
Academie des Sciences, 88
Adams, Brooks, 290
Adams, Henry, 11, 280, 290
Adams, John, 24, 52, 168, 291
Adams, John Quincy, 60, 92
Adler, Mortimer, 99, 100
Administration: effect of scientific revolution on, 15–16; Administrative Class in Great Britain, 59–62, 78, as U.S. academic model, 94; development in U.S., 60–62; scientists in career civil service, 60–62, as policy initiators, 68; responsibility in, 68–69; value-free nature of, 95; influence of industrial management on, 95–96; differences between U.S. and British concept of, 96; policy in, 96; purpose in, 183–184; relation of issues to, 185. *See also* Administrators; Civil service
Administrators: distinguished from professionals, 133–134; political control of, 137; military policy responsibilities of, 148; role in technological planning, 149–152; autonomy of, 193; relation to science, 196; as advisers, 234; Continental, 286
Advice: role in constitutional affairs, 229–233; strategies of, 233–237; in oceanography program, 238–241;

public accountability of, 242–257; in interagency programs, 247–248; and presidential authority, 251–256; scientific, for Congress, 262–264; for the President, 260–262, 265–269
AD-X2 (battery additive), 202–204
Aerospace Corporation, 42
African states, control of scientific and professional societies in, 174
Agricultural sciences: extent of influence, 48, 54; in policy initiation, 63–64; and land-grant colleges, 97
Agriculture: federal grants in, 63–64, 74; Department of Agriculture, 128, 186, 237
Alaska, 57
Air Force, U.S., 42, 75, 223, 254
American Association for the Advancement of Science, 29, 111, 112
American Chemical Society, 30
American Institute of Biological Sciences, 112
American Medical Association, 53, 143
American Revolution, 79, 89, 167; mentioned, 18, 175
American Philosophical Society: history, 28; goals, 87; Jefferson and Franklin as presidents of, 88, 169; comprehensive nature of, 112; mentioned, vii
American Society of Biological Chemists, 112
Amery, L. S., 299

Index

Index

Index